For Both Mazrui,
highest regard

Development Planning and Decolonization in Nigeria

Development Planning and Decolonization in Nigeria

Toyin Falola

University Press of Florida
Gainesville/Tallahassee/Tampa/Boca Raton
Pensacola/Orlando/Miami/Jacksonville

01 00 99 98 97 96 6 5 4 3 2 1

Library of Congress Cataloging-in-Publication Data

Falola, Toyin.
Development planning and decolonization in Nigeria / Toyin Falola.
p. cm.
Includes bibliographical references and index.
ISBN 0-8130-1422-0
1. Nigeria—Economic policy. 2. Nigeria—Economic conditions—To 1960. 3. Great Britain—Colonies—Economic policy 4. Decolonization—Nigeria. I. Title.
HC1055.F35 1995
338.9669—dc20 95-46423

The University Press of Florida is the scholarly publishing agency for the State University System of Florida, comprised of Florida A & M University, Florida Atlantic University, Florida International University, Florida State University, University of Central Florida, University of Florida, University of North Florida, University of South Florida, and University of West Florida.

University Press of Florida
15 Northwest 15th Street
Gainesville, FL 32611

For Dolapo Omobola Martin Falola, my son

Contents

Tables

Preface

This is the first comprehensive book on the foundation of economic planning in Nigeria, the beginning of finding an intelligent solution to the intractable problem of underdevelopment. In the late colonial period, 1940–60, the belief was that a planning model based on a project-by-project strategy within the framework of a mixed economy would provide a "big push" to transform a "traditional" society into a "modern" one.

The book starts with a general discussion of the colonial economy, developing the thesis that long-range planning was not an important aspect of British rule before 1940. The origins of planning are explained, with a focus on how World War II provoked far-reaching political and economic changes. Three chapters are devoted to a lengthy discussion of the first plan, the Ten-Year Plan, including its revision in the early 1950s. The conclusion reflects on the economic history of the last years of colonial rule and connects the period with the postcolonial economy.

This study furthers an understanding of the economy in Nigeria through an analysis of the origin of planning, the broadening of the database to trace the process of economic growth, and the discussion of the impact of economic reforms in the country. Its importance to modern Nigeria lies in its perspective of how late colonial development planning profoundly shaped Nigerians' thinking about the role of the state and their continued implementation of development policies (despite much criticism) up to the International Monetary Fund's entry on the scene in the 1980s. Thus, the book is crucial to understanding the historical roots of the contemporary crisis of the Nigerian state.

This study is based both on official documents obtained from several archives and on extensive fieldwork conducted in Nigeria over a period of two years. Specific archival records are cited in the notes and bibliography. I also consulted various official publications, including specialized reports, minutes, annual reports, debates in the Legislative and Regional Houses of Assembly, and commissioned works on different aspects of the economy. The range of my fieldwork is greater than can be reflected in this study, given the official nature of planning and my emphasis on the central/federal level. For many years I have been concerned with the analysis of change in colonial Nigeria, and that interest has yielded considerable fieldnotes. In drawing on oral sources here, I have focused on the public reaction to planning, the interpretation of development, and on assessing the major development schemes of the period. I located a good number of people who served on the Development Committees mentioned in the study and career civil servants in units concerned with planning. I also located people who lived in areas with major schemes such as oil mills or who were victims or beneficiaries of major schemes such as farm resettlement projects. Many contemporary observers were also interviewed. In locating informants and conducting interviews, I was privileged to direct a talented field staff which was keen on knowing the past and on using my study to reassess themselves and their country.

The idea of writing this book was conceived in Nigeria in the mid-1980s, the research began in Canada, and the writing was completed in the United States. I owe a debt of gratitude to numerous people in these countries. In Canada, my research was facilitated by the support of the University of York by a small grant to undertake a preliminary investigation of available source materials for the project. Sultan L. and Wazir K-F. made Toronto a pleasant place in which to live and work, in addition to assisting me with financial support from their grant made available by the Canadian Social Sciences and Humanities Research Council.

My relocation to Austin, Texas, was facilitated by Professor Brian Levack, the amiable chairperson of the history department, and Professor John Lamphear and his kind wife, Diana. John, Diana, a host of others, notably "awo̱n 'je̱bu gidi" (Samuel Osisanya's family of Norman and Femi Owoseni of IBM), and the clan of Manuel Callahan provided a social network that minimized the boredom of going through over twenty thousand pages of documents and notes. Hugh O'Hear and his wife, both formerly based in Ilorin, Nigeria, offered friendship and intellectual stimulation that sustained my interest in my research. Florence O'Bisi, my wife, and my children, Dolapo, Bisola, and Toyin, were as supportive as ever: without them, nothing would be possible. The library of the University of Texas at Austin is a source of pride, not to mention the outstanding scholars in the University's department of history.

The list for those who assisted in Nigeria is extensive. Many people spent enormous amounts of time with me. I am afraid that many will be annoyed that I have not repaid them by at least mentioning their names here. I must, however, acknowledge the special debt I owe those who facilitated my research, including Labi Adeyemi and Uyilawa Usuanlale of the Nigerian National Commission for Arts and Culture, Abdulahi Maradun of the Arewa Center for Historical Documentation, Dr. Ademola Babalola, Akin Alao, Dr. Femi Akindele, and all my in-laws based in Lagos and Ilawe-Ekiti. In combing the three principal archives, I was privileged to obtain the assistance of my friend and colleague, Yinka Banwo of the University of Ilorin, in addition to many diligent field research assistants and translators. Segun Faleye and Remi Akinade of Ibadan were permanent pillars of support. Other people served as couriers of important research materials at very critical moments: Mama and Baba Joli of Iwo Odo Oba, Dr. Iheanyi Enwerem of the Dominican Institute, Ibadan, Nigeria, Femi (Oko Rose, Baba Ayo) of "Ibadan and Abroad," Dr. Tola Pearce of Awolowo University, Ile-Ife, and my brother, Idowu Falola of Chicago. In my two major research trips to Nigeria, Kayode and Bola Odeleye were excellent hosts, always excited to see me and to provide help. As my "director of research" in Nigeria, this book would not have been completed without the invaluable assistance and support of my long-standing friend, Kayode Odeleye, an engineer by profession and a man of great intellect and warmth.

In the final preparation and revision of the manuscript, I benefited from the generous comments of several prominent scholars, notably Professor John Peel of the School of African and Oriental Studies, University of London, Professor J. B. Webster of Dalhousie University, Halifax, Dr. Jane Guyer, director of the Institute of African Studies, Northwestern University, and Dr. Bola Dauda, director of the Center for the Study of Public Order, University of Leicester, United Kingdom. Two anonymous readers added their encouraging comments. All these scholars have set high standards of intellectual rigor and clarity of exposition from which I have benefited. Felipe Campos of the University of Texas at Austin assisted with computer formatting, at no charge and with a dedication that is worthy of emulation. Many thanks to my friend and student, Joel E. Tishkin, for compiling the index and for assisting with the neverending pile of "housekeeping tasks."

At the University Press of Florida, I have been aided by the skillful ministrations of Dr. Walda Metcalf and her able colleagues for their wise counsel and interest.

Introduction

Since the 1970s, the performance of the sub-Saharan African economy has discredited development planning as a creative invention. Development economics as a discipline also began a swift retreat, as scholars and the general public became both cynical and skeptical about its tools, diagnoses, and prescriptions.[1] Economic planning proved ineffective as the continent experienced growth without development—negative growth, depression, and decay.[2] Since the early 1990s, the possibility that fresh ideas might transform the continent has provided something of a boost, once again, to development planning. Knowledge is in the process of renewal: a few new case studies indicate possible extensions to earlier development policies, while the collapse of the Soviet Union dented the socialist model and called into question ideas based on its ideology. Some theoreticians of development planning are beginning to fight back, by attributing Africa's failure not to their ideas but to the problems of politics and governance.[3]

The Colonial State and Economic Planning

This book is an attempt to focus on an ongoing problem in a totally different manner. It is neither about the current images of decay, decline, and stagnation nor about theoretical reevaluations. It deals with the very beginning of coping with underdevelopment through planning, an important historical phase that has been slighted in most research.

In the last years of colonial rule and the years immediately following independence from European powers, development planning was introduced and became popular as a means to accelerate the rate of economic growth, raise living standards, and reduce dependence on external markets. Officials expected successful planning to lead to a "takeoff,"[4] when a country would become able to generate, from its diversified economy, domestic savings and income for economic growth programs and then be independent from the outside world for capital and manpower. The country would also have possessed all the necessary facilities, institutions, and industries to provide conditions for permanent growth. To reach the takeoff point, all available resources would have to be harnessed through completion of many capital projects; there would also be an honest partnership among all government levels, basic essential services for the entire population, law and order, an expansion of productive machinery in savings, investments, and local industries, an expansion of agriculture for both exports (to earn revenues) and domestic needs, more schools to produce capable workers, more medical services to ensure a healthy and productive population, government support of the private sector, and the acquisition of external capital and skills. In all these, the state could not be neutral or allow things to fall haphazardly into place: it would dominate society by deliberately shaping the economy and its future and by speeding up progress. Justified by the imperatives of development, however, state intervention increasingly developed into political authoritarianism.

Planning is a conscious effort by a state to achieve a number of development objectives at a future date. The significance of planning to Nigeria cannot be overstated. The twin problems of political instability and underdevelopment have engaged the country for the entire twentieth century. Although British colonial rule generated significant changes from the onset, until 1940 Nigeria's colonial government primarily ignored the mobilization of resources for rapid economic transformation and enhancement of living standards for the population. Very limited money was committed to welfare services, and there was little interest in industrialization, research, or production improvement methods.

The British government was of course aware of the need for development. Yet for many years, the Nigerian colonial state did not believe in or pursue the concept of planning as a formal exercise. Indeed, economic planning as theory and practice was criticized in the 1920s and 1930s as a communist device intended to destroy private enterprise and establish political dictatorship. Attitudes changed during and after World War II, when Britain itself became increasingly committed to a welfare state and used planning to ensure economic stability, alleviate poverty, and cope with the limitations of market mechanisms.

The dominant thought on planning at this time was influenced by Keynesian economics, which advocated state intervention to rationalize resource allocation. Changes in economic thought in Britain were dispersed to its colonies. Other significant sources of inspiration for colonial planning included the rise of Britain's Labour Government, with its interest in a welfare state, as well as the cold war, which instigated a search for an antisocialist approach to development.

The idea that there must be a plan to guide economic behavior and governmental activities stimulated an enduring policy of planning in the last years of colonial rule. Concrete experiences were gained from the colonial plans that enabled the newly independent Nigeria to modify those plans, create bigger and perhaps better development institutions, and further understand economic problems.

Notwithstanding the motive that influenced the British to introduce planning in the first place, the Nigerian political elite quickly imbibed the idea in the 1950s and has remained committed to it, if only to gain credibility among the populace. To the Nigerian elite who inherited power from the British, the belief in planning owed its popularity to a variety of factors. First, there was the great lesson offered by the rapid transformations of the Soviet Union and Japan, which many African nationalists and leaders attributed to those countries' conscious planning efforts. Second, the elite believed that, given a shortage of capital, only the state had the ability and resources to mobilize so that the dynamic sectors would be developed. Still on rationale, planning has always been justified by the need to ensure the expansion and correct allocation of resources and promote desired changes.[5] The postindependence African socialist countries have added other reasons such as altering the configurations of social classes and attacking foreign domination.

The colonial state did not have to contend with many of these reasons for economic planning or the multitude of theories that were propounded after the 1950s on development. Nevertheless, the colonial state also had a rationale, theory for, and concept of development planning. The reason for planning was limited to achieving a minimum economic growth in such a way that the objectives of colonial rule were maintained and people's aspirations for change were cleverly controlled to prevent violence and widespread resistance to colonial rule. The theory was to implement planning strategies in the context of a free market regulated primarily by the interests of the state. The colonial state rejected socialist planning, with its centralized and mandatory guidelines. The colonial plans operated within the ideology of a capitalist mixed economy, characterized by the recognition of the political subordination of the colony to an imperial power, the existence of a "static traditional" and modern sectors, and the dualities of private and public investments and of indigenous and foreign enterprises. In such a mixed economy, the state believed that planning would bring rapid social and economic development, correct the structural inadequacies in the economy, and modernize the "static traditional" sector. To the colonial state, development was the progression of Nigeria from a lower, undesirable "traditional" condition to a higher, better, "modern" one similar to industrialized societies in Europe.

The conception of development was based on the prevailing view that the "primitive" society must seek to break the barriers imposed by tradition, expand the market, and increase both the levels of investments and the real per capita income.[6] For a country with a low per capita income (like Nigeria), formal planning must achieve a "big push" or a "critical minimum effort" to propel growth beyond the vicious cycle of poverty. The big push must ensure a massive increase in investments. Capital formation became the key to development: "The central fact of economic development is rapid capital accumulation (including knowledge and skills with capital)."[7] Success would be measured by economic growth in some sectors and the overall gross domestic product (GDP) growth rate. Acceptable rates of investment were discussed. In the 1950s, the United Nations called for an increase from a current level of 5 percent of the national income to a minimum of 10 percent.[8]

Although the colonial state depended on agriculture for the bulk of its revenues until the last years of its rule, various development theoreticians and officers argued that the use of capital accumulation for industrial expansion would propel development. Unlike agriculture, which reinforced traditional values, industrialization would promote changes in traditional values and attitudes, instigate technical progress, increase labor productivity, and transform agriculture with new technology. In the 1950s, the Nigerian power elite in the various regions were concerned about how to bring this industrialization about, either by mobilizing surplus agricultural labor for the industrial sector[9] or by concentrating on one or a few major industries with high growth potential.[10]

The planning models in Nigeria since 1940 fall into three categories, two of which were utilized during colonial rule: the project-by-project approach, integrated planning, and comprehensive planning. The choice of a model is based on the objectives and methods for achieving them. From 1940 to 1955, the colonial state adopted a project-by-project model that was an aggregate of public investment projects unrelated to one another or to any broad policy objectives or priorities. The project-by-project approach tends to plan for an immediate present and fails to develop a vision of the future with any clear economic targets. This model attracted foreign investments over a short period of time and was successful for societies in unstable political environments.

In the last years of colonial rule, the model changed to an integrated approach that comprised a set of individual projects combined into a few sectoral programs that constituted the public sector investment plan. These sectors were transportation, energy, education, and agriculture. As in the project-by-project approach, the state did not relate the sectors to a set of income or production targets.[11]

The early years of planning in Nigeria were marked by optimism and a belief in planning. Those who challenged the validity of the assumptions on planning were ignored. Even the Nigerian power elite who criticized the colonial plans in the 1940s followed a similar orientation in the 1950s, thus accelerating the pace of change with additional funding and projects. The post–World War II period was the golden age of the social sciences (boosted by the New Deal and neoclassical economists, especially John Maynard Keynes's ideas on deficit budgeting), when most people believed that economists had valid answers to the economic problems of the future and could indeed plan to avert those problems.

The prescriptions and assumptions in the early plans (increased trade, enhanced productivity, improved communications, expanded access to education, establishment of local industries, and so on) were among the conditions for the takeoff. To the planners, colonialism itself was regarded as an engine of growth, because it opened the country to the world market, provided training, and stimulated production. In the 1950s, the dominant economic philosophy was that the society would grow rapidly as productive opportunities expanded. The colonial changes of the preceding decades were assumed to have laid much of the necessary groundwork. Independence would empower the Africans to grow along a capitalist path. The country had to aid the rapid growth of domestic and foreign private investments by removing unnecessary government controls and restrictions to the expansion of the market, providing incentives to the local entrepreneurs to behave like rational "economic men," and attracting foreign investments. Many of these ideas were carried forward into the 1960s and beyond.

As a policy instrument, planning has now acquired the negative reputation of running into trouble or of producing insignificant results. With the benefit of hindsight, we are now in a position to affirm that while a development plan can bring about growth in some sectors, it does not necessarily ensure enduring growth or structural transformation. Since the mid-1970s, the concepts and strategies of development that underpinned the earlier plans have been questioned by both the Left and liberal scholars. The Left believes that planning has expanded the reproduction of domination and dependence and intensified the exploitation of the poor. To the liberal scholars, the initial planning exercise achieved little respectable growth, the majority of the population failed to benefit, and the gap between the rich and poor countries widened.

The colonial state was hampered by, for example, its own political and economic objectives, low levels of investment, multiple demands by the people, physical and infrastructural inadequacies, and labor constraints. The colonial plans were able to assess many of the problems of the country, list all the necessary and desirable projects, and lament the poverty of the people. While the colonial state formulated and published the plans, it did not judge itself on the basis of their success or sacrifice its long-standing objectives. Writing in the late 1950s, at a time of great faith in planning, Arthur Lewis, one of the leading theorists of the fast growing and prestigious discipline of development economics, compared a planner to a doctor looking for vulnerable points: "The planner is rather in a position of a doctor who is called upon to make a general medical examination. He has a list of things to look for, which experience has suggested as the most vulnerable points. This list has been compiled on the basis of experience. It has changed from time to time, and now includes items, such as symptoms of cancer and liability to heart attacks which were not included a very short time ago."[12]

This book will examine how the colonial state chose to combat a crisis that was prone to sudden attacks of cancer and heart attacks—to use Lewis's metaphor. In interpreting the plans, however, I do not exonerate the planner, as Lewis did, since we are dealing with a doctor (that is, the colonial state) who was equally as sick as the patient.

Inadequacies of the Literature on Colonial Planning

The subject of colonial planning is submerged in the literature on either economic development or post–World War II changes. The bulk of the literature on both themes, whether original or derivative, relegates colonial planning to the footnotes or at best dismisses it as a gross failure undeserving of scholarly attention. The fact that development planning began at the most intense period of nationalism and decolonization has also tended to divert attention away from it to the more dramatic issues of constitution-making, political party formation, emergence of the first generation of leaders, and power rivalries. Thus, the literature on the last years of colonial rule has focused more on the politics of decolonization.[13]

In addition, no serious attention has been paid to the ideas generated by the discussions on economic planning at the earliest stage, both by the colonial officers and the emerging Nigerian politicians and scholars. This serious omission may result in part from the presentation of planning as a modern phenomenon without any serious historical antecedents. Indeed, the economic history of the end of colonial rule in Nigeria (and in most of Africa) is poorly documented. On the one hand, we have the intensification of colonial exploitation after World War II. On the other hand, there was a climate of reformism, of which development planning was a part and the transfer of power the climax. The details of this curious chemistry, as well as the impact on the state and people, deserve extensive studies, at both micro- and macro-levels. By ignoring the economic history of this period, we ensure an extremely poor understanding of such important elements as a society in transition, the economic basis of political competition, the politics of revenue allocation and their consequences for power politics, economic ideologies, and the foundations of the postcolonial economy.

In the broad context of colonial literature, planning as a theme of study is poorly integrated into the discussion of economic change. The majority of the commissioned works that reported the state of the economy from time to time could not have mentioned planning before 1940 because such a policy had not yet been pursued, while post-1940 studies tended to focus more on aspects that sustained the colonial state. Many of the scholars who wrote about the nature of the colonial economy did so not so much to understand the planning process but to elaborate upon the legitimation and operations of the colonial state. With a few exceptions,[14] the literature on the colonial economy is dominated by a discussion of change in the principal sectors, such as agriculture, transport, and mining, mainly before World War II, and the assessment of change is limited to the extent to which Nigeria was transformed or retarded by British contact.[15]

On the whole, the richness of the literature on colonial Nigeria disguises the obvious: our knowledge of development planning is poor indeed, in spite of its potential contribution to the understanding of the state and development, as well as to the nature of economic and social transition in the last years of colonial rule. The understanding of this transition is a crucial task for modern Nigeria historiography.

In the 1960s (declared by the United Nations as the "Development Decade") and thereafter, economic development became a flourishing academic enterprise, generating a vast amount of literature, as part of a global concern to understand the third world.[16] The scholarly contributions on Africa focus on the new nation-states, with minimal attention to the origins of development planning. Many other studies are overgeneralized or are based on statistical analysis and formal growth models, offering a wide variety of ideas on planning with little regard for history and practical experience.

The few works that show some awareness of previous planning efforts tend to mislead in some way. First, there is a body of literature that briefly dismisses colonial plans because they deem them unimportant.[17] Yet the plans are significant for both colonial economic policy and the country's intellectual history. Second, another body regards them as a "bourgeois exercise" to consolidate imperialism and deliberately underdevelop the country.[18] In the words of one such author, planning was a "sham interest" in welfare to make colonial people forget the ruthless actions of the past and thus make it acceptable to employ further exploitation.[19]

The dependency school, which argues that unjust international trade and external domination constitute the leading obstacles to Africa's development, grew in importance as a mode of analysis after World War II,[20] almost at the same time as development planning was gaining popularity. To the dependency school, colonial (and indeed postcolonial) plans were doomed to fail as long as the continent failed to sever its relations with the West.[21] The a priori dismissal of economic planning's importance may have theoretical merit, but it is no excuse to ignore the details of a major phase in colonial economic history. Finally, there is a body of literature that attributes too much positive impact to the colonial plans. A leading example of this exaggeration is R. O. Ekundare's *Economic History of Nigeria* (1973), a synthesis that regards the plans and other colonial policies as contributing to the rapid growth and development of the country. Ekundare notes that the plans and other colonial policies definitely pushed Nigeria toward the takeoff that it attained ten years after independence, transforming its previous subsistence economy into a sophisticated one.[22] The present study challenges Ekundare's conclusion.

In summary, the idea that the very foundation of the concept and process of conscious economic planning in Nigeria was laid during the colonial period has been largely ignored. When the newly independent country formulated its plan in 1962, it was hailed as the First Plan,[23] in spite of the fact that it was built on the earlier colonial plans of the forties and fifties. The pioneer economists who were interested in development planning also took 1962 as their starting year, because of a mistaken assumption that there was no "national" plan before this date.[24] By ignoring the colonial attempts at development planning after World War II, many extant works on the subject predicate their key assumptions on the following ideas: planning began with independence, intellectual discussions of and interest in development problems are postcolonial, and the colonial economy fell into one homogeneous phase of exploitation from the late nineteenth century to 1960, with few or no reforms. These three impressions, well entrenched in many primary and derivative studies, are misleading. The colonial plans of the 1940s and 1950s provided the intellectual and technical foundations for the plans of independent Nigeria.

Until the oil wealth of the 1970s injected substantial capital into Nigeria and compelled some innovations in planning, the postindependent plans and policies in fact borrowed extensively from the colonial ones. Without attention to these early plans, any effort to understand the post-1960 economy is partial and sometimes calls into question the creativity and ingenuity attributed to the postindependent political elite. Moreover, discussions on the impact of petroleum—the major source of revenue since the late sixties—that fail to recognize the changes in the country's postwar economy have exaggerated either the contributions of oil revenues or the intellectual ideas that have been generated since the oil boom.

The Reevaluation of the Nigerian Economy

This book attempts to rescue colonial plans from oblivion and remedy the lack of historical treatment of the subject of economic planning in Nigeria. It is limited to a twenty-year period, from 1940 to 1960, during which the colonial state initiated planning as part of its economic policy. Acting on instructions from the Colonial Office in London, Nigeria designed its first development plan in 1941, upgraded in 1946 to the Ten-Year Development Plan. The Ten-Year Plan was revised in 1951 to accommodate new demands and respond to the introduction of a federal system of government in the 1950s that was less conducive to central planning. Following the 1953 report by the International Bank for Reconstruction and Development's (IBRD) commission, the "Economic Programme" was approved in 1955. This program, revised after independence in 1960, lasted until 1962 when a new plan was published. In the 1950s, following the transfer of power to the three regional governments, new bodies became active in development efforts; at the same time, there was a plethora of regional plans, reflecting the aspirations of the elite of each region and the recommendations of the IBRD's mission. My primary aim is to analyze and assess the first plan and the subsequent revisions.

I have not set out to present a generalized discussion of either the colonial economy or the economics of decolonization. Rather, my concern is limited to a single aspect of change and economic policy: development planning. In a sense, what I have done is to isolate planning from a broad range of post–World War II colonial economic policies.

While there was a plan designed to cover the entire country, each region also had a plan in the late 1950s. The regional plans are beyond the scope of this book and deserve separate investigations, locating them in a slightly different context of political and bureaucratic indigenization, the rise of a Nigerian power elite, and a competition fueled by aggressive regional self-assertions. The major theme of my presentation, therefore, is the planning conceived and executed by the central government in Lagos, under the supervision of the Colonial Office in London. The central government had the sole responsibility for national planning until 1954 when the revised Constitution imposed decentralization and transferred many responsibilities to the regional governments. Throughout the 1950s, the federal government continued to be involved in planning and played a leading role in a number of sectors, especially the provision of an infrastructure. During most of this period, a portion of the former German Cameroons was administered as part of Nigeria, first as a mandated territory and later as a United Nations trust territory. My analysis is restricted mainly to Nigeria without the Cameroonian portion.

The book is organized into seven chapters. Chapter 1 is a general discussion of the colonial economy up to World War II, with an emphasis on development. Chapter 2 is an explanation of the origins and implementation of development planning in Nigeria in the early years. Chapters 3 and 4 comprise an examination of the first plan, the Ten-Year Colonial Development and Welfare Plan. Its philosophy and performance in the first five years and the early development institutions are examined. Chapter 5 analyzes the Ten-Year Plan, which was revised in 1951 and terminated in 1955. From 1955 to 1960, the federal government formulated its last colonial plan, the Economic Programme, which forms the subject of chapter 6. Chapter 7 summarizes the history of planning over a twenty-year period and reflects on its short- and long-term implications.

CHAPTER ONE

Investment in Colonial Nigeria before World War II

> We have also failed in our duty to promote the economic welfare of the people. There remains their social welfare, and here it is beyond question that lack of funds has sadly retarded progress, and that further expenditure would produce immediate results. It is also, I fear, beyond question that both educational and medical facilities are seriously inadequate to the needs of the people. . . . In the case of education, not only is it impossible to satisfy demands for extended facilities, but the impossibility of fulfilling our obligations in the shape of grants to missions . . . is making it exceedingly difficult for them to obtain properly qualified teachers. On the medical side, not only is there a constant demand for an extension of hospital and dispensary facilities, but there is a staggering annual loss of life and efficiency, caused by a large number of diseases, endemic and epidemic, which experience elsewhere has shown to be susceptible to attack by intensive campaigns of a nature which Nigeria cannot at present afford.
>
> Bernard H. Bourdillon, *Economic Development of Nigeria*

The Colonial Development and Welfare Act of 1940 initiated a sustained policy of economic planning in Nigeria. A long-range plan to achieve an expansion in welfare services, education, and local industries represented a major policy shift during the last two decades of British rule. This chapter will trace the historical antecedents to this important measure. While this period witnessed profound changes, arising from the new administration's policies and Nigerians' quick responses to them, these changes were not achieved because of the adoption of any planning model.

While the colonial state had objectives and ideology that directed these changes, it did not set goals (and how to achieve them) in terms of the rapid development of the country and its people. Many officers were committed to change (as studies on slavery, pawnship, and the judiciary have all revealed) and even to development, but such a focus should not be confused with the concept of development planning. The officers who were opposed to development planning were by no means opposed to development. On the contrary, they believed that development or change would occur without state planning. No one was opposed to investment, at least in those sectors that would aid the colonial objectives, but every form of investment or even of social engineering should not be confused with planning. In what follows, I shall provide a brief synthesis of the colonial economy, analyze the state's attitude toward development, and then conclude by describing the conditions that made possible the changes of the post–World War II era.

The Economy and Society before 1939

The contacts between Nigeria and Britain predated the colonial conquest. From the fifteenth to the nineteenth centuries, Nigeria was involved in both the transatlantic slave trade and the so-called legitimate trade in raw materials. During the late nineteenth century, trade relations gave way to colonial domination. Among the primary objectives of imposing colonial rule were the need to obtain a cheap and constant supply of raw materials for European industries, secure a market for the products of these expanding industries, and create new outlets for investments. The purpose of British rule was thus to initiate a transformation of Nigerian society and its economy in order to meet these objectives.

The Nigerian territorial state evolved piecemeal, beginning with a crown colony in Lagos in 1861, followed by the penetration into the hinterlands in the last quarter of the nineteenth century, the amalgamation of the northern and southern protectorates in 1914, the breakdown of the south into the eastern and western regions in 1939, and the establishment of triregional federalism in the 1950s.[1]

The dominant economic theory that influenced colonial rule before World War II was Adam Smith's laissez-faire. Although Smith believed that a poor colony could borrow from the mother country, he advocated that every colony should manage its own affairs on the basis of its own resources.[2] A colony must be financially independent and strong enough to support its own government. The British taxpayer, the undersecretary of state for colonial affairs said in 1926, should not be called upon to pay for recurrent services in the colonies.[3] Generosity in the form of financial assistance could be extended in emergency cases (for example, earthquake, hurricane, and famine), each to be considered on its own merit. The alternative source of revenue for a colony was loans in the British capital market.

The post–World War I governors, such as Hugh Clifford and Donald Cameron, did not see themselves as "development administrators." To them and to the majority of the colonial officers, the government's role was to ensure conditions favorable to private enterprise, to provide services in the areas of health and communications since the private sector did not have the means to pay for them, to maintain law and order, and to accept existing class structures. As for economic growth or development, there was nothing urgent about it, even if it was desirable in the long run.

With its policy so clearly stated, the colonial mission prior to World War II was to create the basis for limited change through a capitalist ideology and then to reap the rewards by way of surplus extractions. The details of the changes that followed have engaged scholarly attention. After ending the sovereignty of hundreds of kingdoms and chiefdoms, a new administration was established. Whether as a direct or an indirect system of rule, the goal of the administration was to subordinate indigenous authorities to the British officers who derived their legitimacy from conquest, coercion, and racism. Major legislation affecting Nigeria was passed in London, and the country was bound by the treaties concluded and obligations set by the British government.

While the local colonial authorities in Nigeria were allowed to initiate legislation, such action required the approval of the Colonial Office before it could become law. Other notable changes were the introduction of English common law, the doctrine of equity, and the statutes of general application. Local customs and laws were retained if they did not conflict with British-imposed rules. Indigenous authorities were allowed to retain some power in order to serve the ends of policing, collecting revenues, and administering the small units. In 1914, the country was unified politically—the separate colonies of northern and southern Nigeria were amalgamated in order to centralize the colonial administration, facilitate the construction of a countrywide railway, and merge the key elements of the fiscal system in a way that the north would benefit from the ports and the revenues generated in the south, instead of relying on grants from London.

A colonial civil service was introduced to establish a unified bureaucratic system. In order to ensure its own hegemony and achieve its economic goals, the colonial state established an army and police, who worked hand in hand with the civil service and judiciary. Public complaints against the forces were many, but a law-and-order regime was effectively founded. To finance the administration, the colonial state developed a fiscal system that relied on customs duties, loans, and taxation (after 1902 in the north and 1918 in the south).

An infrastructure—roads, railways, and telecommunications—was established to facilitate the mobilization of people and goods. By 1939, a total of 20,990 miles of roads (mainly dirt), had been built to connect production centers with the railways and administrative centers. A rail system begun in 1898 with a sixty-mile route reached its peak of 1,903 miles in the 1940s. Postal and telegraph services were established with post offices first in the south and later in other parts of the country. In addition, as part of the primary measures to create a colonial economy, a new currency was introduced, as well as commercial banking from 1891.

The consequences of these measures were many, as different studies have already indicated. Combined with the activities of the Christian missions that had embarked upon a policy of vigorous penetration and conversion by the mid-nineteenth century, colonialism produced a new elite with formal education and exposure to many aspects of Western culture. The faults of the missionary and colonial education system were in its denial of the history and culture of the people, its emphasis on a limited number of disciplines, and its slow production of the educated workers necessary for development. Western education, in spite of its limitations, became part of the aspirations of Nigerians who sought new opportunities in the modernizing sector of society and who desired key political positions.

A system of wage labor was also introduced, gradually replacing older forms like slavery and pawnship, and became the major way to recruit workers into the modern economy and bureaucracy. The colonial state attempted to control the radicalization and protests of this labor force through regulations and the use of its security forces. To those who were able to earn a cash income, wage labor was attractive. Their lifestyles encouraged many to emulate them in tastes, language, and migration to the towns where "modern" jobs were available. Each time they demanded a better welfare system, wage earners increasingly became a sharp nuisance to the colonial administration. With their migrants and an army of job seekers, the towns and cities offered opportunities to make demands for change and to express anticolonial feelings.

The backbone of the colonial economy was agricultural production. Agricultural work was performed by small-scale cultivators who relied on their ancient methods and tools, not by any foreign-dominated plantations or settlers as in the case of other colonies in east and southern Africa. The state blocked European entrepreneurs' efforts to take land. The production of export crops was assured by Nigerians' desire for imported items and for education of children, by pressure by the state, taxation, price incentives, and provision of an infrastructure.

Colonial export-oriented agriculture was a success story, as virtually all the desired crops—palm products, cocoa, cotton, rubber, groundnuts—did well as key items of trade. According to G. K. Helleiner, by 1929 the value of exports had increased sevenfold, export volume by fivefold, and export production accounted for 5 to 7 percent of gross domestic product (GDP).[4] Mineral production was important, too, including tin in the Plateau (central Nigeria) and coal in Enugu in the east. Mining was lucrative, controlled by the government (in the case of coal) and big business.[5]

By 1940, the colonial economy and society had reached a high degree of maturity. The economy grew rapidly, though without any policy of formal long-range planning and in spite of the decline during World War I and the depression of the early 1930s. In the first two decades of colonial rule, capital was injected into the colonial economy to develop ports and railways and to open mines. Retail companies were expanding their operations. Attractive prices were also paid for raw materials. All of this fostered change and exploitation of people and resources. Indeed, most sectors of the economy underwent twenty years of steady growth, with contributions mainly from the peasants in production, private enterprise in distribution, and the government in public finance.

With roads, railways, currency, banks, schools, civil service, and police—some of the visible signs of the new era—there were already elements of a new economy and the conditions for future change. R. O. Ekundare summarizes the growth rate up to 1945:

> The railway mileage increased from 124 in 1905 to 1,903 in 1945. . . Mileage of roads maintained by the Public Works Department . . . increased from 2,800 in 1925 to 6,225 in 1945. . . . Population increased from an estimated 16.8 million in 1900 to 27.4 million in 1945. The value of total foreign trade also increased from £3.9 million (4s. per head) in 1900, to £35.2 million (£1 6s. per head) in 1945. The total value of imports increased from £1.9 million (2s. per head) in 1900 to £15.9 million (10s. 6d. per head) in 1945. Similarly, the total value of exports increased from £2 million (2s. per head) to £19 million (15s. per head) in 1945. The Nigerian government revenue also increased from £2.7 million in 1900 to £13.2 million in 1945.[6]

These changes notwithstanding, the economic signs for the 1930s and beyond were troubling. First, while Ekundare and Helleiner are right about the considerable changes and the growth indicators, these meant little in relative terms for the majority of Nigerians. Most areas remained rural, lacking in all the modern indicators of progress. Every social service was inadequate. The colonial state ignored all issues unrelated to its objectives, even if they were important to the people. For instance, industrialization received practically no attention—from the very beginning, the government had no desire to support industrial modernization. Neither were foreign investors interested in industries, since trade and transport businesses were quite lucrative. By 1940, under the colonial state the extent of industrialization was limited to a small number of cotton ginneries and sawmills, a cigarette factory in the west, and a few soap factories in the east.

As another example, through a discriminatory policy of granting licenses, leases, and location sites, the state was less active in promoting indigenous entrepreneurship. The state failed to grant loans to emerging local groups, instead favoring foreign investors. As a consequence, the influence and power of foreign capital became heavily entrenched in this period—foreigners came to dominate the commanding heights of the colonial economy and, with the support of the state, they won huge and generous leases, as well as sole rights to import and distribute consumer products. They also benefited from tax breaks and state patronage.

Second, public revenues and expenditures were both inconstant and somewhat unpredictable, as both fluctuated with the fortunes of the economy. From 1918 to 1939, little capital was injected, and there was a constant outflow of profits. The bulk of the revenues was from customs and excise duties. For instance, the post–World War I boom in exports ended in 1921, rose again in 1927–28, and fell from 1929 to 1934. Revenues were small to begin with and diminished further in the depression years. Expenditures rose and fell, depending on the amount of revenues. The budgetary allocations for so-called development schemes were too limited. The budgets were balanced at a very low level, since surpluses were uncommon. In the words of I. Nicolson, this was an "administration on a shoe-string,"[7] and in the 1930s it had to cope with the problems of penury.[8] This dismal financial status affected all levels of the economy and social services. The number of administrative personnel was inadequate and, with some budgetary cuts in the 1930s, there was little money committed to future development.

The government resorted to external borrowing, which had major consequences for the economy and public revenue. Public revenues had to cover the service charge on loans; in 1934, the percentage of debt charges was 19.1 percent of the total export proceeds. In relation to overall annual public revenues, the percentage of debt charge was as high as 32.8 percent in 1934 and 26.9 percent in 1935.[9]

On the eve of World War II, the country had acquired a huge debt of £24,764,599,[10] paying an annual interest of 4.7 percent on outstanding loans, in addition to existing loan charges of 25 percent of its revenue.[11] Worried by this debt, the governor remarked to the Legislative Council in 1939 that his government had borrowed to the limit of its capacity, without local capital to rely on. With a per capita revenue of 5s. 11d., Nigeria was the poorest country in British West Africa and had few resources available for development. The governor noted that the country was in a vicious circle from which it could not emerge without spending more money on development services, but the needed money would not be available until the country was developed. Nigeria was not in a position to expand, progress, or even stand still.[12]

Third, foreigners dominated the economy, as control of the leading sectors was held by Europeans and Lebanese. The exploitation of the country's mineral resources was entirely in private hands. It is true that foreign companies contributed to the circulation of new currency and expanded the market, but their interest was limited to investments in trade, transport, and mining—investments that offered immediate profits. Moreover, those profits in large part left the country. There were few indigenous entrepreneurs with the capital and facilities to contribute to rapid development. By and large, Nigerians occupied the lowest place in the economic and social hierarchy, working, for example, as petty traders, low-wage earners, mine laborers, and small-scale producers of cash crops.

External dependency was yet another drawback. As the case of World War I demonstrated, political and economic upheavals in Europe brought hardships, scarcity, and revenue reductions.[13] The economy was also hard-hit by the depression of 1929–32 when prices fell, export trade deteriorated, living standards declined, revenues diminished, and export and import duties were raised.[14] The colonial administrators, who had always opposed development projects, were able to use the effects of the depression to support their argument that a colony with an unpredictable revenue base should only live from hand to mouth.[15]

Producers and traders, who suffered from the market contraction during the depression, were forced to adjust to lower living standards; they complained about and criticized the government and resented the foreign firms. Their protests were joined by the wage earners, who condemned the arrogance of their white superiors and demanded higher wages. The survival strategies adopted by foreign firms (cutbacks in the number of retail stores and combining to prevent unnecessary competition) generated further resentment from their indigenous rivals who blamed foreigners for failing to halt the decline in trade and for controlling the largest share of the market. The official response was to "wait and see," in the hope that time, never a scarce commodity in these early years, would end all problems.

There were other disturbing economic tendencies. Development was uneven among the regions and even within each province. New services were concentrated either in the administrative centers or in those areas where raw materials were available. Other locales suffered neglect, and many of their people chose to migrate in search of a better income. For people in areas with exploitable resources, the quality and quantity of services they received depended on the exportable worth of their crops or minerals. The implication of this was the segmentation of society between the city and village and between areas with resources and those without. Lack of uniformity would become a factor in future discord. Since each product was transported abroad from a production enclave, building an integrated national economy for the benefit of all was difficult. In any case, the infrastructure to service the economy was designed for the export sector, not for domestic needs. Neither was the majority of producers able to earn much with their small farms and limited capital.

The state did not pursue a program of extensive creation and expansion of social and economic services. This attitude was reflected in its annual expenditures. For instance, in the 1938–39 fiscal year, 55.9 percent went to administrative services, 22.9 percent to social services, and 18.5 percent to economic services.[16] The nonadministrative expenses concentrated on the maintenance of the infrastructure and offices concerned with facilitating the export trade. Indeed, in 1939 the colonial government claimed that it did not have much money for social services, research, industries, and programs that would promote welfare and development.[17]

Although revenues from agriculture were substantial, the colonial government invested little in this area and showed even less commitment to the producers by way of land improvement or introduction of better farming techniques and management. By focusing attention on the devastation caused by famine in northern Nigeria, Michael Watts's *Silent Violence* demonstrates the failure of agriculture and government policies.[18] In 1939, at least six provinces were without any agriculture officer, the Co-operative Societies were performing poorly, and the Forestry and Veterinary Departments were not making any important progress.[19] In spite of its poor record, however, "development" was part of the vocabulary of the colonial state well before World War II. The missing element was "planning."

"Undeveloped Estates" and "Imperial Assistance": Economic Ideology before 1929

The colonial state occasionally claimed that one of its goals was to develop Nigeria. Contrary to this declaration, the actual goals of the state were to extend and consolidate its hegemony, maintain political stability and order, exploit the colony, and integrate it into an external economy. For many years, development planning was not one of the aims of the state.

There are four phases in the evolution of modern Nigerian economic development: 1860–1895, 1895–1929, 1929–40, and 1940–60. In the first phase, from the British occupation of Lagos in 1860 to the extension of Britain's power in 1900, social and economic expenditures received no consideration. Initially, the economic basis of the administration was very narrow, confined mainly to the revenues from customs duties. Expenditures on administration consumed the bulk of the resources, almost 50 percent of total revenues. The philosophy of Adam Smith reigned supreme: "Laissez faire ruled in every colony, however slender its resources."[20]

The second phase, from 1895 to 1929, was associated with Joseph Chamberlain's doctrine of investing in the colonies for the benefit of Britain. On August 22, 1895, Chamberlain, the influential Colonial Secretary, broadened colonial economic policy when he declared that: "I regard many of our colonies as being in the condition of undeveloped estates, and estates which can never be developed without imperial assistance. . . . I shall be prepared to consider . . . any case which may occur in which, by the judicious investment of British money, those estates which belong to the British Crown may be developed for the benefit of their population and for the benefit of the greater population which is outside."[21] Chamberlain admitted that some colonies had seen no progress over a period of a hundred years: "British rule has done absolutely nothing, and if we left them today we should leave them in the same condition as that in which we found them." His solution was to aid the development of a colony as a state enterprise in a way beneficial to it and to Britain, without, in the words of a distinguished apologist of the British Empire, creating "pest-holes."[22] Assistance should be rendered and aids approved in cases of need, but all must be carefully considered to assist development.

Some scholars have praised Chamberlain for his policy of accepting responsibility for the development of the colonies.[23] He is credited with introducing the doctrine of "imperial responsibility," that is, of using money raised in Britain for development projects abroad. As subsequent events would show, however, the intention was actually to fulfill the colonial objectives of developing agriculture for export. In Chamberlain's doctrine, the colonies would rely on loans and taxes, railways to open up the hinterland, systems of land tenure that would make land available to those who needed it, and the farmers persuaded or forced to produce. As Chamberlain himself conceived it, the best customers of the British were in their colonies, and the government had to do its best "not to kill the goose that lays the golden eggs."[24] What he advocated was not charity; he expected investment abroad to yield great returns.

The first concrete manifestations of Chamberlain's policy were the construction of the railway from Lagos to the hinterland and the improvement of the Lagos port, both financed with external loans. The motive was to facilitate the movement of goods to the ports for transportation to Europe. The Colonial Loans Act, passed in 1896, encouraged the use of loans for measures that would enhance the export trade in a relatively short period, although only a total of £1.4 million was provided to all the colonies over the period from 1896 to 1916.

In his celebrated book, *The Dual Mandate in British Tropical Africa,* Lord Frederick John Dealtry Lugard, Nigeria's first governor-general (1914–19), restated the goal of the colonial economy much more clearly and forcefully after World War I: Britain should govern well and promote the development of its subject people, in an arrangement beneficial to both. Europeans would use African products that "lay wasted and ungarnered" in return for providing manufactured goods and "the substitution of law and order for . . . barbarism." Both in theory and practice, however, the economic interest of Britain took priority over the philanthropic.

Most of the economic and social changes associated with colonialism were pursued in the spirit of this so-called dual mandate. While the motive was restrictive, there were incidental gains to Nigerians—paid for by their labor, taxes, and profits—such as roads and railways that passed through their villages and towns and a limited number of schools, dispensaries, and hospitals mainly in the administrative centers. As much as possible, recurrent expenditures on social and welfare services were kept to a minimum.[25] If the situation was poor in the colonies, to the extent that they could not meet their public debt, social services was the first item to get cut from the budget. Thereafter, the country had to seek financial assistance from abroad. While the most generous assistance would be grants-in-aid, these were in general difficult to obtain.[26]

The Colonial Office popularized the option of loans in the British capital market. The regulations implemented through the Colonial Stock Acts of 1877–1900 made loan acquisitions dependent on the repayment capabilities of a colony.[27] There was a restrictive principle guiding loan approval: poor colonies were denied because of the difficulties of debt servicing and repayment while potentially wealthy ones like Nigeria were considered undeserving because they should be able to generate adequate internal revenues. A 1925 proposal that the British government should assist the colonies with interest payments in the first five years of the loan was rejected. It was not that the colonies did not have access to loans after demonstrating that they were qualified, but the interest rates increased by 1-3 percent after World War I, and the money had to be spent on sectors that promoted colonial interests, such as railway construction.

Nigeria had utilized loans and grants since the late nineteenth century, but in general its people benefited little from them.[28] According to a governor with firsthand experience, the external assistance was not aimed at development but at countering the unavoidable deficiencies in revenues and balancing the budget. The governor stated:

> Colonies in receipt of such assistance were regarded as poor relations who could not, in all decency, be allowed to starve, but whose first duty was to earn a bare subsistence and to relieve their reluctant benefactor of what was regarded as a wholly unprofitable obligation. While they were in receipt of a dole, their finances were subject to a strict Treasury control, which, since its main objects were to ensure that the receipt of the dole did not encourage overindulgence and that a position of financial independence was attained as soon as possible, was scarcely conducive to a forward policy of development. The doctrine of individual self-sufficiency held undisputed sway. It was regarded as the first and most important duty of every colony to attain equilibrium between local revenue and local expenditure as early as possible, and having attained it, to maintain it.[29]

"Undeveloped Estates" and "Imperial Assistance": The Colonial Development Fund, 1929–1939

The first step to embark upon formal planning may have been the Colonial Development Act (CDA) of 1929, which begins the third phase of my periodization of the history of economic development. The CDA provided grants or loans from imperial funds to the colonies and protectorates for the purpose of developing agriculture and industry and thereby promoting commerce with Great Britain. Before the CDA, although assistance for specific development projects (like railway construction) was provided by guaranteed loans or otherwise, there was no act to allow a colony to obtain funds to pursue any active policy of development or to expand services beyond the limits of its local revenues. The methods intended to achieve the purpose of the CDA included

> the promotion of scientific research, instruction and experiments in the science, methods, and practice of agriculture and industry, and the organization of cooperation and instruction in the growing and marketing of produce; encouraging the adoption of improved machinery and equipment for cultivation; the improvement of internal transport and communications; harbors; fisheries; forestry; surveys; drainage and irrigation; water supplies and water power; the production, distribution and supply of electricity; promoting the development of mineral resources; and the promotion of public health.[30]

The Colonial Development Act's background was not unconnected with the search for solutions to the problems of the depression in Britain. The Labour Party, which assumed power in 1929, enacted the CDA in July of that year to authorize the British government to spend annually a sum of £1 million to aid agriculture and industries in the colonies in order to promote commerce with, and relieve economic depression in, the United Kingdom.[31] The act sought measures to improve trade relations between the colonies and their mother country with the expectation that this would stimulate aggregate demands at home and increase revenues and consumption of manufactured goods abroad. Although the CDA was couched in the philanthropic language of developing the colonies, the aim was articulated as seeking a solution to the unemployment problem in Britain[32] rather than as a serious commitment to helping the colonies, as some have interpreted it.[33]

All the colonies were encouraged to submit proposals for projects that required financial assistance from the Colonial Office. The projects were to promote purchasing power in the colony "to the general benefit of the trade of the Empire."[34] Large projects could only be financed by loans from the fund, but only a few applications were approved because of the need to avoid the burden of interest and repayment charges. Small projects for schemes of public health and research that required small capital outlay were favored. Applications were allowed on a continuous basis; a colony must wait for opportunities and avoid getting discouraged by previous failures. Twice a year, a colony had to submit progress reports in connection with all works undertaken with the assistance.

Although it was not enthusiastic in applying for assistance for reasons that are explained below, Lagos discussed a number of possible projects including infrastructure, agriculture, and public health facilities. Heads of departments responded with long lists of projects needing funding with loans and grants, but the governor rejected most of them. All the applications by individuals and private companies were also rejected.[35]

No funding priorities were stated, but the railway and public health took precedence, judging by the extent of discussions on both issues and by the various applications for assistance.[36] By 1932, Lagos had decided on the items it would support (table 1.1) and a limited amount of funding was obtained. In 1935, the government described the promotion of public health as its best achievement under the 1929 CDA. The Nigerian government applied for a substantial free grant of £107,300 in September 1930 to fund public health initiatives, including establishing training schools for midwives and sanitary inspectors, improving dispensaries, undertaking research, purchasing ambulances, and building a leper colony and a mental hospital. While the Colonial Office was interested in health and encouraged the application, it was unwilling to recommend any amount exceeding £55,000 and that only with the condition that the Nigerian government would undertake to meet the remaining expenditure from its own resources.[37]

Inevitably, most of the public health projects were abandoned because they involved heavy annual recurrent expenditures in addition to other expenses such as staff accommodations. Projects that received attention during the 1930s are listed in table 1.1. A few training facilities for indigenous public health personnel were added. Three maternity centers were built in southern Nigeria (at Ilorin and Aba in 1935 and at Calabar in 1936). In April 1935, training centers for sanitary inspectors opened at Ibadan in the southwest and Kano in the north, both with a capacity of forty-six students. Ten ambulances were purchased, but the distances to be covered were so long that they were of limited use to anyone in an emergency. In the Benin province, a leper colony was maintained with 187 patients. Part of the grant was also used both to purchase health propaganda films to teach basic hygiene and to conduct investigations on food deficiencies and toxins. Research work on sleeping sickness did not begin until 1937, with the object of controlling it in the northern provinces through improved treatment and a special control service to prevent infection. In 1939, the sleeping sickness teams examined and treated many cases in different dispensaries.[38]

The public health schemes included divergent aspects of medical work, such as providing maternity training centers, dispensaries, ambulances, leper

Table 1.1. Expenditures for assisted schemes (in £)

Schemes	*1930–31*	*1931–32*	*1933–34*	*1934–35*	*1935–36*
Railways	18,422	10,500	21,721	13,100	16,300
Veterinary scholarships	105	885	338	126	190
Nutrition research	1,969	917	747	—	317
Tsetse fly research	1,075	—	—	424	—
Maternity training centers	—	11	2,876	4,694	—
Training centers for sanitary inspectors	—	—	5,455	1,219	—
Dispensaries for NAs	—	3,515	4,652	32	135
Ambulances (10)	—	—	4,626	—	—
Leprosy settlements	—	3,000	3,000	—	—
Research on schistosmiasis and guinea worm	—	88	426	1,534	—
Sanitary improvements	—	478	2,469	759	277

Source: NAI, CDF, General Papers, Estimates, vols. 3–4.

relief, and schistosomiasis and guinea-worm research. A few people were trained, and medical facilities spread to a few locations. The dispensaries and maternity centers were popular.[39] None of the facilities was adequate for its locale, and the majority of the population had no access to facilities of any type.

The relaying of the 98.5 miles of 45-pound track with 60-pound rails between Minna and Kaduna was part of the subsequent relaying of all the northern lines. The Minna-Kaduna line was the busiest section of the line in the north and the most useful for trade in kola, groundnuts, cotton, hides, and skins. The project was economically viable, especially as the aim was to increase the trade in groundnuts by improving the railway system. The project was completed in 1935.[40]

By the time the CDA was terminated in 1940, Nigeria accomplished very little. True to its primary goal, the loan money was spent on a limited number of projects (table 1.2). Of the £330,000 received, the sum of £114,450 (or 34.7 percent) was granted to pay the interest on loans for the construction of the Minna-Kaduna railway, £51,000 funded the organization of ground facilities for air services, and £95,000 facilitated research and treatment of sleeping sickness. Agriculture received £3,400 to encourage mixed crop farming and another £1,500 on tsetse fly research, while the rest went for other small expenses. The CDA made no funds available for general education. It minimized recurrent expenditures and ensured that assistance from other sources was sought and used before its own funds were spent.[41]

The 1929 Colonial Development Act failed to fulfill most of its goals. From the very start, the loan program was doomed. A sum of £1 million per year for ten colonies was a miniscule amount, both for the advantages that were anticipated for the "mother country" and the changes expected in the colonies. What each colony received was small, as every annual report on the fund clearly indicates.[42] The assistance per person was small, too, less than two shillings. The annual disbursement was slow because of the complicated application procedure.[43] By 1940, total allocations fell short of the £1 million per year, as all the colonies combined received only £8.8 million. Of this amount, loans totalled £3.2 million and grants £5.7 million.[44] Nigeria received less than half a million (£330,000) over a period of ten years. The fund was distributed so sparsely that it produced little or no significant result in the colonies.

Even if it had been possible for Nigeria to request more money, such a request would not have made much economic sense because the country would have been further encumbered with loans. Assistance from the fund was either by grants or loans to meet the cost of a specific project or grants or loans to defray the interest on a loan.[45] Only loans could be obtained to finance large undertakings. Loans were intended to assist a colony in defraying either in whole

Table 1.2. Grants to 1938

Completed schemes	*Grant type*	*Amount received (£)*
Nutrition research	Full cost	3,543
Tsetse fly research	Full cost	1,500
Public health improvement	5/6ths of total expenditure	40,057
Air Services	Half the expenditure on the Ground Organisation of Aerodromes (up to £51,000)	51,000
Uncompleted schemes		
Veterinary scholarships	Nigeria's contribution was double the grant	1,926
Agricultural scholarships	Nigeria's contribution was double the grant	2,002
Ilorin Stock Farm	£3,400 on condition that the recurrent cost of the scheme was met by Nigeria	2,538
Sleeping Sickness Service	Funding up to £19,000 a year for five years provided Nigeria supplied the balance under the scheme of £11,000 per annum	7,500

Source: NAI, CDF, General Papers, Estimates, vol. 4.

or part interest payable during the first ten years of the debt. The reason for using the fund provided by the CDA was to encourage a colony to borrow on its own credit in open markets wherever possible. As the burden of public debt was already heavy by the 1930s, the Nigerian government wisely reckoned that it made no sense to obtain loans either for new projects or to finance old debts.

In 1930, Lagos declined the offer of a loan to finance projects for bridges and houses in the city and for the Lafia-Chad railway. In rejecting this loan, Sir Graeme Thomson, the governor of Nigeria (1925–31), provided persuasive reasoning. While pointing out that straightforward donations would be of the greatest benefit, he questioned whether the guarantee of interest on a short-term loan was of any service, since it introduced an unwanted element of speculation. There was no assurance that the country would be in a position, after five years, to be able to pay the interest on the loan, since its revenues depended on both general trade prosperity and a number of local factors that were unpredictable.[46] Since the country was careful not to enter into more debts, the fund was not useful in financing large projects.

The Nigerian secretariat was also careful to avoid making any application that would ignore the interest of the "mother country." When Sitterbert Herbert Pearse, representing the Egba division in the Legislative Council, proposed that the government should apply for a free grant "(following the precedence of Sierra Leone) for street drainage and for clearing and deepening the rivulets leading into the Ogun River," the chief secretary said that this was impossible because the projects would not promote industry and relieve unemployment in Britain.[47]

In an attempt to use the fund for smaller undertakings, Nigeria realized early that this was difficult, again because of the administration of the CDA. Sir Bernard Bourdillon, the governor from 1935 to 1943, who was more critical of the 1929 CDA than his predecessor, narrated his experience with respect to the fund and small undertakings. In September 1930, the CDA Advisory Committee in Britain, while considering Nigeria's application for a grant to meet the capital cost of specific health projects, insisted that "in all projects of this nature, the Colonial Government concerned should, wherever possible, be required to bear a reasonable proportion of the cost involved." The committee therefore decided to provide only 65 percent of the capital cost of the seven approved projects, insisting that Nigeria provide the remaining expenditure from its own resources and complete the funding and all the seven projects. Incidentally, the schemes involved the country in quite considerable additional recurrent expenditures. Due to the fact that the country was in a difficult position, it decided to accept the aid. Hoping to save money, one of the projects' budgets was reduced by two-thirds, but the grant was quickly reduced proportionately.

Governor Bourdillon provided another example. In 1937, he applied for a grant of £30,000 per year for five years to cover the cost of an important anti–sleeping sickness project. The CDA Advisory Committee allowed him to appear before it and took the view that £11,000 of the £30,000 represented the cost not of new services but of an extension of existing services and was not a proper charge on the fund. The Committee agreed to provide £11,000, even though the governor pointed out that this would involve the curtailment of other necessary health measures. The governor had to cut all expenditures to the bone and reduce the amount of allocations to health measures.[48]

In addition, Bourdillon had other problems with the CDA funds. As he explained, the problem was in the administration of the CDA funds, which was simply an attempt to tackle a severe problem without a decision on broad policy goals. With the 1929 Colonial Development Act, the British government in effect communicated that "it [was] about time we did something to develop the colonies; we ought at the same time to be able to increase our own exports and give some relief to unemployment; let us give them a million a year and see that as much of it as possible comes back to this country." To the governor, casual assistance would not produce any satisfactory progress while the doctrine of individual self-sufficiency was retained. The interest of the Colonial Office was not in development of the colonies but in the restoration, maintenance, or attainment of an equilibrium between local revenues and local expenditures.[49]

Since colonial policy remained unchanged, the instructions on how to spend the fund tended to be restrictive. The administration of the fund followed the principle that a colony should enjoy the services that it could maintain with its own resources.[50] Small-scale public health projects such as improvements in drainage and water supplies and the erection of hospital buildings and laborers' dwellings were preferred to any undertaking that would consume money on a continuous basis. The Colonial Office was also interested in surveys of roads and railways. Of course, public health and infrastructures were projects that had been part of the general colonial program before 1929 because of a belief that they enhanced the production of export crops and the purchasing power of a healthy population.

In 1941 when the 1929 CDA was terminated, the Colonial Office admitted that the Act had been limited by its inability to allocate money to schemes of a capital nature, and this in turn hampered the material development of the colonies.[51] Until the beginning of World War II, development planning was still an insignificant aspect of colonial policy. The Colonial Development Act of 1929 achieved very little in its eleven years. The orientation was not toward welfare. The colonial officers were committed to their narrow objective of promoting exports, although they too complained that the fund provided under the CDA was inadequate to meet the gargantuan problems of underdevelopment. In general, the 1930s witnessed little progress in social and economic services. The combined sector of agriculture, veterinary, and forestry saw a drop in annual expenditure from £427,000 to £388,000; that of communications dropped from £161,000 to £139,000; and public works dropped by almost 50 percent, while the slight increase in education and public health was accounted for by spending on a sleeping-sickness project. Using the figures for 1938–39, the expenditure per person was 4s. 8d., an amount too small to achieve any development of substance.

The senior administrators in Lagos placed the blame for low performance on the constricted budget and called for external assistance.[52] Bourdillon, who put more emphasis on development, demanded a "radical change of policy" to abandon the doctrine of self-sufficiency.[53] As far as the governor was concerned, Nigeria was a poor country, spending the bulk of its income on public debt service, the military, pensions and gratuities, administration, and the maintenance of internal security, but little on social services. Contrary to popular opinion, the country benefited little from external financing.

By 1936, total investment was £75 million, 46 percent of which was public capital on which the Nigerian government had to pay full interest. This was a small amount for a country of 20 million people; none of it was expended directly on improving the quantity or quality of produce. All of the capital was spent on communications and the organization necessary to transport produce to the world market. Concerning external financing, the governor recorded the "actual amount of the concrete financial assistance," which a policy of self-sufficiency had allowed the British Treasury to give to Nigeria: The total sum (including grants-in-aid, grants from the 1929 CDA, and an appropriation to compensate the Niger Company) was approximately £6 million (included as part of the £75 million mentioned above). In his frank conclusion, the governor remarked that Britain had received full value for its investments in Nigeria by way of trade and payments to its officers:

> Of nearly £2,000,000 which is paid every year to British officials and ex-officials by the Nigerian Government, less than half is received in Nigeria, and even of that a good proportion is spent on imported goods. In the year 1937–38 a sum of £1,876,336 was paid to European officials by way of salaries, personal allowances, gratuities and pensions. Of this amount no less than £1,067,050 was paid in the United Kingdom, in the shape of pensions, family allotments, and leave pay. Some of this is used to finance the importation of goods by officials; nevertheless the transactions unmistakably represent invisible exports from Great Britain to Nigeria of something in the neighborhood of a million pounds a year. In addition, the Nigerian Government pays over £100,000 a year to a British Shipping Company on account of the passage of British officials and their wives.[54]

In the late 1930s, the officers in Nigeria were already convinced that paying attention to welfare and the development of the country was in the best interest of Britain because it would increase the supply of raw materials and expand the market for British manufactured products. The thesis was a simple one: if production was increased, the people's purchasing power would increase, with a corresponding increase in the demand for imports. To increase both production and purchasing power, however, Britain must invest in "developmental services."

To conclude on the development trend by about 1939: for the country to move forward, the inflow of capital must exceed the outflow. To maintain an equilibrium, the flows must be equal. From 1900 to 1914 there was evidence of prosperity in that there was more inflow than outflow of capital. The political scene was quiet while Nigerians were, perhaps, traumatized by conquest, although some derived benefits from the initial colonial investment. From 1914 to 1939, there was a steady capital outflow, and benefits were not spreading fast enough to the majority of the population. Thus, Nigerian politics began to focus more on demands for change.

The Pressure for Progress

Both internal and external pressure paved the way for the reforms inaugurated during and after World War II. From the very beginning, the imposition of colonial power was resisted. When the administration unfolded its programs, protest changed to grievances on specific policies and demands for reforms. Colonial rule had produced a category of wage laborers who, conditioned by their working environments, salary, and knowledge about the outside world, became increasingly restless and radical. The workers began to demand better pay, faster social change, and a role in the government. They were joined by a number of educated people who were eager to penetrate the colonial administrative system. Indigenous entrepreneurs were not left out. The increase in capital accumulation by some entrepreneurs, and the desire to expand their activities and secure better access to trade, sometimes in competition with the expatriate firms, encouraged them to seek reforms in the colonial system.

There were broadbased demands beyond the narrow interest of vested groups. More people began to seek wage employment in the urban areas and thus wanted the system to open up. In general, there were requests for more social services in health and education. Based on their knowledge of export revenues, some articulate citizens were even calling for wealth redistribution.

Much more widespread than these protests was a concept of progress that had been advanced by the educated elite since the nineteenth century. Missionary education had produced an intelligentsia that had occupied a prominent role in the country's history since the mid-nineteenth century.[55] With an initial interest focused on trade, the civil service, and the church, the role of the intelligentsia broadened during the colonial period to embrace such other spheres as politics and professions like law and medicine.

As I mention in a later chapter, this intelligentsia also provided some answers to the underdevelopment problem. During 1940–60, they were critical of some of the economic policies of the colonial state. On the one hand, the intelligentsia spoke for itself, advocating its desires as members of a middle class in the process of formation. On the other hand, it saw itself as an intermediary between the colonial state and Nigerians—for instance, between the farmers and the foreign firms or between taxpayers and tax spenders. In the late nineteenth century, the elite were worried about the gradual disappearance of African "merchant princes" (like King Jaja of Opobo and Madame Tinubu of Lagos) because the British encouraged foreign firms like the Royal Niger Company to flourish; they were also displeased with the initial takeover of some land by the government because they thought that the survival of Nigerians depended on farming. Early in the twentieth century, the focus of protest changed to empowerment, protection of small-time traders, and economic equality between the races.[56]

The grievances of the intelligentsia inspired the formation of political parties with broad objectives.[57] Acting on the premise that the country belonged to them, and that they were qualified to represent the uneducated people and serve in the administration, the elite demanded reforms. As the literature on protest and nationalism has pointed out, the elite received additional support from the Pan-Africanist activities of blacks in the United States. Initially, protest was organized on the basis of opposition to certain policies, such as the 1895 demonstration against taxation in Lagos, against land expropriation and increased water rates in 1908, and against land control in southern Nigeria in 1912. In these demonstrations, the elite used the press as a major ally.

In 1913, a short-lived umbrella organization, the National Congress of British West Africa, was conceived, although it did not hold its first meeting until 1920. The Congress was ambitious in its demands, calling for such things as a West African Dominion, a university, better general education, and health services. While the concern in the 1920s was to use constitutional means to achieve reforms, there were significant changes by the 1930s. The youth movements and political parties of the 1930s demanded more power, sought to involve several segments of society, and reached out to those in the rural areas.

The most successful of the movements was the Nigerian Youth Movement. Founded in Lagos in 1934, it involved such future leaders as Obafemi Awolowo and Nnamdi Azikiwe, a combative press including the *Daily Service* and the *West African Pilot,* and a vision that was radical and hostile to British rule.

The interactions between the colonial state and its critics had become predictable by the 1930s: the state granted only a limited number of concessions without compromising the core of its policies. To the officers, the colonial economy would continue to exist as it was, while political independence was not in sight. However, some events in the same decade began to indicate the necessity of change for both groups. The grievances of Nigerians began to focus on such issues as favoritism to foreign firms, demands for welfare and social services, and the creation of more jobs. Anticolonial feelings were heightened not only by the activities of political parties but also by other internal and external events.

Within Nigeria there were deep problems of increasing unemployment in urban areas, poverty, social disruptions caused by colonial changes and increasing urbanization, ethnic rivalries, and inadequate schools, as well as the fact that development was in general too slow to meet the aspirations of a population that was becoming better informed. The annual per capita revenue of the country in 1940 was small,[58] public revenues and expenditures fluctuated,[59] expenditures on development schemes were too small, and the debt charges on external borrowing exceeded 25 percent of annual public revenues in the 1930s. Certain sectors of the economy were in decline.

Externally, the Italo-Ethiopian crisis of 1935 intensified Pan-Africanism worldwide and enhanced the status of Nigerian critics of the colonial state. To many analysts the immediate catalyst of change was the series of riots in the West Indian colonies from 1935 to 1938, which shook the British Empire and called into question its strategy, motives, and ability to maintain control for a long period. Under severe pressure from the colonies and political groups at home, the British government was forced to do some critical rethinking. In 1938 it established a Royal Commission of Inquiry in the British West Indies,[60] which produced a bleak report that set the stage for the Colonial Development and Welfare Act in 1940.

Even apart from the events in Ethiopia and the West Indies, there was an increasing number of critics of the colonial state in Britain itself as well as among the administrators in the colonies. In his Marshall Lectures at the University of Cambridge in 1950, W. K. Hancock, author and influential observer of the British Empire, informed his audience that he and many others had been worried since 1939 about the poor conditions of the colonies, and he called for "a vigorous state action to promote colonial development and welfare."[61] Hancock was correct, as the contemporary writings of influential critics and colonial observers such as R. Coupland, Lord Hailey, W. W. Macmillan, W. H. McLean, and Margery Perham reveal.[62]

J. D. Hargreaves pointed to a view current in the 1930s that to reduce political grievances there should be an international effort to "guarantee equal opportunities in tropical Africa."[63] Such a view promoted an active discussion in colonial welfare and proposed suggestions that the government should "experiment with new techniques for state intervention and planning of economic development."[64] The "impulses towards reforms" led to many ideas, including the views that economic development could only come with social development and welfare, scientific and technological knowledge should be extended to Africa, methods of agricultural production and nutrition should be improved, the environment should be protected, and research should be conducted on many aspects of African life. These proposals incorporated ideas on the rights of the colonies (for example, self-government), economics (for example, planning for the future), and social welfare (for example, the provision of more hospitals).

In Lagos, Governor Bourdillon had written a provocative memorandum to the Colonial Office to establish that the country had a limited borrowing capacity, could not attract any huge foreign capital, and failed to spend on social and development services; moreover, progress was retarded.[65] To the governor, there was no way the country could generate funds for its development.[66] In making recommendations for change, the governor strongly believed that Britain's starting point should be to abandon the policy of self-sufficiency and provide external aid in two forms: capital and assistance for recurrent expenditures. Rather than go to the open market for loans as designed by the 1929 Colonial Development Act, a colony should be able to approach the Imperial Exchequer to avoid the heavy burdens of interest. In addition, the British government should offer assistance toward "developmental projects" either by capital grants or loans on easy terms and finance the services of the key departments of agriculture, veterinary services, geology, and cooperative societies.

World War II brought home the need for "a vigorous state action," as suggested by Hancock, Bourdillon, and others, even if most of what they said was considered too radical at the time. The war paved the way for a new colonial policy on development and welfare. Although the major theaters of war were far away, Nigeria was involved, both in its contributions to the success of Britain and in the impact of the war itself.[67] There was widespread discontent by many Nigerians with the colonial administration. Indigenous entrepreneurs believed that their failures or poor performances were due to an administration that was hostile to them. Demands for change came from urban dwellers because of inflation, scarcity of goods, and poor living conditions, as well as from those who wanted to obtain salaried jobs. The critics of the colonial system were emboldened by the war. Intense interactions between the Nigerians and Europeans in war situations dispelled the myth of white superiority. Aspiring politicians had a crowd of discontented people from which to draw support, and they were no longer happy with slow political changes.

Beyond the shores of Nigeria, there were governments like the United States and the Soviet Union and individuals who challenged the basis of colonial rule, calling for the right of the colonial subjects, like free citizens elsewhere, to choose their form of government. The Fabian Colonial Bureau in Britain was vociferous in its anticolonial rhetoric, and it put the issues of colonial freedom and development before the British Parliament. One solution to the hostile mood of colonial people was to initiate changes to improve welfare with better education and health services and to liberate the people from poverty.[68] The need to curtail protest by restless and angry people made reform a wise strategy to pursue.

CHAPTER TWO

Colonial Development and Welfare, 1940–1945

History will regard the death of the doctrine of individual self-sufficiency as one of the most important landmarks in the whole story of the Colonial Empire.

Bernard H. Bourdillon, on the passing of the Colonial Development Act in 1940

Circumstances have so far altered as a result of the intensification of the war that I am afraid that the Bill may for some time at any rate appear somewhat out of tune with the more instant and immediate military pre-occupations of the present time. I am afraid, therefore, that much that we had hoped to do under this Bill when it became law must wait for happier times.

Lord Lloyd, *Parliamentary Debates,* House of Lords

In February 1940, the Secretary of State for the Colonies presented to the British Parliament a policy paper entitled "Statement of Policy on Colonial Development and Welfare,[1] subsequently read in both Houses of Parliament and approved with little modification in July as the Colonial Development and Welfare Act (CDWA). Many British politicians hailed the Act as the beginning of a new era in colonial administration. It instituted a new economic policy for the colonies, superseding that of 1929. The change was partly to meet the recommendation of the West India Royal Commission that there should be a central organization for the development of the West Indies. The Colonial Office chose to move beyond this recommendation by looking at its colonial empire in general in relation to "broad questions of development and welfare."[2]

The 1940 CDWA, like other acts legislated by the colonial power, was not free of paternalism: "His Majesty's Government are trustees for the well-being of the peoples of the Colonial Empire, and the spontaneous and whole-hearted support given by the inhabitants of every territory to the common war effort is the best testimony to their appreciation of the way in which this trust is being discharged."[3]

The aim of the new policy was to protect the interests of the colonies by "developing" their natural resources in order to provide opportunities for an improved standard of living. While some colonies could develop themselves by utilizing revenues from heavy taxation, most required external assistance because they were poor, dependent upon agriculture, and heavily indebted. The quality, efficiency, and ability of the governments in these poor colonies made them incapable of coping with the problems endemic to social and economic underdevelopment.

The solution to the problems of underdevelopment in the colonies, concluded the Secretary, was to provide them with external assistance. In a new package under the CDWA, the British government would spend £5 million annually for ten years on capital and recurrent expenditures in the areas of agriculture, education, health, and housing. The Colonial Office was to plan the expenditures, assisted by a Colonial Development and Welfare Advisory Committee comprised of government and nongovernment members. Research in the colonies would attract greater attention, with an allocation of £500,000 per year and the establishment of a Colonial Research Advisory Committee.

By deciding to set aside this fund for financing a wider scope of economic and social programs, the British government accepted an obligation to contribute to the development of its colonies. The concern was to improve the "economic position" of the colonies so that they would be able to satisfy the interests of their people. How the British support would improve the "economic position" was not clearly stated; instead, the policy was to provide funds "related to what the colonies can do for themselves." The policy demanded the "coordination of efforts" between the United Kingdom and its colonies.

For its part, the Colonial Office appointed an additional assistant under-secretary of state and created a social services department. In addition, the Colonial Office would be active in the supervision of the colonies by sending technical advisers and other staff. The Secretary promised more "co-operation between the Government at home and the Governments overseas," although what he meant by this was in reality close supervision of planning in the colonies. The policy also called for cooperation among officers in the colonies, especially between the administrative branch and the technical staff in medical, agricultural, and veterinary services, so that their activities would be better coordinated. The procedure for disbursing development funds was that the Colonial Office would invite the colonies to submit their plans for scrutiny by the Advisory Committee, "who will be able to take a comprehensive view of the proposals for the Colonial Empire as a whole." To allay fears of external control, the Secretary promised that the Colonial Office would not dictate any particular plan to the colonies.

The inclusion of a package on welfare in the 1940 CDWA was a major departure from the former colonial policy.[4] This inclusion was probably inspired by the West India Royal Commission, which recommended the establishment of a West Indian Welfare Fund.[5] The addition of "welfare" had a number of implications. First, the colonial regime, while still emphasizing its goal of exploitation, would pay attention to services that could uplift colonial subjects' standards of living. Second, these services would be planned for, with regular budgetary allocations. Third, some attempts had to be made to procure the money for a welfare program.

The 1940 Act differed from that of 1929 in several other ways. A larger fund, £5.5 million per annum, was allocated for it, representing a fivefold increase. Also, the allocation was for development purposes; a colony would no longer be required to spend its own money on the limited services it could afford. This was broader than the 1929 Act, which allowed aid to be spent on projects that would improve commerce and industry in Britain. In other words, the 1929 Act had a narrow objective: material development. The separate allocation to research was yet another difference.

As part of the welfare scheme, education also received attention, with a commitment of £500,000 to research. The provision for education and research would be met by operating charges from grants, another deviation from the 1929 Act. On the whole, the 1940 Act had a wider scope and a clearer, more explicit pronouncement on the role of the state in development. The admission that some colonies required external grants for development was at least a minor modification to the thesis of the colony as a self-supporting project.

Perhaps the most important aspect of the 1940 CDWA—that laid the foundation of modern planning in Nigeria—was the recognition accorded to economic planning as a strategy to achieve change within a foreseeable future. In responding to the CDWA, every colony had to submit a plan to be implemented over a period of at least five years. In the earlier act, the colonies were only expected to apply for money from time to time for "short-range" schemes likely "to give the greatest and speediest benefit."[6] Most of this chapter deals with the Nigerian response to the introduction of economic planning. Since 1940, the idea that the country must be able to determine ahead of time what it requires to grow and to provide for its people has become one of the goals of the state.

In a memorandum to the colonies on economic planning, the Colonial Office provided additional details of the policy. Part of the fund was to be in the form of a loan that involved assisting a private concern to start a new project or to make a capital expenditure that could generate revenue. Grants, too, would be provided after the determination of suitable schemes and the knowledge of the resources available to a colony to execute them. The Colonial Office promised to approve the appointment of additional staff in the secretariats in the colonies to facilitate implementation. In September 1940, technical details were issued on the procedures for submitting proposals, qualifying for money, and assessing progress.[7]

The Response by the Nigerian Government

Bernard Bourdillon saw the 1940 Colonial Development and Welfare Act as a victory for those who had called for more assistance to develop the colonies. To this enthusiastic governor, the act marked the "death of the doctrine of individual self-sufficiency."[8] He wasted no time in instructing his subordinate officers and the press to advertise and commend it to the public. More important, he set a deadline of two months for all the provinces to submit their proposals.

The short deadline for the submission of proposals is important to understanding the plan formulation process in the early years. Lagos did not provide clear, detailed guidelines or a philosophy to guide the provinces. The method adopted by the Resident (the administrative head of a province) was to request departments and his subordinate lieutenants, the District Officers, for a statement of their needs, including "all [that] they had considered most urgent and of vital importance."[9]

The Oyo province provides a good example of this procedure. Each department quickly reviewed its progress and problems in order to create a catalogue of demands for capital and recurrent expenditures. The Forestry Department wanted money to demarcate reserves, improve water supplies, build a depot for timber, buy a lorry, and do research. The Agriculture Department wanted more research on mixed farming and the establishment of five experimental unit farms. The District Officer of Ile-Ife/Ilesa demanded water schemes and assistance for Oduduwa College. In Oyo province, requests were filed for the tarring of roads in Oyo and Iseyin, construction of new roads, and water supplies for all the major towns in the province. Ibadan made even more demands: the extension of the Adeoyo hospital, improvement of town roads, water supplies for Ede, Iwo, and Osogbo, tarring the district roads, building an abattoir, improvement of sanitation in all the towns, and new buildings for education.

Following the instructions from Lagos, each department justified every demand and provided estimates. All proposals were "ambitious," again following instructions, and they were projects that officers believed would lead to the development of either the towns or the departments. Later in 1943, this initial ad hoc approach by departments was abandoned in favor of the deliberations of standing committees on development.

Development was broadly defined to cover all governmental activities. The proposals submitted by the departments and districts touched upon almost every sector of government operations. The private sector was not included because nobody requested its participation. The attitude of the Nigerian government toward planning was itself a reflection of that of the Colonial Office, which failed to define precisely what it meant by development. In its important memorandum to the colonies in April 1940, the Colonial Office issued the most direct statement: "Economic advance in the Colonial Empire is dependent to a greater or less extent upon an improvement in conditions of life among those engaged in production and industry, and the expansion of certain branches of the social services is an essential preliminary to any economic development. . . . The first emphasis should be placed on the improvement of the economic position of each Dependency, in the hope that it may be able to an increasing extent to provide out of its own resources the social and other services which its people should enjoy."[10]

All projects in such areas as health, education, and agriculture, regardless of their likely consequences for people's lives, were regarded as contributing to development under the 1940 CDWA. One other influential idea was that development could be brought about by increased spending, made possible by external funding. The role of the private sector was undefined, and the opinion of the general population on its future was ignored.

The Emergence of a Planning Bureaucracy, 1943–1945

The initial response to the request by the Colonial Office for development schemes was uncoordinated because there was no established structure to respond to such a new policy. Moreover, planning was added to the routine administrative functions of colonial officers. In both London and Nigeria permanent standing committees had to be established primarily for development and welfare purposes.[11] After much delay, in September 1943 the Colonial Office established the Colonial Economic Advisory Committee to advise the

Secretary of State on the general development of the colonial dependencies.[12] Although the Colonial Office issued guidelines on the general principles to follow, it encouraged the formation of similar committees in the colonies, who could then devise plans reflective of their local circumstances.

In Lagos, development committees were approved in 1943. Prior to that, action had preceded thinking in collating proposals. The so-called pre-1943 development and welfare activities were performed as part of the normal functions of government—for instance, conferences were held in the south in 1941 and 1942, and temporary boards were created in the north in 1942.[13] The government needed the new bodies to advise and coordinate the proposals submitted throughout the country.

New development committees were established countrywide in 1943. The overall coordinating committee, the Advisory Committee on Economic Development and Social Welfare (hereinafter referred to as the Advisory Committee), located in Lagos, was established in August. The Advisory Committee did not have much impact on planning in these early years because the schemes for the early 1940s had already been proposed. It did begin a more active discussion on the nature of development and embarked upon fresh proposals that would become part of the future Ten-Year Plan.

The various development committees were a crucial component during this period. They were the first major semibureaucratic planning organs for the country, laying the foundation for similar committees throughout the colonial period and later. Moreover, the committees generated a considerable amount of data on development, with particular reference to what they thought the country should do. Most of what they recommended during this period was integrated into the post-1945 plans.

Apart from two educated Lagos men, all the other members of the Advisory Committee were high-ranking government officers. At its first meeting, August 5, 1943, the Advisory Committee considered the agenda prepared by Chairman T. Hoskyns-Abrahall, Acting Chief Secretary to the government.[14] His extensive agenda laid out governmental ideas on development, as well as its priorities. In addition, it defined the scope and topics of the Advisory Committee, even before it met, leaving the members with very little to discuss or suggest at their first meeting. Thus, a committee established to assist the government spent its entire time discussing and approving what one high-ranking officer brought before it.

In the covering memorandum to the agenda, Hoskyns-Abrahall used the complexity of running a country as large as Nigeria to justify the establishment of the Advisory Committee.[15] It was not an executive body with power over departments, and it had no money to spend. The work of the Advisory

Committee fell into three categories: the settlement of ex-soldiers; the coordination of existing government organizations and the creation of policies for the administration of the country where these were required under the terms of reference of the Committee; and the examination of all works and projects proposed by any governmental department and held to fall under "postwar reconstruction."[16]

Listing the settlement of soldiers as the first priority of the Advisory Committee was no doubt an indication of the government's concern that the demobilization of World War II soldiers could create social and political problems when the war ended. Lagos also intended to use part of the development fund for the settlement of soldiers. The government wanted the Advisory Committee to find ways of creating more avenues to recruit labor and to give the ex-soldiers the first preference.

Next, the agenda provided the guidelines on the disbursement of funds. Of the £5 million for all the colonies, Nigeria could expect no more than £850,000. The Advisory Committee was asked to consider proposals beyond this amount. The agenda reflected the position of the governor, who believed that voting a fixed sum of money every year was not the right approach; rather, the country's needs should first be determinied. The determination of needs became the guiding principle of the central and provincial development committees (PDCs) during the 1940s. By encouraging the Advisory Committee to be ambitious, however, the agenda requested a classification of projects into three groups: the first group, if they were to be undertaken at all, could be undertaken only under the Colonial Development and Welfare Act; second were those that were not suitable for an application under the CDWA and therefore should be undertaken by the Nigerian government; and third were those that the Nigerian government should first consider and, if it could not finance them, only then should application be made for assistance under the CDWA. The Advisory Committee was not provided with any principle with which to organize the various schemes.

Finally, there was a great deal of discussion in the agenda on land, agriculture, mineral, and local industries. The Advisory Committee was to define the meaning of rural land planning, suggest improvements to land utilization, and find answers to problems such as soil erosion, high population density in some areas in the east, and food shortages in some parts of the country. The Advisory Committee was also to recommend ways of improving irrigation, mineral, and livestock, and local industries, and other aspects of the economy and society. From the comprehensive agenda and the notes on each item, the briefs to the Advisory Committee were rather broad, encompassing virtually all the activities of many governmental departments. The briefs limited the power of the PDCs to an advisory and supervisory role and agreed to give preference to ex-soldiers in the recruitment of labor and to promote a few chosen local industries (tanning, wool, fishing, soap, and woodworking).[17]

Thus, the second organ was the provincial development committees (PDCs), established for each of the twenty-three provinces. It included senior administrative officers, and representatives of the Christian missions, firms, indigenous authorities, and the Health, Education, and Public Works Departments. Membership was divided into two categories: the official members, comprised of department heads, and the nonofficial members, mainly Nigerians chosen by the Resident to represent different interest groups. The PDC was to coordinate the activities of the various departments, reduce the workload of the Resident in matters relating to the Colonial Development Fund, make suggestions on projects and prepare schemes on its own initiative. The PDCs received instructions and guidelines from the Advisory Committee.

The decisions of the first meeting of the Advisory Committee were communicated to the provincial development committees. They were asked to supply information on areas where soil degradation was a problem, suggest schemes to combat famine, coordinate the submissions of the main departments on rural land planning, and examine all previous schemes for the tarring of highways and roads in larger towns. The PDCs were not allowed to take over the roles of departments or duplicate the works of the Native Authorities. They were to be more concerned with projects of great magnitude or those requiring the employment of many demobilized soldiers. They also considered proposals submitted by the districts. After a slow start, while trying to understand their functions and power, the PDCs grew enthusiastic and ambitious in their proposals and demands. A list of their many demands included the development of local crafts, industrialization, schools, road construction, expansion of health facilities, water and electricity supplies, and employment for most people.[18]

Below the PDC was the divisional development committee (DDC), comprised of a few high-ranking chiefs, the District Officer, and senior officers of the Health, Agriculture, and Public Works Departments. The divisional development committee also involved interest groups, such as the Christian missions, foreign firms, and a few educated elite. By January 1944, many DDCs had held their initial meetings. Their minutes constitute one of the richest sources of information on local economies during the early 1940s. I will touch upon some of their discussions to indicate their general concerns and approach.

The District Officer usually served as chairperson; he informed the other members of instructions from either Lagos or the Resident. Proposals could be suggested by any member. These were then discussed, including rough estimates of costs. The meeting ended by establishing priorities. In almost all cases, DDCs were unable to find the answers to questions as to what sums of money to expect or who was to bear the maintenance cost. In establishing a priority, projects were divided into two categories: those to be financed by the Native Authorities and those by the Colonial Development Fund or the central government. Every item had to be justified to attract funding and meet the requirements of Lagos. All districts made wide-ranging demands for virtually everything.[19]

Most districts were concerned with water supplies, markets, roads, health services, education, electricity, post offices, and the supply of radio boxes. Some of the projects were new, such as building schools and roads and promoting local industries. Many concerned maintenance services, such as repairing bad roads and marketplaces. In establishing priorities, every district considered its most essential needs. Most places in the western provinces demanded the following in order of priority: purification of water supplies, improved sanitation (building laundry slabs, seater latrines, incinerators), market enlargement and repairs, construction of health centers, Native Authority offices, and sawmills (in Ife and Ilesa), tarring of roads, extending the available electricity supply, and the distribution of radio boxes.[20] In the eastern provinces, the most proposed priorities were the provision of water supplies, land surveys, land use regulations, provision of health and medical facilities, establishment of new primary and secondary schools, electricity supply, and the provision of roads and other general amenities.[21] The priorities were similar in the north.

Although each district stressed different items, all the projects fell into four categories. The first was sanitation, mainly the provision of safe water, public latrines, and incinerators. In many areas, the construction of abattoirs and the tarring of roads were regarded as part of sanitation. Next was the improvement of markets, which included establishing new market sites, expanding older ones, and creating regulations on cleanliness. The third was the development of local industries. On this, the divisional development committee merely prepared a list of local crafts and requested technical assistance. Finally, there were schemes of "general development," reflecting local circumstances: many proposals included the building of more schools, trunk B roads[22] and railways, Native Authority offices, civic centers, libraries, cinemas, football and cricket fields, swimming pools, tennis courts, and the provision of telephone and telegraph services. Some districts wanted hospitals, others desired roads. At the level of the PDCs, "minor items" such as rural and urban planning, land development, and tree planting in towns were added. In general, the minutes of the DDCs contained hundreds of projects that died on the drawing board.

While the Nigerians in the various committees contributed to the discussions and raised a number of questions about finances and the sincerity of the government in executing the projects, it was clear that the ideas about development and the prioritization and justification of the projects were provided by the colonial officers. One chairperson informed his committee that they could not alter the priorities put before them.[23] Sanitation, improvements of markets and local industries, and general developments were arranged in this particular hierarchy by the colonial officers. These were not the priorities of most Nigerians, especially the elite. Education, employment, road construction, agriculture, health facilities, and loans to traders were their primary concerns.

In justifying the development schemes, colonial officers did not deviate from the broad goals of the state. Most District Officers put sanitation before education and justified it in ways that were incomprehensible to most people. The officers were interested in prohibiting hawking and street trading, both "undesirable from the health point of view."[24] They called for new market sites that were far removed from traffic. Nigerians wanted the exact opposite: hawking to allow children and women to make some money, street trading of items to buyers who were in a hurry, and markets close to traffic to minimize the use of head porterage.[25]

Consider another example: officials wanted to spend money on village development by providing a meeting hall, safe water, incinerators, and public latrines. People who were drifting to the cities and towns for job opportunities were less interested in such projects. In suggesting the abolition of existing markets and relocation of the important ones to new areas, the administrators demonstrated their lack of understanding of the linkage between the markets and political power. In the west where this proposal was routinely made, markets had been traditionally located close to the compounds of chiefs and *Obas* (kings). While not opposed to the creation of new markets, indigenous political authorities resisted the relocation programs.

While most proposed projects emphasized social welfare (for example, sanitation and village and town planning), most people's demands involved the economy or education. Officials justified their preference for social services by pointing to a lack of technical knowledge that would support industries and to the need for greater expenditures on economic projects. The social welfare projects were in line with the so-called civilizing mission to upgrade indigenous people's minds and environments. The colonialist assumption was that most Nigerians were "extremely primitive and conservative" with many "social problems," including living in an "insanitary huddle of small, roughly built huts and stores."[26]

The essentials of planning were also provided by the colonial officers who touted three major ideas to most committees: (1) "Planning must stimulate the enthusiasm of the people. This could be achieved if a satisfactory economic condition and a reasonable standard of living was maintained"; (2) a pool of European staff must "supervise and train Nigerians"; and (3) "the policy of allowing Africans to develop along their own lines must be rejected. There should be no hesitation in preparing schemes which might interfere with the normal routine of people's lives."[27]

Of these three groundrules, the first was the least controversial. To the administrators, public health and the use of such goods as shoes and mosquito nets constituted the enhancement of the standard of living. Nigerians thought otherwise, emphasizing instead education, which would allow graduates to earn regular salaries. The third idea was at the root of many unpopular suggestions, such as relocating people, village remodeling, and so on, which would meet with failure in the years ahead.

With respect to the role of the European staff, a commonly held view among the officers was that the country was lacking in men and women with the ability and intelligence to move it forward. The people had to be educated and led in the correct manner. In 1944, one officer went so far as to suggest that rather than spend development funds on concrete physical projects or welfare services, it was better to use it to pay for the salaries, pensions, and passages of an all-imported European staff that would instruct Nigerians.[28]

When we shift from the issue of priorities to that of needs, the aspirations of the majority of the population and the proposals put forward by many committees tended to coincide. All the committees mentioned roads, education, agriculture, and jobs—all improvements desired by the people themselves. Perhaps the officers were trying to please everybody by including these items. However, from the people's point of view, every item that the district development committees mentioned was part of what they associated with progress. By the 1940s, individuals' expectations centered around money (obtained through wages or trade), acquisition of imported European items, education, and so on.

The average cost of all projects in a small district was £30,000 and in a large district was £300,000. Although these sums would be spread over five years and jointly contributed to by the Native Authorities, the central government, and the Colonial Development Fund, they were generally large and beyond the expectations of the Colonial Office.

While many of the indigenous members on the DDCs expected rapid changes, the colonial officers did not. In submissions to Lagos by the PDCs, the Residents stated clearly that they were aware that many of their proposals would not be executed anytime soon and that costs had to be revised. No senior officer suggested a date by which the schemes they put forward would be executed. As the Resident of Oyo province concluded in December 1943, any tentative deadline on project execution was contrary to the idea of economic planning.[29] His counterparts elsewhere encouraged grandiose proposals, based not on available financing but on community needs.[30] Funding became an indeterminable factor, creating yet another factor in future failure.

Both the PDCs and the DDCs became talking shops not only on items covered by the 1940 Colonial Development and Welfare Act but on virtually all issues. The committee members, including officers and chiefs, demanded everything possible and called for improvements in virtually all sectors of the society, with each area emphasizing local interests.

The administrative officers either provided the focus, edited the minutes, or simply limited themselves to aspects relating to the CDWA in their reports to Lagos. In some instances, the minutes were minimal revisions of a lengthy agenda put before the committees, and there is no evidence that the illiterate members understood all the deliberations. The meetings of the DDCs and PDCs were irregular. They had neither executive power nor funds to spend. The issues they dealt with were either referred to them as part of the development projects or were their own suggestions as to how to improve the welfare of their constituents. Although all committees issued proposals and estimates, each committee interpreted its role and power in a different way.

The committees did not achieve their goal of public involvement in their work. They remained elitist in composition, dominated by government officers and handpicked Nigerians. The official belief was that since the Native Authorities were rudimentary and most people were primitive, the British officers must provide guidance.[31] In many cases, the development committees made recommendations in areas where they lacked understanding. In some cases, they did not have the data required to support their conclusions or to "formulate any schemes based on a long term policy."[32] The activities of the committees were unknown to the general public, a problem that worried a number of officers.[33]

Plan Performance

The achievements of the 1940 Colonial Development and Welfare Act were very limited. There was much talk about many things but in concrete terms, only a few projects were ever executed. I shall examine both the ideas and the few schemes that received attention. The focus in the early forties was largely on discussing various proposals. In responding to queries from Lagos or in preparing proposals for discussion or approval, the development committees generated many new ideas and proposals. Although not executed during this period, the ideas reflected the official solution to the country's problems.

As might be expected, agriculture was a leading priority, a cornerstone of development. For the entire colonial period and later, agriculture supplied the bulk of export items, recruited the majority of the people, and sustained the financial basis of most local authorities. The colonial officers were keen on measures to increase the productivity of export crops and ease the difficulties of farmwork.[34] The indigenous farmers and chiefs, on the other hand, wanted a strategy to combine export with food crops, in addition to the development of local agro-allied industries.

The preferences for the development of food crops and local industries, on the one hand, and for export crops, on the other, were partly an indication of the differences in the perception of and approach to planning. Whereas the colonial government favored export crops, many Nigerians demanded a shift to food crops. At the Fifth Conference of the Chiefs of the Western Provinces, held at Ijebu Ode on June 5, 1941, the chiefs from areas with little cocoa and timber production were critical of the agricultural policy of the government and demanded that more practical measures be applied to food crops.[35]

While the governor and the director of the Agriculture Department were interested in food production, they did not believe that it should be a priority. The director told the chiefs that they should present proposals on how to create a balance between production for external markets and local demands. For example, he advised them to grow rice because there was a market for it. The governor supported the director. The chiefs should cultivate rice, cocoa, coffee, palm products, citrus fruits, yams, and cassava. Except for yams, the crops suggested by the governor were required by the government either for export or to feed the army. The campaign for inreased rice production was intended to get more food for the military and that for cassava production was intended for starch to be exported.[36] After 1941, many proposals were submitted on food crops and new industries, both in response to the CDWA and to changes in the general economy.

Next to agriculture was research work in areas such as land use, soils, crops, and forest reserves. Research thus occupied a distinct place in the 1940 Act. To ensure that research funds were not diverted, a separate budget was passed for just those funds. Research interest was primarily in agriculture, to improve crop yields and minimize crop diseases. All provinces gathered information on their soils, which reflected the then limited scientific knowledge of soil productivity,[37] erosion,[38] and irrigation.[39]

Some minor research was focused on other issues. The West African Institute of Industries, Arts, and Social Science conducted research on the textile industry.[40] Increased information was acquired on the techniques of making locally used items such as mats, cloth, raffia bags, baskets, and soap, with a view toward enhancing their production. Most reports emphasized the need to spend more money on improvements and to develop new technology for the mass production of locally used crafts. The government, however, was more interested in their potential as export items, with the result that more interest was shown in those products that could generate higher revenues. As part of some joint projects with other British West African colonies, the government contributed some funds to the West African Institute for Oil Palm Research, established at Benin in 1939, and to research on cocoa in Ghana.

The third major active sector was the livestock industry, which until the 1940s received very little attention. Promoting this industry at a faster pace became a goal of planning. From the government's point of view, the industry could boost revenues and increase the living standards of those in animal husbandry. In spite of yearly estimates by local authorities, no reliable statistics on the livestock population were available.[41] The major products of the industry were milk, butter, and slaughter animals for butterfat, meat, and hides and skins. There was a large demand for meat: an estimated 300,000 cattle were slaughtered annually in the north and 120,000 in the south. In addition, the country supplied the Gold Coast with cattle. An estimated 5.5 million goats and sheepskins were traded yearly, suggesting that a large number of these animals were slaughtered.

The goals of the development schemes for the livestock industry were to expand it, improve weight gain, introduce new breeds and selective breeding of local cattle and sheep, and reduce the price of beef so that more people could afford it. Thinking that southern Nigeria had suitable grazing lands and that there were sufficient entrepreneurs who would undertake animal production, the plan in 1942 was to promote this industry in that part of the country. The Veterinary Department suggested the creation of large farms (1,000 acres plus) to run a livestock industry along mass production lines.[42]

This goal for livestock production failed in the south, confirming what indigenous people already knew and revealing the ignorance of some officers. The 1945 reports noted that animals were wandering around the streets of southern villages.[43] For the majority of southern farmers, animal rearing was not a full-time occupation but a supplement to crop farming. In the north, where the livestock industry was better developed, the results were different.

Before 1940, concerns had focused on the eradication of the tsetse fly (responsible for sleeping sickness), leading to the establishment of the Sleeping Sickness Service. New proposals attempted to attract more money to combat the tsetse fly through a program of rural planning.[44] Other proposals were to send cattle to areas uninfested by the tsetse fly and to attract pastoralists to such areas.[45] If successful, the Veterinary Department would establish camps in such areas and take other measures to encourage cattle farmers.

The favorable response to development schemes in the north encouraged the Veterinary Department to suggest other new ideas. It called for the expansion of the poultry industry by introducing European fowl. Apart from the small numbers of fowl kept by the church missions and some southern migrants, however, the industry made no progress.[46] A request was made to increase horse breeding, but nothing was done during this period. During the war, Vom and Kaduna became small-scale centers of hog production. The successful trade in prime pork, bacon, and ham to foreigners encouraged support for this proposal. The administrators were opposed to it, in order not to offend the Islamic population, and the idea was dropped.[47]

Overall Assessment

The extent of the development efforts before 1945 was limited to the ideas contained in the various proposals and to establishing priorities that reflected official interpretations of different localities' key needs. By putting welfare and development on its agenda, the colonial state accepted some responsibility for the people's welfare. Nigerians who were interested in progress received a great opportunity to assess and criticize the performance of the government on the basis of its promises. The proposals under the 1940 Colonial Development and Welfare Act did not promote improvements in communications, the infrastructure, education, health facilities, cooperative societies, or many other sectors included in the minutes of the district development committees. For average citizens, the CDWA and the subsequent schemes existed only on paper. The early forties was a period of inflation that led to a general strike in 1945. Why did the planning during this period have such a limited effect?

As a reaction to intense pressure, the CDWA was a political move to use minimal economic reforms to calm agitators, contain the worsening crisis of colonial rule, and signal a change in colonial administration. In private correspondence, the Colonial Office was clear about its intention: to seek the means to achieve "minimum relief required to alleviate distress" and to "ensure quiet and contentment and maintenance of morale."[48] The CDWA was not a tool for change that would be so radical and profound as to disrupt Britain's long-standing goal of deriving benefits from the colonies. When the colonies were asked to submit proposals, the Colonial Office was at the same time clearly warning them not to expect too much money, to be aware of the need to spend more of what they had on the war, to consider the shortage of personnel and capital goods, and to be cautious in preparing long-term development programs. Some of the conditions to be met before receiving or spending money under the Act revealed unambiguously the concerns and priorities of the Colonial Office. The colonies must relate their proposals to the war effort and limit their expenditures to the sterling area. A project must be "urgent and important to justify the expenditures of money in the present circumstances."[49]

W. K. Hancock concluded that the CDWA "had some immediate propaganda value."[50] This is an understatement: the propaganda value was more useful than anything else in the colonies throughout the war years. The Act was passed at a time when Britain needed the loyalty of its colonies in order to be victorious in World War II. In 1940, the Colonial Secretary had anticipated difficulties when he stated that the outbreak of the war would "inevitably affect the rate of advance" but that Britain would proceed with the program "as far and as fast as the exigencies of the times permit."[51]

By 1943, Bernard Bourdillon, who had welcomed the Act with great enthusiasm, was becoming disillusioned because the expected funding did not materialize. Not long after the Act's passage, the Colonial Secretary warned that all the schemes should be executed with whatever local resources were not required for the war effort—and only those projects that were urgent enough to justify funds "in present circumstances" should be pursued.[52] Correspondence between Lagos and the provincial and district administrations warned them to be careful with expenditures and to conserve materials like petrol and stationery.[53]

The war years were unfavorable to welfare schemes. Britain itself was too financially weak to be of much assistance to its colonies. In Nigeria and other colonies, the economic objective of the war economy was to reduce imports, curtail expenditures, and divert resources to the war effort. Thus, the war imposed severe limitations on the economy and society. Available funds and personnel were greatly diminished because of diversion to war-related demands.[54] The country's supply of goods and services fell. Revenues diminished. The number of staff was reduced and the attention of those remaining was diverted to war-related concerns.

The Nigerian government had hoped that the 1940 CDWA would provide funds for a "steady, progressive economic expansion."[55] Although the budgetary allocation was the largest in Britian's history, the colonies did not receive the entire amount. Part of the funds was in the form of loans that colonies were required to repay with interest. In addition, the projects approved under the 1940 Act had to be supported by substantial domestic resources: grants were expressed as a percentage of total expenditures. Indeed, the policy statement warned that the allocation of £5 million and £500,000 per annum were maximum figures that would not be attained immediately. The

Colonial Office waited for projects to be carefully framed before allocating money. There was another major defect: the Act had a fixed annual maximum allowance that prevented money not drawn upon in one year from being carried forward to increase the maximum in later years.

Of the annual £5.5 million promised to all the colonies, only £178,000 was released in the first year, with a total of £1 million by 1943. As table 2.1 shows, the number of projects and the funds spent on all the colonies were far less than anticipated. By the time the CDWA was terminated on March 31, 1946, the entire capital flow to all the colonies was £10.5 million, instead of the estimated £33 million.[56] By 1944, Nigeria had received a total of £479,855. This included £230,000 for a dredger, £104,000 for workers' housing at Enugu, £50,000 for an airport and roads, £50,700 for veterinary training, and £12,000 for a geological survey.[57] Most of these projects were actually in support either

Table 2.1. Summary of schemes for all colonies, 1940–1945 (in £)

	Development and welfare			*Research*		
Type	*Number*	*Grants*	*Loans*	*No.*	*Grant amounts*	*Total*
Administration	4	46,434	—	—	—	46,434
Agriculture and Veterinary	79	1,832,044	289,384	12	128,470	2,249,898
Communications and transport	30	814,991	101,000	—	—	915,991
Education	38	546,114	—	—	—	546,114
Fisheries	3	4,965	—	4	18,820	23,785
Forestry	9	437,355	—	1	150	437,505
Housing and land	12	457,235	44,600	—	—	501,835
Industrial dev.	3	10,395	2,600	—	—	12,995
Labor	1	3,450	—	—	—	3,450
Medical and Health	55	704,179	5,742	2	11,218	721,139
Nutrition	5	9,353	160,000	—	—	169,353
Social services	31	499,947	—	5	18,975	518,922
Surveys	2	9,800	—	3	39,700	49,500
Telegraph and telephones	7	20,455	14,900	—	—	35,355
Water and irrigation	34	689,143	995,230	1	45,000	1,729,373
Miscellaneous	3	23,200	—	2	35,000	58,200
Total	316	6,109,060	1,613,456			
		7,722,516		30	297,333	8,019,849

Source: UK, *Colonial Development and Welfare Act, 1944*, 16.

of the war (as in the case of the airport) or of export trade, as in the construction of the dredger and the geological survey.

During the time the grant was doled out, a vigorous "Win the War" campaign was launched in Nigeria, soliciting financial assistance, labor, and food supplies. The war took more time and energy than the implementation of the 1940 Act: the propaganda emphasized methods of obtaining resources for the war effort, not for any development project.[58] By 1945, a total of £409,255 in monetary contributions had been collected from individuals, social and religious organizations, firms, and others for the various war funds. If these contributions were deducted from the development grant, the remainder was £70,600. Productive labor also was diverted to the war effort. About 16,000 people joined the army and hundreds of others were recruited to construct airfields, barracks, hospitals, and roads. As the economy mobilized for war, farmers worked to meet demands and, in some cases, target figures.[59]

Official assessments of the CDWA's five years in operation were negative. Very little was achieved by way of expansion in economic and social services. The 1940 Colonial Development and Welfare Act did not alter in any significant way either the objectives of the colonial state or the standards of living of the majority of the population. Indeed, the country and its government hierarchies were repeatedly warned to be fiscally conservative.[60] To complete the schemes proposed by all the provinces, the country required more financial allocations, staff, and time. Time was the only available commodity in 1945.

The Impact of World War II

To confine discussion to the 1940 Colonial Development and Welfare Act provides only a beginning to understanding the Nigerian economy during this period. The plan did not exhaust the range of government activities. Neither did it include those of the private sector nor provide the only factor of change. The war economy itself was in fact much more significant than the plan, while the private sector continued to operate with an overriding quest for profit. The number of salary earners increased by 63.9 percent from the 1939 figure of 183,000 to 300,000 in 1946. During the same period, the value of imports more than doubled from £6.8 million to £19.8 million as did that of exports, from £10.3 million to £24.6 million. The currency in circulation increased threefold.[61]

The basis of expanded economic activities was laid during the war years. In the attempt to win the war, meet the problems of general shortages of supplies, and prevent smuggling with enemy territories, the government established a number of new regulations to control production and trade.[62] New currency regulations were imposed on the colonies in order to strengthen sterling against the dollar. Nigeria was forced to conserve hard currency by importing only essential items. The government decided to impose some control on foreign firms, acting as an agent to dictate prices and supply goods. Some restrictions were imposed on imports: while goods from the British Empire could be freely imported, licenses were required for other countries' goods. While it is true that the control measures reduced the power of the foreign firms to decide where to buy and what prices to pay the farmers, the measures eventually worked to their advantage. They received generous licenses and quotas and dominated the supply of goods from Britain. While it is also true that the government fixed prices below the international level, the firms again benefited. Thus, the merchants, many of whom belonged to the powerful Association of West African Merchants, had cause to celebrate. They collected huge profits and the state received an income based on the differential between local prices and those of the Ministry of Food, although many of the profits did not leave England. After the war, these control measures became integrated into the economy.

A notable example is the West African Produce Control Board established during the war. Although it was disbanded after the war, it was replaced by a number of commodity boards such as the Cocoa Marketing Board. The boards had control over the marketing of crops; they stabilized prices to underpay producers, and they accumulated capital, some of which admittedly was spent on development planning.[63]

During the war, the government extended its control over the economy. Lagos established ties with several other African countries to obtain scarce goods and exchange ideas.[64] The production of raw materials like rubber and tin received a boost because Britain lost its far eastern colonies. Import scarcity also encouraged the establishment of small-scale industries for dairy, meat, butter, potatoes, sugar, beer, soap, and so on.[65]

The infrastructure expanded during the war years, primarily to facilitate the war economy. The closure of the Mediterranean route to Britain and her allies made West Africa an alternative highway to the Middle East. Within Nigeria, facilities such as harbors, airfields, railways, and army camps were built within a short time. Thirty large airfields were built and many roads were improved to "correlate the military requirements in the way of additional or improved roads with the general plan for the development of the road system."[66] The road network was expanded by five thousand miles. Social services, notably military hospitals, were built or expanded. Some of these were converted to civilian hospitals after the war. As Britain provided part of the money for the construction of these projects, such projects represented a transfer of capital to the colony. As projects that would never have been undertaken, or at least not until later, they represented visible, rapid changes. Such construction provided a boost to business activities. The large number of troops using these facilities also increased the quantity of money in circulation.

The scarcity of foreign imports induced an expansion in domestic production of alternative commodities. The producers and traders of goods not needed in large quantities had to divert their efforts to producing other commodities. At the same time, the demand for products needed for the war contributed to expansion. Thus, for two reasons, production was expanding during the war. The Colonial Office instructed Nigeria to produce more timber, rubber (a tenfold increase), and tin (twofold),[67] among other products. The domestic dairy industry and light industries involving the production of rope, building materials, and textiles grew rapidly to cater to the military. These industries survived the war. Export receipts increased, due to more demands for oil and rubber, in a way favorable to the country's international trade and balance of payment. The Agriculture Department intensified its campaign for higher production. To obtain income and meet the shortfalls in the prices of established crops, producers responded by experimenting with new products, such as sugar cane[68] and rice in many areas in the southern provinces.

Without any prior plan, at least one hundred thousand people received training as "tradesmen" in roles connected with the war (for example, electricians, fitters, carpenters, clerks, and hospital dispensers). New "military schools" were established to train these people. After the war, they were demobilized but many of them continued to work and improve upon their skills, becoming part of the semiskilled force utilized in the development schemes after 1945.

During the war the demand for economic and political changes intensified.[69] By asserting control over the economy—regulating transport, setting wages and prices, establishing marketing boards, and so on—the government made itself the main source of attack. Before 1940, it was accused of inaction. After 1940, it was accused of inadequate performance and discrimination, as the focus of grievances shifted from the foreign firms to the government.

The control measures of the war years put the foreign firms at the forefront of Nigerian business. Nigerian competitors deepened their hostility toward these firms. The enterprising Nigerians who had hoped to establish direct links with foreign manufacturers were disappointed that government control made this difficult, as they needed licenses. What these Nigerians believed was that the government, in alliance with the European firms, was out to destroy them and, according to James S. Coleman, the Nigerians were willing to sponsor political movements to fight their cause and attain power.[70]

The government control during the war forced others to contend with the state's power as well. Lower prices for export crops meant lower incomes for many. Wage ceilings and price controls hit the salary earners and market women.[71] During the war, appeals for self-sacrifice were not appreciated by all, perhaps because they were far away from the battlefield. Citizens' grievances, exacerbated by years of neglect, played into the hands of nationalists who presented self-rule as an alternative to colonial autocracy.

The labor and nationalist movements became combative by attacking colonial policies and demanding radical changes. In more subtle ways, the intellectuals in these groups began to write about alternative goverments and methods of development. Many of these educated people complained that the country's social and economic advance was limited despite its enormous economic resources. Almost everywhere, people demanded roads, schools, and medical services. Either to attract attention or to express their frustration, or to simply find solutions to their problems, many areas embarked upon self-help development schemes, building community schools and roads, holding meetings on public welfare, and so on. No doubt, this great urge for progress moved far beyond the speed anticipated by the colonial administration.

The most visible threat to the colonial state was posed by the demobilized soldiers.[72] Military service during the war widened Nigerian soldiers' horizons, expanded their tastes, and politically radicalized a large number of them. Many soldiers aspired to maintain or increase their living standards. So concerned was the colonial state with these ex-soldiers that it gave priority to the development of their gainful employment. From 1944 when demobilization began, the problem of absorbing ex-soldiers became a national concern. Many were angered by either unemployment or low wages. During the war, soldiers received from 1s. 9d. to 3s. 9d. per diem; after the war those who were lucky enough to find jobs received on the average 1s. per diem. Those who had acquired training as mechanics, motor drivers, carpenters, fitters, and so on were initially interested in salaried jobs. The common suggestion by most district development committees was that the men should be used as laborers in the completion of development schemes and other projects, until they found other jobs.[73] The Native Authorities hired a fortunate few, but jobs were, in general, very scarce in most provinces. To the administration, those who had no jobs and who had spent their gratuities presented a real danger.

The colonial state thought that it was only the ex-servicemen who posed a threat, but their view proved too narrow: there were thousands of people who were either jobless or living in very poor conditions. During the war, hundreds of people abandoned their farms to migrate to military locations, hoping that the army would recruit them. The majority of them were then stranded far from home with no resources or family support.[74]

World War II contributed not only to the economic problems but also to the social tension of the period. Imported items were limited to the most essential—and those were scarce and expensive. Those who were able to sell their produce or earn wages had an excess purchasing power that produced inflation. The unequal distribution of available resources was an additional source of anger to the poor. Rationing was introduced with the so-called Pullen Scheme, which attempted to distribute scarce materials such as salt and petrol.[75] In a number of areas, the recruitment to and the purchase of food for the army caused deep grievances.[76]

Prices were high. To a population that was used to cheap food, its scarcity and high cost became a major trouble spot.[77] In 1944 and 1945, crop failures and severe shortages were reported in many parts of northern Nigeria.[78] The problem of food scarcity was further complicated by a combination of factors: the activities of food speculators who traveled widely to buy and sell food at high prices in the towns, the large-scale buying by the Supply Board for the military, and the abandonment of farms by young men to work in the towns or serve in the army. Extensive food thefts occurred in places such as Zaria and Ilorin provinces and the Kabba division.[79] In Bauchi, imported goods were scarce. In Benue, the war years brought economic disruption mainly because 8,000 men left for the army.[80] In the neighboring Plateau province, the decrease in tin production produced high unemployment in 1945. This compounded economic problems including inflation and created a land shortage in areas like Birom. Prices for yams and *gari,* two important staple crops, skyrocketed.

Some provinces responded to the inflation by increasing general taxes (for example, Benue province raised taxes by 25 percent and Sokoto by between 6 and 14 percent), cutting the size of the administration, and finding other means to increase revenues.[81] Whatever steps provinces took were additional burdens on their citizens, who had to go to great lengths to obtain money.[82]

In June 1945 the hardships of the war years culminated in the General Strike by the African Civil Service Technical Workers Union. This was the first major postwar strike. It highlighted the workers' radicalism, cooperation between labor unions, and the general negative reaction to the troubled colonial economy. The strike was successful, especially in areas with high proportions of civil servants. While this strike deserves its own study, I will mention a few cases that illustrate its impact.

The strike affected the Post and Telegraph and veterinary services in Katsina. It caused a great disturbance in Zaria because, as the officials said, it involved "educated men who could think at times in terms of Nigeria's welfare."[83] The official provincial report stated that "local employment in Zaria and Kaduna was adversely affected, and markets and food supplies to some extent dislocated in the greater centers of population."[84] The case of Niger province was worse because Minna and Zungeru in the Bida division had large numbers of railway workers who joined the strike.[85] In many other areas, the civil servants and technicians marched in the streets, essential services were restricted, communication was disrupted, and the Nigerian police and the Nigerian Regiment were drafted to maintain emergency services.

The end of the war and the nationalism generated by the strike brought about much change. The discussion about progress was no longer confined to the elite. Many expected the colonial economy to be restructured. Almost everywhere, the expectation was that controls would be relaxed and consumer goods imported. Dispelling the widespread feelings among Nigerians that the end of the war would bring prosperity became a difficult task for the colonial administrators. After a lengthy observation of the people's mood, a reflective senior administrator concluded in 1945 that "the problems of peace will be incomparably more difficult to solve than any which arose during the war years."[86] Nevertheless, by 1943 official circles had accepted the need for change. Between 1943 and 1945, leading British officials, including Winston Churchill and Arthur Creech Jones, Secretary of State for the Colonies, were already planning a new policy with the objective of the "fullest possible political, economic and social development."[87]

Both official criticisms of the 1940 Colonial Development and Welfare Act and the domestic pressure for social and economic change prepared the way for the revision of the CDWA in 1945 and the publication of a more elaborate plan the following year. The major achievement of the 1940 Act was to provide preliminary ideas and schemes that would receive priority consideration after 1945. The anticipated rapid changes in the postwar economy made 1945 a transition year, with people's doubts turning to hope.

CHAPTER THREE

The Ten-Year Plan: Content, Philosophy, and Development Institutions

> We all agreed that we could not either justify or indeed maintain our Colonial Empire unless we were prepared in the next few years, when the end of the war removed any physical handicaps which now stood in our way, to make very great developments, developments not only on the political and social but also on the economic side. . . . The Colonial Office had developed a much greater body of principles for dealing with political and social questions than it had for dealing with economic questions. And yet of these three fields . . . it was most urgent and most important to develop in the economic field, which would shortly be presenting the Colonial Office with all sorts of new problems.
>
> Arthur Creech Jones, British Secretary of State for the Colonies, address to the Colonial Economic Advisory Committee

> The main purpose of development planning should be to ensure that all the resources available are used to the best advantage, that the whole field of possible development and welfare is surveyed, and that the sums to be devoted to each project are determined, so that the programmes form a well-balanced whole.
>
> Sessional paper no. 21/45, *Colonial Development and Welfare*

In 1946, Nigeria published its first planning document, *A Ten-Year Plan of Development and Welfare,*[1] which covered the period from 1946 to 1956. This document required revision by 1951 because of political changes and to correct its inadequacies in several areas. In this chapter, I examine the background factors that shaped the first plan, its contents and philosophy, and the bureaucratic machinery established for its implementation. In chapter 4, I shall discuss the implementation, achievements, and limitations of the plan. In chapter 5, I shall discuss the revision of the plan, which made official assessment possible and influenced the orientation of the economy during the 1950s.

The Context of Development Planning

The Ten-Year Plan was formulated against the background of three factors: the impact of World War II, a colonial economic ideology, and guidelines from the Colonial Office. Each of these factors is examined at some length in order to fully comprehend the plan's objectives and details.

The war economy and ideas generated during the war years provided part of the plan's background, and the anticipated behavior of the postwar economy provided one of the guides.[2] The government expected the scarcity of imported items to continue after the war.[3] Demands were likely to expand for household goods, clothes, cement, and other goods that had been expensive during the war. Scarcity of personnel was likely also to continue until the government was able to recruit additional workers. Demands for raw materials were expected to increase, but contraction of supplies of commodities produced in response to the war was expected.

In addition, the government was unwilling to drop several of its control measures established during the war. The continued shortage of imported goods had to be solved by a system of rationing and import control that was in force throughout the forties. Control was imposed on exports, too, with the marketing boards fixing prices and the quantity of crops to purchase, as well as keeping their reserves in British banks to invest at low interest rates. The government also resorted to higher taxation and price controls in an effort to curb inflation.

Four other urgent issues were considered. First, the demand to promote local industries and food production that had originated during the war years could no longer be ignored. The relaxation of shipping restrictions and increased imports might kill these industries. One way to help the indigenous enterprises was to block importation of similar goods. This had to be balanced with the interest of foreign companies that profited from imports. To satisfy both the indigenous entrepreneurs and foreign interests, local industries would be allowed to grow only at a slow pace.

Second, the country faced the issue of the employment of the large pool of labor released from the army. At the same time, educated Nigerians demanded that ex-soldiers be trained for skilled jobs instead of recruiting personnel from Britain. Third, the international market for products from the colonies was expected to increase. What was unclear to the colonial government was both the scale of this international demand and the best policy of control to pursue.

In responding to the increased demand, a policy of production for export might have negative consequences on domestic food requirements. To the colonial state, an ideal plan would be to continue to focus on export crops while taking some measures to increase food production.

Finally, Britain had to continue to profit from its colonies in order to recover from the economic disasters caused by the war.[4] Its strategy was to help the colonies while at the same time benefiting from them. Officials were no longer hostile to the idea of planning. Moreover, a strategy of promoting social welfare could be implemented without hurting British interests.

Britain was indebted to the United States, and the dollar was the only strong currency. Since the United States needed tropical products—minerals, cocoa, coffee, and so on—Britain could obtain these from its colonies and sell them for scarce dollars. Britain's postwar strategies, therefore, were to invest in the colonies so as to obtain more raw materials and to retain political control, at least until sufficient profits were garnered. Development planning became part of this investment. A social welfare program was intended to produce a healthier population that would produce more for export. Part of the profits from exports would then pay for new development projects.

The aforementioned economic calculations and projections shaped the attitudes of the Colonial Office and the Nigerian government. The effects of scarcity, cessation of wartime industries, shortage of personnel, need to create alternative sources of income and employment, increase in demand for the traditional export commodities, and assurance of surplus transfer to the metropolis were all considered in postwar planning and in other economic measures pursued after 1945.

The Ideology of Development: "All-in" versus "Outline" Planning

The second factor that influenced the orientation of the Ten-Year Plan was ideology. The broad principles that guided development planning were established toward the end of the war. Unlike the initial implementation of the 1940 Colonial Development and Welfare Act, the Ten-Year Plan was preceded by a consideration of political ideology. Within Nigeria, several radical elites were already talking about the Soviet model, referring to the Soviet Five-Year Plans as well as Italy's and Germany's wartime plans, which radicals believed brought rapid developments to these countries. Socialism was considered, even though it was not debated with any rigor. Socialists in Nigeria and elsewhere called for the direct intervention of the state in all sectors of the economy: the government should determine the shape and power of the infrastructure and the quantities of goods to produce, export, and import, and so forth. The official characterization of socialist planning was described in 1944 as an "all-in" system that excluded the participation of the private sector.[5]

The Colonial Office rejected the all-in system in preference for what it called "outline" planning. In outline planning, the government would provide a general framework for state involvement and yet leave substantial power to individuals who would then determine consumption and production. The government would harmonize individual decisions without controlling the quantity of goods for production or consumption. It would also provide the "foundations and conditions" of production (for example, system of law and order and public communications) and allow individuals to make decisions on the basis of market prospects. When necessary the state could offer incentives for, or alternatively restrict, the production of certain items; the state could prohibit or compel the consumption of certain commodities or provide the use of services such as water and roads, but it would allow individuals to determine their preferences. In essence, outline planning was a capitalist ideology.

The colonies were given only the option of outline planning by the Colonial Office, and the Nigerians who wanted an alternative ideology channeled their energies into criticisms. Each colony was called upon to find a suitable mix between state and private activities. A colony must stimulate, rather than restrict, private initiatives and promote a partnership between the state and private enterprises. The provision of basic services was essentially to enable private interests to function. It was, however, realized that the private sector would avoid unprofitable or new and risky ventures. In anticipation of this, the government had to be more active in providing basic services and promoting such enterprises, either financing such enterprises or providing incentives or information about them.

As a basic tenet, an outline strategy also pursued the development of human resources: "The greatest permanent asset of a country is the industry, skill, intelligence and enterprise of a healthy people."[6] Deficiencies in human resources had to be remedied, and the government should consider such issues as the availability of information on resources, the land tenure system, how to improve nutrition and education, promotion of private investments, and how to minimize exploitation of the people.

The final concern was finance. Since finances were limited, a colony must decide where to obtain and allocate its money for urgent and fruitful projects. The three sources of funding were the surplus funds generated by the colony, public loans raised locally or in London, and loans or grants made available under the Colonial Development and Welfare Act. London expected a colony to utilize its own surplus first, before taking loans or grants. This attitude came from the belief that some colonies had accumulated money because they postponed their expenditures during the war.

In formulating the ideology and implementation of development planning, the Colonial Office insisted that the objectives of planning must be well defined to avoid financial problems for Britain. Economic development must be "dependent on opportunities of sale of produce externally."[7] The colony should move at a pace dictated by its internal funds, even if limited external funds were available. While Britain would render assistance, the colony must aim at "only those economic and social services which it can afford from its own resources . . . [because] it would be quite impossible for the British taxpayer to assume the sole burden of raising colonial standards of living or to continue indefinitely the subsidization of the greater part of the Colonial Empire on even a limited scale."[8] In practice, British taxpayers provided few of the funds for the development projects of the 1940s and 1950s.

In spending external grants, colonies must focus on how to achieve economic efficiency and increased production. To raise standards of health, education, social services, and general well-being, the economic position of a colony had to be enhanced, its natural resources utilized to the greatest extent possible, and opportunities widened for human enterprise and endeavor.[9] While a colony would, no doubt, benefit from these anticipated changes, the basic orientation was still to maintain a dependent economy.

A distinction was made between expenditures on economic and social projects. The economy was the key to progress: if the colony improved economically, it would be in a position to fund social projects. Meanwhile, the goal was to improve social services in such a way that they could contribute to economic development. While the benefits of social projects were immediate and apparent, the effects of the economic schemes were always difficult to determine.

The Colonial Office and Development Planning

The third factor that shaped the Ten-Year Plan was the role played by the Colonial Office in providing guidelines. As in 1940, the need to embark on planning was enforced from London. The 1945 revised Colonial Development and Welfare Act authorized expenditures of £120 million on development in all colonies, to be spent over a period from 1946 to 1956. While the £120 million was a "forward" capital grant to be spent over a decade, the previous grants had been on a year-to-year basis. This long-range view became one of the revised Act's most distinctive elements.

Colonies could draw on the fund at any time during the ten-year period, subject to an annual maximum of £17.5 million of which a maximum of

£1 million could be spent on research. The colonies were not prevented from using other funds, such as surplus balances, public loans, and revenue surpluses, to supplement development grants.[10] The realization that money was available from year to year encouraged more consistent policies in the colonies and a belief in planning for and implementing specific projects. The element of continuity, as W. W. Rostow later pointed out, is as important as access to a large amount of aid.[11]

Economic motives were behind this colonial policy that would consume £120 million, an amount regarded as substantial by many colonial officers. The Colonial Office stated that dependence on revenues from agriculture was a constraint, since prices fluctuated resulting in colonial revenues that were "an unreliable basis for a policy of steady development."[12] Even if colonial governments and their economic administration were capable and efficient, they still would not have the resources to embark on major capital projects. The only solution, concluded the 1945 Act, was for the colonies to seek external assistance.[13] The Act advertised an "enlarged policy of colonial development" with the sole aim of improving the economic positions of the colonies by promoting their resources and the welfare of their people.

The Act had a self-imposed limitation: it did not set out to achieve "definite quantitative targets."[14] The proffered financial resources were limited, in spite of the promise that "any purpose" likely to enhance development would receive funding. The colonies were advised to supplement the grants with public funds and assistance from private enterprise. The Colonial Office did not intend to assist the colonies beyond placing administrative, technical, and social services "at proper standards." In fact, it was clear that the colonies themselves would have to seek the means to develop, without imposing a burden on British taxpayers. In Lagos, the Secretariat noted that it had to convince Nigerians that there were two ways of moving forward: either through gifts from Britain or through domestic creation of wealth. Nigerians were told to forget the gifts and seek internal funds for development, although the country would receive its share of the Colonial Development and Welfare Fund (CDWF).

There was, however, a built-in danger in this financial arrangement. As a single grant—in the form of a "stock"—that might be consumed over a certain period, colonies had to consider what they would do after the British funds ran out. This became a real concern in 1947 when the Colonial Office announced that it would commit funds for the Medical, Forestry, Agriculture, Veterinary, and Education Departments' proposals for only the first six years of a plan; the colonies would have to find money to complete their projects.[15] The awareness that funding would be exhausted after a certain period constituted a limit to what could be achieved. In a sense, the situation called for caution in raising people's hopes.

As the various development committees discovered, much of the time they spent on developing proposals was wasted, either because of limited funds or because the recommendations were too wide-ranging and comprehensive. Inflation could also affect a block grant. Indeed, while the CDWF was fixed over a ten-year period, changes in the world economy, especially postwar inflation, reduced its actual value. For example, in 1950 Nigeria had to reestimate the cost of its plan, with a monetary increase of £35 million, a substantial increase within a short period.[16]

The Colonial Office and Development Financing

Not only was the idea initiated from abroad, it was also partly dependent on the aid promised by the Colonial Office. The colonies were allowed to draw a maximum of £17.5 million per year, instead of the previous £5.5 million. A sum of £20 million was added to this amount in the 1949 amendment to the Colonial Development and Welfare Act, increasing the annual allowance to £25 million from 1950 to 1956. Every change was made by amending the 1940 Act and obtaining the authorization of the British parliament.

Central allocations covered common services that were provided by the Colonial Office to all the colonies, including expenses on research. The central schemes covered a broad range of expenditures that individual colonial plans could exclude, notably geological surveys and other important research on agriculture, industries, education, and training. What this meant in practical terms was that the colonies would not receive the entire £120 million because of the need to keep a reserve against unforeseen expenditures and because of the allocation of funds to joint projects.

In distributing the funds among the colonies, the Colonial Office considered each colony's size and population, known economic possibilities and resources, current state of development, and available local resources. The allocation to a colony did not, however, constitute an authority to spend. Rather, it allowed economic planning for a decade on the basis of estimated funds. In other words, colonies could propose schemes, as long as those schemes were suitable for assistance and within the approved general guidelines developed by the Colonial Office. Both external and internal financial resources should be pursued fully for possible development and welfare schemes.

The total allocation of £85.5 million to all colonial territories fell into three types: loans, grants, and grants of interest on loans raised from other sources. As all sums from the CDWF, either as loans or grants, counted equally against the allocated sum, a colony benefited by procuring grants rather than loans. However, the Colonial Office did not encourage acceptance of grants for the entire cost of revenue-earning schemes that were considered suitable for loan financing. Upon acceptance of a publicly issued loan, a colony could apply for a grant from the CDWF to meet the cost of interest on the loan over a short period of time.[17]

A colony could not have more than the maximum allocated to it, regardless of the type of funding. To the Colonial Office, insisting that a colony should shoulder a heavy burden helped ensure "that those persons who obtain direct benefit from schemes should be made to pay at least part of the cost."[18] Schemes that were considered appropriate for revenue-earning included housing, electricity, and urban water supplies. As much as possible, a colony must consider the maintenance cost of all its major schemes after the end of the plan period. One consequence of this was that a careful plan could not overload the budget with recurrent charges on works and services, especially those services that did not yield revenues.

The procedure for fund distribution was established by the Colonial Office. Each colony must integrate the grant into its public sector expenditures, and every scheme required justification. London informed each colony of the amount available to it and requested a prepared statement of its expenditures according to that amount plus revenues from other sources. The colony prepared a comprehensive development plan detailing all expenditures on and sources of finances for schemes. The plan could, however, make provisions beyond immediately available funds, although it must establish some priorities that immediate funds would meet.

In London different committees appointed by the Colonial Secretary scrutinized each plan. At this stage, some of the projects submitted might be rejected and money then transferred from one project to another. After approval the colony was responsible for the implementation of its projects, although the Colonial Office could help with personnel and suggestions. In Nigeria, the proportion of the CDWF grants in the overall expenditure of the Ten-Year Plan was 43.1 percent, with the remaining 56.9 percent of the money to be raised internally.

The policy on financing was not without major problems. It is clear that most of the measures apparently designed to protect the colonies and ensure that the schemes continued after the end of colonial aid were in fact intended to minimize the financial involvement of the Colonial Office. The most apparent problem was the distinction between grants and loans and the projects that either could finance. By insisting that the so-called revenue-yielding projects be financed with loans, the burden of the interest inevitably affected other economic sectors in such a way that important social services suffered. Writing in the 1950s, the economists R. F. Mikesell and R. L. Allen correctly noted that the rigidity in the mediation of financing between the economic and social schemes was an unsound component "since quite obviously a country requires different types of capital, all of which contribute to the expansion of the social value product."[19]

The utilization of loans reduced Britain's commitment, because they would be repaid with interest. Thus, Britain was participating in profit sharing, if there were returns on investments, as well as protecting its own funds, even in the event of the failure of a plan. Like foreign aid, the Colonial Development and Welfare Fund included stringent guidelines: it must be spent on projects approved by the Colonial Office. Moreover, by insisting on the allocation amount for each sector, the Colonial Office established political control and directed the pattern of economic development.

Both officials of Nigeria's colonial government and the Nigerian intelligentsia wanted more external aid. The intelligentsia believed that more aid would increase the rate of change. Thus, one of the major issues during this period was the adequacy of the fund. Leading economists of the day, such as Arthur Lewis, considered the amount too small. He stated that the money was less than a third of what was "needed for a reasonable rate of economic development."[20] Writing a few years later, Henry Collins concluded that "the total amounts allocated for colonial development [were] not generous or even adequate."[21] These Western scholars, as well as the Nigerian critics of the fund's size, assumed that there were objective rational factors used in determining the amount of aid.

While the Nigerians made their points on the basis of what Britain gained from their country, the scholars of the 1950s and 1960s, writing when the leading opinion was that the development of Africa depended on foreign aid, were interested in a theoretical discussion of determining an adequate level of aid. Some of the criteria that the scholars developed (such as the level of income per capita, improved standards of living, savings ratio, productivity, and efficiency) were not always deemed relevant by the Colonial Office. The Colonial Office held Britain's interests uppermost and did not intend to sponsor any planning that might be derogatory to those interests.

Resource scarcity in Britain was also an important factor: World War II expenditures had affected many sectors, taxes were high, public debt rose from £351 million in 1938 to £1.7 million in 1943, and capital losses were high. In addition to receiving aid from Canada and the United States, Britain became a debtor nation.[22] In 1947, responding to colonies' demands for additional funds, Arthur Creech Jones, the Colonial Secretary, used the war's impact as the primary reason for the small amount of aid: "For the moment, the condition of our country makes requests for larger grants difficult in the extreme."[23]

The apparent link between the British economy and the CDWF was, however, influential only up to a point: it failed to consider the capital reserves of the colonies in Britain, in addition to other forms of capital flight.

Since all the colonies were supposed to benefit from the CDWF, another issue that generated some controversy was achieving a fair territorial distribution. As table 3.1 shows, the amount varied from one colony to another. Those who sought more grants for their own country criticized the disparity. In the 1950s some economists also reached the conclusion that the territorial allocation was unfair and without a basis in any rigorous sharing formula. Writing in 1959, the economist Douglas Dosser queried the principles of allocation and suggested that gross domestic product per capita and grants per capita were more realistic markers.[24]

While objections about distribution were raised, there were in fact criteria developed to guide the territorial allocations. The Colonial Office explained in 1945 that it used size, population, economic potential, state of development, and available internal financial resources to arrive at the allocations. A loose principle of "a fair proportion of the total amount available" was generally applied.[25] In response to colonial officers' requests for additional funds, the Colonial Office published the revised allocation principles in 1955, largely based upon the "wealth of each territory." The colonies were divided into three groups on the basis of wealth: (1) "the wealthy ones like Ghana, Singapore and Northern Rhodesia," (2) "the average ones like Nigeria, Tangayikka and Jamaica," and (3) "the poor countries like St. Helena, Somaliland and the Windward Islands, so poor in resources and so underdeveloped that they required more funds."[26] The criteria were not rigid or strictly technical. The Colonial Office aimed to respond to the urgent needs of each colony rather than follow a rigid formula.

The Local Response: Nigeria and the Ten-Year Plan

In November 1945, the Colonial Office instructed the colonies to submit their plans. Lagos was enthusiastic about its plan. Given the promise of external revenue, people believed that the funding would break the vicious cycle of poverty by providing "the necessary cushion required to ease the breaking process."[27] With this optimism, the Nigerian government developed its proposal, subsequently approved by its Legislative Council and the Colonial Office, and published *A Ten-Year Plan for Development and Welfare*.[28] This 163-page document was Nigeria's first comprehensive development plan, providing the intellectual and practical basis for those that followed.

The Nigerian colonial government contemplated expenditures of £55 mil-

Table 3.1. Financial allocations to colonies, 1946–1956 (in million £)

Territory	*Total*	*CDWF*	*Loan*	*Local Resources*	*Total*	*CDWF as % of total*
Gambia	2,130	1,500	200	430	630	70.4
Gold Coast	81,400	3,000	23,000	55,400	78,400	3.6
Nigeria	55,000	23,739	15,267	9,905	25,172	43.1
Sierra Leone	11,178	2,950	5,000	3,228	8,228	26.3
Kenya	42,450	3,500	23,450	15,500	38,950	8.2
Tanganyika	24,450	5,349	10,000	9,101	19,101	21.8
Uganda	28,500	2,500	2,000	24,000	26,000	8.7
Zanzibar	1,902	1,275	—	627	627	67.0
Aden	6,270	850	2,385	3,035	5,420	13.5
N. Rhodesia	52,000	2,778	—	—	49,222	5.3
Nyasaland	32,999	3,872	n.a.	n.a.	29,127	11.7
Somaliland	900	900	—	—	—	100.0
Mauritius	8,192	2,039	4,538	1,615	6,153	24.8
Seychelles	325	250	—	75	75	76.9
St. Helena	245	245	—	—	—	100.0
Fiji	4,504	1,226	1,176	2,102	3,278	27.2
Cyprus	7,497	2,020	287	5,190	5,477	26.9
Falkland Islands	275	150	—	125	125	54.5
Barbados	3,437	208	1,250	1,979	3,229	6.0
Guiana	14,680	6,625	6,794	1,261	8,055	45.0
Honduras	1,382	852	530	—	530	61.6
Jamaica	21,263	6,243	6,558	8,462	15,020	29.3
Antigua	995	699	296	—	296	70.2
Montserrat	219	188	19	12	31	85.8
St. Nevis	1,613	327	240	1,046	1,286	20.2
Virgin Islands	107	107	—	—	—	100.0
Trinidad	9,483	1,000	5,654	2,829	8,483	10.5
Dominica	973	773	200	—	200	79.4
Grenada	1,416	478	312	626	938	33.7
St.Vincent	1,047	446	200	401	601	42.5
Malaya	44,800	4,724	28,700	11,376	40,076	10.5
N. Borneo	8,700	2,500	1,300	4,900	6,200	28.7
Sarawak	9,352	1,950	642	6,760	7,402	20.8
Singapore	53,00	2,775	13,417	36,808	50,225	5.2
Total	526,595	88,038	153,415	206,793	438,557	

Source: Compiled and calculated from UK, *Colonial Development and Welfare Act, 1944,* table 1.

lion. A sum of £2 million was withheld for unforeseen projects. Apart from the police and military, the plan touched on virtually all aspects of public activities. The funds were drawn from three sources: CDWF (£23 million), loans to be raised by the Nigerian government (£16.2 million), and Nigerian government revenues (£15.8 million). The balance by the Nigerian government was to be gathered from all levels of administration from their normal annual budgets.[29] As table 3.2 shows, expenditures were divided by projects and on a year-by-year basis. The central government administered the funds, and guidelines on allocations were issued to each province and department. Communities, individuals, and church missions were expected to contribute financially to development projects, but this was not included in the figures because the extent of their contribution could not be anticipated.

The highlights of the plan were as follows:

1. A sum of £1.1 million would be expended on administration and organization. In order to improve the marketing of export products and develop internal trade, a Department of Commerce and Industries would be created. It would encourage local industries, as well as improve the methods of extracting palm oil, develop fisheries, and assist the expansion of peasant textile industries. Development officers would be appointed to assist administrative officers in the planning and execution of development schemes on a regional basis and to aid the Agriculture, Veterinary, and Forestry Departments in the extension of their activities.

2. A sum of £1.8 million was provided for physical planning, which included town planning, village reconstruction, and expansion of electricity supplies. Most of the towns and villages required replanning and a number of preliminary schemes had already started; others were in the planning stage. The proposed contribution to the cost of these schemes was 33.3 percent for urban areas and 10 percent for the villages. An extension of electricity supplies was also urgently needed, and steps had already been taken to bring electricity under public ownership and control.

3. A total expenditure of £11.3 million was recommended for the area of communications. The extension of the road system was necessary for the development of internal trade, for the transport of export produce, and to aid the general movement of the population and its food supplies. Improved telephone, telegraph, and wireless facilities were critical to administrative and commercial concerns, and the improved system would be designed to fit any general West African system of telecommunications that might be introduced. Proposals also included upgrading the Marine Department, improving existing waterways, and opening new ones. New dredging and sand-pumping craft would be purchased for the development of Lagos and other ports and also for land reclamation and antimalarial work.

4. Economic development would receive £4.2 million. The country was in great need of widespread improvement in agricultural methods and animal husbandry. By greatly expanding the existing agricultural and veterinary

Table 3. 2. Expenditures by annual phasing and projects, 1946–1956 (in £)

Projects	*1946–47*	*1947–48*	*1948–49*	*1949–50*	*1950–51*	*1951–52*	*1952–53*	*1953–54*	*1954–55*	*1955–56*	*Total*
Rural water supplies	153,500	248,500	450,000	450,000	450,000	450,000	450,000	450,000	450,000	450,000	4,002,000
Urban water supplies	210,000	250,000	450,000	450,000	450,000	450,000	450,000	450,000	450,000	450,000	4,060,000
Road development	272,300	497,400	636,300	670,500	726,400	764,000	802,600	840,800	898,000	938,000	7,046,300
Electricity development	187,400	476,800	216,000	97,000	111,800	256,400	60,300	50,700	50,800	37,000	1,544,200
Telecommunications	50,000	50,000	80,000	80,000	80,000	80,000	100,000	100,000	100,000	100,000	820,000
Marine development	810,868	655,784	374,994	124,024	120,054	306,900	287,974	286,504	284,464	266,374	3,517,940
Malaria measures, Lagos	20,000	24,000	24,000	24,000	22,000	—	—	—	—	—	114,000
Medical and health services	102,609	156,744	215,972	281,424	363,015	577,879	657,804	821,470	878,861	1,006,999	5,062,777
Leprosy control	83,530	96,410	104,280	98,220	100,000	100,000	100,000	100,000	100,000	100,000	982,440
General education	306,300	382,100	387,000	409,400	416,800	432,200	405,500	385,440	441,580	492,420	4,058,740
Technical education	63,832	74,495	92,448	104,515	107,238	129,880	118,286	147,763	137,940	139,056	1,115,453
Hausa Lit. Bureau	93,000	28,350	13,500	2,500	2,500	2,500	2,500	2,500	2,500	2,500	152,350
Agricultural development	69,074	88,148	105,852	157,206	175,710	190,784	233,308	250,282	268,056	285,280	1,823,700
Veterinary development	52,020	64,040	73,205	64,195	53,315	52,535	52,605	52,025	51,785	64,070	579,795
Forestry development	16,500	40,670	43,462	58,870	73,825	88,296	104,850	119,109	134,280	146,274	826,136
Commerce and industry	12,000	12,000	12,000	12,000	12,000	12,000	12,000	12,000	12,000	12,000	120,000
Fisheries development	15,400	16,940	21,940	24,480	18,070	12,000	12,000	12,000	12,000	12,000	156,830
Peasant textiles	20,045	29,130	13,850	13,690	13,970	10,000	10,000	10,000	10,000	10,000	140,685
Social welfare organizations	32,000	32,000	40,000	40,000	40,000	40,000	40,000	40,000	40,000	40,000	384,000
Town planning and village reconstruction	20,000	34,000	34,000	34,000	34,000	34,000	34,000	34,000	34,000	40,000	332,000
Development Officers	49,525	71,575	73,250	75,800	105,350	80,350	83,050	86,350	85,350	180,900	895,500
Statistical branch	10,000	10,000	10,000	10,000	10,000	10,000	10,000	10,000	10,000	10,000	100,000
Building program	212,800	324,500	412,000	635,500	1,041,500	1,271,500	1,272,500	1,283,000	1,276,000	1,305,000	9,034,300
Sleeping sickness	28,070	49,000	49,000	49,000	49,000	49,000	49,000	49,000	49,000	49,000	469,070
Outstanding from old fund	22,100	3,000	3,000	—	—	—	—	—	—	—	28,100
Veterinary training	11,950	10,000	10,000	10,000	10,000	10,000	10,000	10,000	10,000	10,000	101,950
Local development schemes	250,000	250,000	250,000	250,000	250,000	150,000	150,000	150,000	150,000	150,000	2,000,000
Loan charges	70,769	150,424	212,267	268,241	335,365	419,649	492,976	563,417	634,539	711,336	3,858,983
Total	3,245,592	4,126,010	4,408,320	4,494,565	5,171,912	5,979,873	6,001,253	6,316,360	6,575,155	7,008,209	53372249

Source: Nigeria, *Ten-Year Plan,* 38.

services and by providing better training for local staff, these goals might be met. In forestry, the government policy aimed at maintaining and improving the natural vegetative balance by maintaining properly distributed reserved forest areas. The forestry training school would also be expanded, and sawmills would be built and operated under commercial conditions. The development of deep-sea fishing would be researched and undertaken. New techniques and improved methods would be introduced at spinning and weaving centers, in addition to instituting a system through which workers might purchase their raw materials and dyes at reasonable prices and market their products. The further development of pottery and brick and tile industries would also be investigated.

5. Considerably increased sums would be allocated toward the expansion of social services. A sum of £7.7 million was provided for education, £10.4 million for medical and health services, £8 million for improvement of water supplies, and £384,000 for social welfare.

6. In general education, the lack of teachers and suitably trained Africans prevented quick expansion. Emphasis was therefore given to the development of secondary education in order to provide teachers for an extension of primary education, assistants for the government's technical services, and students for the West African University College when it was established. Primary education would be expanded as fast as circumstances allowed and would be financed locally, possibly with government grants-in-aid. Funds were provided for the training of an increased number of artisans, as well as for a wide range of extended training of selected students in technical institutes. Handicraft centers would also be established; the expansion of the Hausa Literature Bureau at Zaria was contemplated in order to provide an adequate supply of reading matter in the vernacular, a resource essential for the development of education in the northern provinces. Medical and health services would be expanded, as it had long been recognized that existing provisions were inadequate. The hospital and dispensary system would be developed, as well as mobile epidemic units for the mass treatment of disease, rural health centers, and training schools for doctors, pharmacists, nurses, midwives, and sanitary inspectors. Schemes for leprosy control and antimalarial measures in Lagos would also receive funding.

7. Nigeria suffered acutely from the lack of adequate safe water supplies; improvement was essential for the advancement of general health. The rural water supply scheme aimed at making available one water point for every five hundred people in the rural areas. Urban water supplies needed improvement

as well, and in the more heavily populated areas new or improved piped supplies were necessary. Financial assistance would be allowed to cover the cost of the staff and water plant, up to approximately one-third of the capital expenditure—the remainder of the cost being borne by local authorities, assisted if necessary by loans from the Nigerian government.

8. The plan made provision for the appointment of staff to deal with social welfare and a special performance-monitoring organization in Lagos.

9. Provision was also made in the plan for a building program to cost £4.2 million exclusive of the buildings required for the departmental schemes, for local authority development schemes to the extent of £2 million, and for £4 million toward loan charges and sinking funds.

10. The increased services resulting from the plan would entail residual extra recurrent charges at the end of the ten years, about £3 million annually, but there was every expectation that the revenues of the country would be able to bear this extra charge without difficulty.[30]

Tables 3.3 to 3.6 summarize the planned expenditures, sources of funding, and annual phasing. In most cases, the total planned expenditures were shared among grants from the Colonial Development and Welfare Fund, external loans, and internal public financing. The CDWF contributed a different amount to each project, covering all costs in the case of rural water supplies and only a little of the expenditure in others.

Based on the financial commitments, we can make a number of deductions about the size of the plan. The planned expenditures indicate that social services and the infrastructure would consume £35 million (58.4 percent); administration claimed £10 million (19 percent); interest charges claimed £3.9 (7.2 percent); and agriculture and industry received a small sum of £3.6 (6.8 percent). The overall plan failed to explain the basis of financing of many projects, that is, why one attracted a loan or grant while other sectors received very little. Projects that the Colonial Office deemed to be revenue-yielding, like electricity and marine improvements, were financed by loans. Finally, the anticipation of funds from the Colonial Office and from local revenues encouraged the Nigerian government to propose what it regarded as a comprehensive plan.

The Nigerian plan accepted almost all the guidelines of the Colonial Office. The plan contained not just a list of desirable new projects but virtually all of what the government needed "for the fullest development" of material and human resources, services, and organization. It did not obscure the role of private enterprise, although it provided no guidelines. The plan was designed as a joint partnership between the colony and Britain, utilizing external funds and focusing on projects that would enhance productivity. The plan was based on the belief that the future development of the country rested upon improvements in agriculture, animal husbandry, internal trade, and the expansion of the indigenous industries, which utilized locally produced raw materials. The state's role included expanding available resources for new investments, allocating and managing resources, and removing obstacles to growth. Change was assured if production increased and health improved.[31] To achieve both, producers in the rural areas should be able to benefit from better hygiene, access to roads, and some limited education. The encouragement of rural crafts and industries should enhance their participants' earning power and, combined with new welfare services, discourage them from migrating to urban areas.

A Critique of the Ten-Year Plan

The Ten-Year Plan served as a document that would shape Nigeria's future and serve as a base on which to assess the government's performance. The key governmental officers became "theoreticians" not just on the subject of power but on such things as enhanced productivity, water supplies, electricity, and village planning. Many of the officers were of course too eager to proclaim success or excuse failure, but there were a few who began to think that the administration ought to do more for the country. The document also laid the groundwork for later plans. It enabled the state to diagnose the problems of development. Even if colonial officers and Nigerians differed in their diagnoses, it was nonetheless a step in the right direction.

To accept the need for state intervention to bring about major improvement to health, education, transportation, communications, and the generation of capital for domestic use was a great change from the long-held policy of laissez-faire. There were disagreements as to how far the intervention should go in seeking external capital, controlling the market, assisting indigenous entrepreneurs, and so on, but there was a consensus in the 1940s that the state must take certain measures to redirect the economy. The state did not, however, possess the autonomy to do whatever it liked. As a colony, Nigeria lacked an independent fiscal and monetary system while its balance of payments was tied to Britain's. Some implications of the weakness of the Nigerian state were that it could neither manipulate growth parameters nor change the ideology behind planning.

Table 3.3. Finances for the Ten-Year Plan (in million £)

	Internal sources	*Grants*	*Loans*	*Total*
1946–47	0.317	1.348	1.573	3.238
1947–48	0.584	1.717	1.790	4.091
1948–49	0.861	2.149	1.355	4.365
1949–50	0.997	2.199	1.244	4.440
1950–51	1.144	2.373	1.492	5.009
Total	3.903	9.786	7.454	21.143
1951–1955	11.617	12.214	8.353	32.184
Grand total	15.520	22.000	15.807	53.327

Source: Nigeria, *Ten-Year Plan.*

Table 3.4. Estimated aid from the Colonial Development and Welfare Fund, 1946–1951 (£)

Projects	*1946–47*	*1947–48*	*1948–49*	*1949–50*	*1950–51*	*Total*
Rural water supplies	153,500	248,500	450,000	450,000	450,000	1,752,000
Urban water supplies	90,300	124,000	213,400	213,400	213,400	854,500
Road development	206,000	375,000	360,000	360,000	360,000	1,661,000
Electricity	127,000	123,000	105,000	—	—	355,000
Telecommunications	50,000	50,000	80,000	—	—	180,000
Antimalarial measures	20,000	24,000	24,000	24,000	22,000	114,000
Medical and health	102,609	156,744	215,972	281,424	363,015	1,119,764
Leprosy control	78,530	91,420	99,280	93,215	—	362,445
Technical education	53,119	59,329	70,280	78,948	80,441	342,117
Gaskiya Corporation	90,500	25,850	11,000	—	—	127,350
Agriculture	61,574	77,348	91,950	141,106	157,410	529,388
Veterinary	52,020	64,040	73,205	64,195	53,315	306,775
Industries	16,500	40,670	43,462	58,870	73,825	233,327
Textiles	9,185	16,530	9,190	9,190	9,510	53,405
Town planning and village reconstruction	20,000	34,000	34,000	34,000	34,000	156,000
Development officers	49,525	71,575	73,250	75,800	105,350	375,500
Building program	116,750	132,050	191,950	315,000	450,500	1,206,250
Sleeping sickness	17,000	—	—	—	—	17,000
Mission advisers on education	3,000	3,000	3,000	—	—	9,000
Numba-Mamfe road	10,100	—	—	—		10,100
Colliery housing	9,000	—	—	—	—	9,000
Veterinary training school	11,950	—	—	—	—	11,950
Total	1,348,162	1,717,056	2,148,939	2,199,148	2,372,566	9,785,871

Source: Nigeria, *Ten-Year Plan,* 39.

Table 3.5. Planned expenditures of estimated loan funds, by annual phasing and project type (in £)

Projects	*1946–47*	*1947–48*	*1948–49*	*1949–50*	*1950–51*	*1951–52*	*1952–53*	*1953–54*	*1954–55*	*1955–56*	*Total*
Urban water supplies	119,700	126,000	236,600	236,600	236,600	236,600	236,600	236,600	236,600	236,600	2,138,500
Electricity development	60,400	353,800	111,000	97,000	111,800	256,400	60,300	50,700	50,800	37,000	1,000,000
Telecommunications	—	—	—	80,000	80,000	80,000	100,000	100,000	100,000	100,000	640,000
Marine development	786,500	626,250	342,250	89,750	84,250	270,250	250,250	247,250	244,250	225,200	3,166,000
Educational	260,000	260,000	230,000	200,000	190,000	130,000	60,000	—	—	—	1,330,000
Building programs	96,050	173,450	185,000	290,500	539,000	749,725	772,350	780,800	798,850	957,800	5,343,575
Grants to local dev. board	250,000	250,000	250,000	290,000	250,000	150,000	150,000	150,000	150,000	150,000	2,000,000
Roads	100,000	1,789,500	1,354,900	1,243,850	1,491,690	1,872,975	1,629,500	1565350	1,580,500	1706600	15807 475

Source: Nigeria, *Ten-Year Plan,* 40.

Table 3.6. Planned expenditures of estimated revenues from Nigerian sources for the first five years of the Ten-Year Plan, by annual phasing and project type (in £)

Projects	*1946–47*	*1947–48*	*1948–49*	*1949–50*	*1950–51*	*Total*
Road development	66,300	122,400	276,300	310,500	366,400	1,141,900
Marine development	24,368	29,534	32,744	34,274	35,804	156,724
Leprosy control	5,000	5,000	5,000	5,000	5,000	25,000
Education development	38,000	86,800	113,300	154,500	158,200	551,200
Technical education	10,713	15,166	22,168	25,567	26,797	100,411
Gaskiya Corporation	2,500	2,500	2,500	2,500	2,500	12,500
Agriculture	7,500	10,800	13,902	16,100	18,300	66,602
Commerce and Industries	12,000	12,000	12,000	12,000	12,000	60,000
Fisheries	15,400	16,340	21,940	24,480	18,070	96,830
Textiles	10,860	12,600	4,660	4,500	4,660	37,280
Social welfare	32,000	32,000	40,000	40,000	40,000	184,000
Statistics	10,000	10,000	10,000	10,000	10,000	50,000
Building program	—	19,000	35,000	30,000	52,000	136,000
Sleeping sickness	11,070	49,000	49,000	49,000	49,000	207,070
Veterinary training	—	10,000	10,000	10,000	10,000	40,000
Loan Charge @ 4 $^1/_2$ %	70,779	150,424	212,267	268,241	335,365	1,037,066
Total	316,880	584,164	860,781	996,662	1,144,096	3,902,583

Source: Nigeria, *Ten-Year Plan,* 41.

Many of the problems with the Ten-Year Plan derived from the fact that its initiators held a narrow view of development and pursued their own interests. The document contained a list of many projects that lacked coordination or a rationale in terms of a particular economic target. Reasons for this may have included that the final document was hastily written, there was difficulty in aggregating the multifarious demands, and the government did not think that the projects deserved any form of coherence. Thus, the schemes were not integrated with each other, nor was there an assessment of their likely overall impact. Also, the document indicated that the plan was not final, as several "subsidiary schemes" might be added because of new demands or "requirements arising from experience,"[32] but how such new projects would complement the previous ones was not addressed.

One colonial officer reiterated that the document was unsatisfactory: "The plan is not so much a plan as a number of quite unconnected proposals."[33] An influential observer, Sir Sidney Caine, head of the Economic Department of the Colonial Office, described the plan as "omnibus schemes designed rather to supplement local expenditures than to undertake a specific project."[34]

The plan touched virtually all aspects of government activity, except defense and domestic security. Most projects were designed to expand current activities of the various government departments in social and economic services. Yet, the plan was ambitious only on paper. The emphasis on increasing production was focused largely on agriculture. Only the minimum would be attained for each sector—a minimum adequate to ensure production rather than substantially improve it. In reality, the funds were small, and financing was primarily conceived as a pump-priming device. As an inventory of proposed public capital projects, the Ten-Year Plan was grossly inadequate. It failed to integrate relevant sectors of the economy; for instance, the private sector was ignored, and no serious attention was paid to industrialization.

The government wanted to utilize external funds as an aid in balancing its budget and to undertake some public works projects. The notion of a plan would then appear to be an effort to increase financial grants and to use the size of the increase as a measure of success. While the shortage of human and material resources was obvious, there was no serious attempt to relate the plan to any technical or economic feasibility. Although its preamble recognized that money, technicians, and artisans were in short supply,[35] the plan nevertheless created projects at a level that required money and skilled labor far beyond available resources.[36] Although loans would be incurred, the plan dealt only briefly with debt servicing and how to raise local revenues to meet various commitments.

A more substantial point of criticism focuses on the Ten-Year Plan's overall objectives. It did not define precisely its economic terms, gave no indication on the economy's direction, and failed to assess its goals. The plan showed little concern for income redistribution, amelioration of poverty, removal of socioeconomic inequality, meeting people's basic needs of shelter, food, and clothes, structural change in the economy and society, capital accumulation, large-scale industrial improvement, or the use of agricultural raw materials within the country.

Rather than talk in quantitative terms (for example, the number of new jobs and the increase in per capita income), the plan provided only a list of proposed schemes. It also made a number of general remarks on the economy but without committing the government to any concrete changes. It may be argued that the schemes listed in the plan were those that would ordinarily have been completed by the colonial government if it had had the money to do so, or that they were projects that should have been completed much earlier.

The Ten-Year Plan's proclaimed goal was to ensure that "certain fundamentals" were corrected,[37] instead of aiming at any "wide economic development."[38] According to the plan, those fundamentals were social services and overhead capital, infrastructure, and agriculture. Social services included education, public health, and water supplies. Social overhead capital included projects for transportation, communications, town planning, and fuel and power. The plan did not, however, establish a rigorous priority for its schemes in relation to the needs of the economy and people. To borrow the words of one prominent scholar, it was "a bit of all the things that everyone would like to have done or that anyone believes ought to be done."[39]

No urgency was conveyed with respect to most of the schemes. The plan was neither a resolution of the many alternative options as to what really was critical in the productive sectors of the economy and the social overhead capital nor an attempt to blend social and economic concerns in ways favorable to the system. Within each of the plan's proclaimed fundamentals, the strategy focused on schemes that would attract financial assistance, without having to explain how one proposed project was superior to or more economically beneficial than another.

The urgency to submit a plan to the Colonial Office and to compete with other colonies in some ways made the prioritization of schemes a luxury. Even when the schemes were combined as a package, they failed to provide a meaningful economic whole.

Writing in a context that is somewhat similiar, Benjamin Higgins coined the concept of "troubleshooting" to characterize a strategy of planning where the sole aim is to remove obstacles to development.[40] Perhaps we may appropriately apply this concept to describe the Ten-Year Plan. To officials, the proposed schemes were probably in those areas that had created most of the problems for the colonial economy, and it was desirable to deal with them as trouble spots. What lends credence to Higgins's thesis lies in the very nature of plan formulation, which relied on submissions by the departments and provinces. If the plan was fully committed to the logic of troubleshooting, it should have gone a step further to anticipate some of the consequences of the new measures and to correct negative ones.

From the perspective of current planning, the 1946 document can also be criticized for its failure to provide information on economic trends. The limited references to economic trends suggest that the concern was to achieve merely a minimum level of growth within a decade. Neither did the document provide sufficient information on the extent of the government's involvement in the economy. Policies on agriculture, trade, the economy, and the roles of government and the private sectors were either excluded from the plan or mentioned only briefly. Perhaps the scarcity of data made it difficult to offer any serious projections or provide any economic trend. Instead, the plan addressed a limited number of sectors—roads, water, health, agriculture, and telecommunications—on which it had some quantitative data with which to set some specific targets around them. Thus, the plan calculated the needs of the future economy in terms of road mileage, water points, telephone mileage, and hospital beds. The underlying principle was to calculate the minimum requirement that could be accomplished with limited money and human resources.

Not all parts of the country stood to benefit. The rural areas were generally excluded except if they were affected by the agricultural projects. Not all cities and towns were chosen as locations for new projects. While most communities were urged in 1943-44 to make development proposals, it was impossible to incorporate everyone's proposals into Nigeria's plan. Moreover, there was little concern to meet most of the demands by Nigerians, not to mention involving them in the planning process. The government provided the draft of the plan to some selected chiefs for their comments, but their responses were not influential.

Indeed, some communities expressed displeasure at being asked to review the draft plan long after the government had made up its mind.[41] The most bitter remarks came from those who felt that their areas had been excluded. For instance, the Owo chiefs (in the southwest) complained that their town was ignored, in spite of its size and its concentration of government and private offices. The nearby town of Oka wrote a similar petition, describing their town "as an outcast of the Nigerian Government . . . totally forgotten," lacking adequate roads, a post office, safe water supply, or a single student scholarship.[42]

The people of the creek and riverine areas were not even mentioned, partly because of the lack of roads to connect them to the rest of the country. In Benin province, the greatest demand by the people in places like Auchi and Agenebode was for their first hospital.[43] Similar complaints of neglect were made in many parts of the east and north.

The Contemporary Nigerian Perspective

Although many of the archival sources are silent on the reactions of Nigerian citizens, responses were expressed elsewhere on the directions in which both the economy and the colonial state in general should go. Here, I focus on the views of Nigerian entrepreneurs, emerging politicians, and educated elite. These were the major groups that had access to the planning documents and that responded by presenting contrary objectives. Many of these Nigerians believed that society could change overnight.

During the war, some Nigerian intelligentsia, like the colonial officers, not only foresaw changes, they also began to develop their own ideas about what those changes should be. There was a small literature on postwar economic reconstruction, with a motive admirably summarized by the established politician Hezekiah O. Davies: "We are living in a new world—a world undreamt of by our fathers. Foreign waves of politics, economics, and culture are breaking violently upon our customs and institutions. Problems such as our fathers never contemplated confront us. If we are to survive at all we must examine those problems intelligently and solve them satisfactorily."[44] The "intelligent" examination was thrust upon them by the war, the new colonial attitude to development, and ideas emanating from the Soviet Union and the United States.

Like the administrators, Nigerians demanded state intervention in the economy. Unlike the administrators, they believed that such an intervention must help them to compete with the Lebanese and Europeans, obtain access to bank loans, deal directly with foreign suppliers, expand their businesses, and improve the working conditions of the middle class. The state had to reform itself in order to empower Nigerians. Nigerians, too, must unite for a common cause, cooperating and helping one another.

The 1940s was also the era of socialism, although the golden age was to come in the 1950s when many more people converted. Those who described themselves as socialists comprised a mixed group of advocates of free enterprise, admirers of the Fabian Society in Britain, and self-declared communists, Leninists, and Marxists. Their main suggestions were that Nigerian entrepreneurs should be protected from competition with the Lebanese and that the state should reduce external debts and provide jobs and education. The nationalization of public enterprises entered the vocabulary, with some calling for nationalization of foreign firms.

The Nigerian Youth Movement (NYM) maintained its charter from the 1930s, calling for a five-year plan to obtain capital for local entrepreneurs and legislation to prevent unequal competition of foreigners with Nigerians.[45] In 1942, the NYM requested the colonial government to develop the country's resources for the "benefit and enjoyment" of its own people.

As the Colonial Office was coordinating its own proposals and Lagos was enthusiastic in its response, so too were some Nigerian intelligentsia considering future plans. Using the press, pamphlets, and books, the intelligentsia began to discuss the economic and political future in "welfare" or "socialist" terms.[46] Some wanted more social services and jobs for all qualified people. They wanted the economy's focus to shift from agriculture to manufacturing. In the words of the feisty nationalist, Mbonu Ojike: "If the people do not industrialize, if they do not produce modern goods within their country, if all the money earned from the soil is spent outside of Africa, just how can people's standard of living rise?"[47]

In this new orientation, the state must redefine itself by planning for

Nigerians, without any profit motives.[48] It should provide free health care and education for all and help Nigerians to establish joint-stock companies. Radical Nigerians rejected the idea that poverty was the "inevitable" fate of the masses: the cure for poverty was to deal a severe blow to foreign domination and find a way to promote common ownership and control of economic enterprises.

The intelligentsia lumped together the 1940 CDWA, the Ten-Year Plan, and World War II in their demands for and construction of change. These three entities, they said, were evidence of imperial collaboration with Nigerians to create a new era of change. Such a change must lead to empowerment, extending liberty, welfare, and freedom to all Nigerians. Their expectations were short-lived. By the 1945 General Strike, and certainly by the end of the forties, there were grave doubts as to whether the colonial government's intentions behind its economic plan were well-meaning.

With the members of the Zikist movement[49] in the lead, the post-1945 mood of some commentators became anticapitalist. The Zikists called for a quick end to economic injustice and inequality and for a just distribution of social wealth.[50] The Zikists and others derided the Ten-Year Plan as a bourgeois document. Imperialism and capitalism were both enemies, destroying hard-working indigenous entrepreneurs and preventing them from competing with European firms.[51] The plan was interpreted as a design to exploit Nigerians, an afterthought to justify the transfer of wealth out of the country, and an admission of guilt that the people had been cheated. In their own campaigns for attention, the politicians among the intelligentsia warned the masses not to expect any positive outcome from the plan.

If the colonial state was serious about improving social welfare, it should be able to draw heavily from the Soviet experience of economic planning. Chief Obafemi Awolowo, the brilliant politician and author, was contemptuous of the plan, dismissing it as "unrealistic, irrelevant, unproductive and generally out of tune with the post-war socio-economic changes."[52] Meanwhile, the Colonial Office had drawn up and approved the plan. In 1946, the Secretariat in Lagos was not listening to criticisms, preparing instead to move forward with its implementation.

Development Institutions

Civil service structures and procedures were established for the administration of development funds and the execution of projects. The previous development committees (DCs, discussed in the preceding chapter) were inherited.

Other units and a new professional civil service were created specifically to meet the requirements of the Ten-Year Plan.

The previous DCs were modified to make them more active. The overall monitoring agency was the Central Development Board (CDB) located in Lagos. It served as the link both between Nigeria and the Colonial Office, and between the central government in Lagos and the regional development committees. The CDB was established in 1945 to replace the Advisory Committee.[53] Below the CDB were the area development committees (ADCs) and the provincial development committees (PDCs). This structure was a replication of the colonial administrative grid, with each lower level responsible to the one above it. The structure was supposed to simplify the plan's implementation, arouse the interest of some Nigerians, and seek the opinion and cooperation of a large number of people. The DCs, however, were dominated by colonial administrators and handpicked Nigerians who did not consult the public.

The CDB became a separate unit in the Nigerian Secretariat in Lagos, with the new title of Development Branch. Initially the Branch was a subdepartment headed by a Principal Assistant Secretary and an assistant with the specific title of Advisor on Rural Development. The changes brought about by the 1945 Act changed the status of the Branch to an autonomous one with its own Secretary, known as the Development Secretary, who was also the chairperson of the CDB. The CDB also included the commissioners of the three regions and the Lagos Colony, the country's Financial Secretary, and the director of Public Works. The CDB's task was to formulate policy and allocate funds to the regions and departments. Its report went directly to the governor.[54]

From 1946 to 1950 the CDB held an average of two meetings per year that were usually well attended; it was sensitive to the ideas and assessments by its members and the proposals submitted by the administrative officers. Most of its time was spent on progress reports for projects and considering and approving annual estimates and methods of making funds available to local authorities. The Ten-Year Plan determined its priorities.

An area development committee (ADC) was based in each region with the chief commissioner of a region as its chairperson. All the Residents and senior representatives of the region's government departments were members. The commissioner could co-opt other persons to represent private firms and local communities. The ADCs's task was to assess the proposals submitted by different provinces and recommend schemes to the CDB in Lagos. With the establishment of the ADCs, the provinces no longer took their proposals directly to Lagos.

Each of the twenty-four provinces in the country had a separate provincial development committee (PDC), comprised of representatives of various government departments, firms, chiefs, and educated Nigerians. Each PDC commented on issues put before it by the CDB and the ADC, prepared proposals for ADC consideration, collated the districts' proposals, and coordinated the activities of development programs in cities and villages.[55]

Often the Nigerian members of the PDCs were not aware of the limitations of the committee. When they were asked to address estimates that Lagos had already approved or a proposal sent to them for information, only the members went ahead to make more demands or request more funds or modifications. In most cases both the ADC and the CDB ignored the minutes of the PDCs. Although the ADCs ignored previous demands, the PDCs continued to make yet more grandiose proposals or repeated old ones.[56] Most of the PDCs did not bother to generate new ideas, since these were generally ignored by Lagos, but they were useful in discussing the progress of development projects and calling attention to important issues.

As before there were divisional development committees, but they were reformed in many areas by dropping the illiterate chiefs in preference for educated men. Three members of each DDC were chosen to represent it on the PDC. The DDC usually itemized and prioritized the needs of its area. Many of their proposals emphasized hospitals, roads, water supplies, and post offices.

One of the post-1946 innovations was the creation of a civil service cadre of Development Officers. In addition to the position of Development Secretary already mentioned, the plan authorized the hiring of one hundred officers to perform several functions primarily connected with planning. Development Officers were appointed all over the country to work with the Residents and Departmental Officers. They were not necessarily technical experts or social scientists but "all-round men with wide experience in many fields."[57] The first set of recruits were non-Nigerians, although eleven out of ninety-four officers were Nigerian by the end of 1949. The officers spent their time drafting proposals, reporting on ongoing schemes, or supervising projects of a technical nature because of the shortage of engineers. In 1947, these officers were praised for contributing to the Ten-Year Plan's success, in spite of the criticism that many of them were unsuited to the job.[58]

In terms of administrative procedures, all parts of the country were involved through these various committees and Development Officers. There was more propaganda devoted to the Ten-Year Plan than on the war effort in the forties. The administrative officers, Development Officers, and members of the DDCs actively discussed their various activities and plans for the future.[59]

Another aspect of the planning bureaucracy was the allocation of development funds to departments and provinces. Financial allocation was centralized. After the schemes had been approved for execution, Lagos transferred funds to the appropriate units of government. Following the introduction of the new Constitution in 1947, the Central Development Board had to meet before mid-November to approve the estimates for the regions that would hold their budget meetings in December. Allocation followed rigid guidelines established by Lagos, in such a way that the power of discretion was curtailed.[60]

All levels of government were expected to contribute financially to development projects. The Development Fund would pay 30 percent of the capital cost of major schemes, and the government would lend the balance with 3.5 percent interest, and twenty years redemption, and payments at 7 percent per annum. In areas that benefited from major schemes, such as the provision of water or electricity, the people had to pay either more taxes or dues.[61]

In March 1946 a new national body, the Nigerian Local Development Board (NLDB), was created to utilize available funds to award loans and grants as a supplement to the major schemes in the Ten-Year Plan.[62] The NLDB received an allocation of £1.25 million for a period of five years at the rate of £250,000 per year. By April 1948, the Board had received its third installment, for a total of £750,000. These funds were revolving, and the NLDB was allowed to retain any revenues accruing from interest on loans, although its total expenditures must not exceed £250,000 in any one year.

The NLDB considered applications for grants or loans submitted by Cooperative Societies, planning authorities, and Native Authorities. Only public bodies or recognized societies were qualified for loans or grants. The Board was authorized to finance six types of projects: (1) "public works, public utilities, town, urban and village planning," (2) "promotion of local crafts and industries," (3) "land improvement, settlement and utilization," (4) "establishment of forest and firewood plantations," (5) "experimental projects for commercial or processing tests of any Nigerian products," and (6) "any project approved by the Governor-in-Council."[63] This was a wide range of activities designed to ensure that the NLDB was active countrywide.

The government believed that the NLDB should play a leading role in fomenting changes in the economy by making capital available to small-scale Nigerian enterprises. Indeed, the Board became one of the most important organs of planning. At its meeting of November 13, 1947, the Central Development Board approved the NLDB's resolution to increase the list of bodies to whom money could be loaned. Companies registered in Nigeria and "groups of persons working in partnership" became qualified for loans, thus extending the funds to private enterprises. The argument for this extension was that the pace of economic development would be increased by including private bodies that did not always possess the collateral demanded by the banks and often lacked the means to raise the start-up capital for an enterprise.[64]

Yearly, the Board determined its priorities before it granted loans. The government was able to focus the activities of the NLDB in its early years by asking it to approve loans and grants to establish pioneer mills for palm oil extraction in the western and eastern provinces. The mills would be established by the Department of Commerce and Industries and later handed over to Native Authorities or Co-operative Societies through loans obtained from the NLDB. It was anticipated in 1946 that a similar arrangement would be possible for the establishment of sawmills and small processing plants for forest products.

The Board was different from the other development committees; its role was unique. The ADCs, PDCs, and DDCs looked to the NLDB to finance schemes through loans. The fund allocated to the Board was revolving, while retaining the interest on loans and relying on the government for its expenses. Its performance was poor in 1946-47 because it received very few applications.[65] Its initial major loans included £60,000 to the Department of Commerce and Industries (DCI) for the erection and operation of twelve oil mills in the eastern provinces, £2,250 to the Ikot Ekpene Co-operative Raffia Marketing Society to cover the cost of new buildings and for its working capital, and a loan of £18,290 and grant of £14,872 to the Calabar-Mamfe Road Area Planning Authority for the resettlement of farmers.[66] The Board began to be more active in 1948 when it received fifty-seven applications for assistance. Of this number, thirty-four loans, five allocations to the DCI, and three grants (of £117,307, £187,000, and £6,595) were disbursed.[67] In 1949, loans and allocations amounted to £220,192.

The Department of Commerce and Industries operated the pioneer oil mills on behalf of the NLDB. By the end of 1948, six mills had been erected and were in operation in the eastern provinces.[68] By early 1950, there were twenty-four mills in the country (nineteen in the east, four in the west, and one in the north).[69] The mills became popular sources of income for producers and traders. As the policy of the Board was to sell the mills, a few enterprising individuals were able to purchase them. The mills became the most important experimental undertaking of the NLDB in its first five years.

At its January 1948 meeting, the Board approved an expenditure of a sum not exceeding £90,000 to sponsor a scheme for the production and export of clarified butterfat, to be managed by the DCI with the advice of the Veterinary Department. Production units were established at suitable places in sparsely populated areas, where there was a heavy concentration of cattle, and operated by locally selected personnel trained in the production of butterfat. The quantity of production was not enough for export, and it was difficult to expand the numbers of milk collection centers. The Board also made grants available to three Native Authorities (Calabar, Zaria, and Katsina) to improve land settlements and build sawmills and markets.

In addition, many loans were granted to promote many of the schemes in the Ten-Year Plan. They included such projects as sawmill development by the Forestry Department, village and urban planning (for example, loans for the Port Harcourt Planning Authority, Sapele market reconstruction, and modernization of Warri market), and local industries (for example, operation of oil mills by the Ibez Trading Company and several others). In granting loans, preferences were given to government departments, Native Authorities, and Co-operative Societies. The interest charges on government agencies were lower than on loans for private companies. The Board spent little on health, sanitation, and other aspects described as "social" in the plan.

Although its ordinance provided for social welfare, in March 1948 the members of the Legislative Council complained that the Ten-Year Plan balanced too heavily on the side of social services at the expense of economic improvements. One of the steps taken to correct this so-called lopsidedness was to use the loans by the Board to stimulate economic projects.[70]

The Board experienced a number of difficulties in its early years. Located in Lagos, it was relatively inaccessible for most of the country. In 1948, the Legislative Council approved a proposition to split the NLDB into three regional boards.[71] In addition, the Board had not been allowed to grant loans to individuals until 1948. Individuals interested in building mills, bakeries, schools, and other facilities applied to the Board for money. While many individuals were disappointed when their applications were rejected, they were optimistic that the Board would eventually assist them.[72]

In assessing the various development institutions, I have examined their adequacy, relevance, and performance. For the Ten-Year Plan and its suggested budget, these institutions were adequate to accomplish its goals. The institutions were not, however, designed to execute projects; this task fell to the Public Works and other government departments. A major weakness in the Ten-Year Plan was the failure of the institutions to monitor performance on a regular and satisfactory basis. With respect to relevance, the institutions were not geared toward mobilizing the general population. Neither were they able to generate useful ideas as alternatives to the direction of the Secretariat in Lagos. The institutions were successful, however, in determining the physical needs of each area, the local industries that could be promoted, and the priority needs of each province or district. In the years ahead, the country was able to build both on the weakness and strength of these early development institutions.

CHAPTER FOUR

The Ten-Year Plan: Implementation and Evaluation, 1946–1950

Although there have been no spectacular advances the rate of progress is quickening. Unfortunately, the foundations are not the most striking part of a house. Those schemes which do not require a great deal of specialist technical supervision, or materials which are still scarce, have begun to show progress. *It is unfortunate, however, that the schemes on which, for lack of staff and materials, it has been possible to make the least progress—particularly urban water supplies, tarred roads, electricity supplies, and hospitals—are those which caught the public imagination when the scheme was launched, and are those by which the success of the plan is measured. In consequence disappointment and criticisms continue and there has been genuine bitterness over the failure to improve main roads and to provide water.*

Annual Report on the General Progress, 1951 (emphasis added)

If the Ten-Year Plan were carried out overnight the improvement in the condition of the mass of Nigerians would be barely perceptible.

Fifth Report from the Select Committee on Estimates, 1950

Beginning in 1946, the Ten-Year Plan had a major impact on colonial administrators' attitudes toward the allocation of funds and the effects of propaganda on change. It was not that the Colonial Office issued new instructions based on the objectives of British rule but that the colonial administrators responded quickly to the plan. The official rhetoric focused on economic planning and social welfare. The requests for more money, plants, and personnel by most of the officers were justified by the need to execute the Ten-Year Plan. The traditional chiefs, who were co-opted into the administration in their various capacities in the Native Authorities, also imbibed the rhetoric of planning. The tone of many annual reports began to reflect a commitment to the

Ten-Year Plan, rather than the stale comments on public security and annual trade. While the development vote was separate, the Native Authorities committed additional funds to the schemes in the plan. The impending transfer of power preoccupied the nationalists, but they did not forget to keep an eye on plan execution, if only to find yet another area where the government would stumble. The implementation of the plan took center stage of colonial activities along with constitutional reforms.

The colonial administrators assessed the plan's performance solely on the basis of the completion of the schemes, while the Nigerian intelligentsia, who compared their country with Europe and the United States, reached the conclusion that planning achieved little. These opinions were fundamentally opposed: each group used a different yardstick to judge performance. The Ten-Year Plan did not provide a useful lead, however, since it scarcely defined its objectives and philosophy in concrete terms. Without an overall quantifiable economic target, it is difficult to measure the performance of the plan. There was no national economy that could be measured. The plan made no explicit statements on how its goals were to be achieved, and it announced no policies to execute and evaluate its proposed projects.

In the 1950s and 1960s, the United Nations provided guidelines to measure the implementation and achievement of development programs in the third world, emphasizing such criteria as per capita income, actual expenditure ratios, the soundness of the assumptions in the plans, and the impact of unforeseen events including bad weather, political troubles, and changing prices in the world market.[1] This approach was also less than entirely helpful, in that it ignored profound changes in the quality of life and the aspirations of a people eager for change.

I will discuss the progress of major schemes, assess their contributions to Nigerian society in the 1940s, and then discuss the limitations of planning as an agency of change. The drawback to this approach is its narrative format: a catalogue of accomplishments is presented, but the evaluation of each one is difficult because it was either ongoing or too limited. Measuring a scheme's value is difficult as well, because the time frame is brief. Nevertheless, the approach has some merits to recommend it. In a model of planning based on the completion of individual schemes, a reconstruction cannot help but examine each scheme. We must not, however, confuse the activities of the plan with other government expenditures during the same period. In what follows, the focus is only on those activities that fell under the Ten-Year Plan, although it should be pointed out that other measures were taken in such key sectors as agriculture and infrastructure.

Cutting across all the schemes was a building program for development, which included a separate administrative official and provided money for new houses and offices. About seventy residential and office buildings were either completed or underway between 1945 and 1950.[2] The expansion was slow and the number of new buildings too limited for a country of Nigeria's size. The building schemes did, however, indicate actions that were possible with planning funds and highlighted those that proved more promising.

Owing to the various construction projects, a few people were beginning to regard public work as a moneymaking opportunity. The use of contractors by the Public Works Department[3] was becoming a source of abuse. Contractors competed to execute projects or supply materials,[4] leading to some cases of shoddy workmanship.[5] Some civil servants, too, began to benefit from the development vote, receiving better offices, use of official property, and access to car loans.[6]

Because of its physical nature, a building, like a road, was an example that people could point to when talking about progress in their communities. During construction, it provided some job opportunities for a few people as unskilled laborers. Food hawking and small trade accompanied these projects, to satisfy the demands of construction workers. As these buildings were eventually occupied, they served in very minor ways to generate employment for people as domestic servants, messengers, and so on. Many buildings became prominent parts of the landscape due to their architectural uniqueness, isolated location, or the significance of their functions.[7] As most of the new buildings were either offices or occupied by Europeans or senior Nigerian bureaucrats, they quickly became symbols of power, with a positive meaning to Nigerians aspiring for power or influence, who began to hope for an opportunity to occupy such buildings and enjoy the luxury and power associated with them.[8] The state certainly did not intend these buildings to acquire this meaning.

As the key source of revenue, agriculture was at the center of most colonial activities. Agricultural exports constituted an average of 85 percent of domestic exports in the 1940s and 1950s.[9] The goal of planning was to expand agricultural services by setting up experimental and demonstration stations and to improve the livestock industry. The strategy was to use these new centers to share with the farmers the benefits of modern agricultural knowledge, research, and investigation.[10]

While the goal of expansion was positive, planning, by promoting exports at the expense of food crops, ignored the basic problem of the forties—diminishing food production concurrent with population expansion. In the strategy of promoting new knowledge, the planners assumed that farmers understood little about their environment and crops. This arrogance doomed many efforts, in spite of the indefatigable character of many of the civil servants involved.

Located countrywide were many small projects such as experimental farms, drainage and irrigation projects, poultry farms, liming and fertilizer demonstrations, palm investigations, a cattle multiplication farm, farm school, soil conservation efforts, and the Bamenda-Cross River/Calabar resettlement scheme. Every region of the country had at least one resettlement project.

In the western provinces the Ogbomoso Farm School opened in January 1949 to provide vocational training in improved methods of agriculture to elementary school boys who were expected to graduate and establish their own holdings as farm settlers. Two sets of students were admitted by 1950, but the school failed to turn these boys into successful farmers, partly due to lack of interest on the part of the graduates and to the project's inability to provide them with land and capital with which to work.

At the Fashola Stock Farm in the Oyo province, the study of the economics of tractor cultivation began; it was not until well into the 1950s that the futility of this effort was admitted since there were not enough tractors to work with. Most of the experiments in livestock in the western provinces were designed to expand the industry, but they were not very successful simply because the majority of the farmers were more interested in crop farming.[11]

There was hope that tsetse resistant cattle could be introduced to the west, following an initial experiment on a number of animals, but the long-term result was overwhelmingly disappointing.[12] The prevention of swollen shoot in the cocoa farms became a major undertaking in 1949;[13] it made many of the farmers very nervous and uncooperative because they thought that this would lead to a loss in revenue if their trees were found to be infected and then cut down. The Oil Palm Research Station completed its facility in Benin and held an international conference in December 1949 that drew researchers from other British colonies.[14]

The Poultry Development Centre was opened at Oyo in October 1946, along with a small piggery three years later, with stock from England, although little sign of successful breeding became evident.[15] A survey of cattle trails from the north to the south was conducted to improve cattle routes and waterholes by setting up troughs and small dams at water points.[16] Lagos's proximity to the sea encouraged proposals for coconut plantations.[17] For most other areas, the only evidence of planning was the campaign for increased production.

In the north, land was cleared and experiments conducted for rice cultivation at Badeggi, with an encouraging result. Experiments in soil conservation were conducted on the Plateau and cattle experiments were conducted at the Kofare Farm at Adamawa, but the findings were insignificant.[18] The Maru Tractor Unit in Sokoto acquired more tractors for rice growing in the Sokoto

River floodplain.[19] Tractor units were set up at Ilorin and Mokwa;[20] however, the machines were too few to make a difference to the scale of production. The livestock industry expanded to the south,[21] with a provision for animal clinics, tsetse fly control, and extension of facilities to treat epizootic and enzootic animal diseases. Persuading the herders to use these facilities proved to be more difficult than had originally been anticipated,[22] because they were not convinced that new knowledge was useful or relevant.

Two experimental farms were established at Yola and Maiduguri—with initial work on tree planting, cattle breeding, and irrigation—all with a limited degree of success. The irrigation project did not commence until 1950 because there was no competent irrigation engineer most of the time and not enough adequate equipment, but some surveys were conducted in the Niger province.[23] Manuring experiments were conducted to determine the best form for phosphate fertilizers for farmers' use. On the whole, the northern provinces pursued a policy of mixed farming and animal husbandry to enable the farmer with an ox and plow to cultivate more acres of land. Reports indicated that close to five thousand farmers in 1950 had adopted the use of the plow; however, as with other ideas, it took some time to become popular. Such projects were too limited to receive much attention, but they did provide the groundwork for larger projects in future years, especially in irrigation and rice cultivation.

In eastern Nigeria, rice production was expanded at Okpoha and Abakaliki. In addition, the government farm at Abakaliki experimented with ploughing and bought new tractors, barrows, and levelers. The government farm received money to build new staff quarters, offices, and workshops, marking a new beginning, even if its tangible contribution would come later.[24] In the riverine swamps of the Cross River, small-scale experiments were conducted on rice, maize, an assortment of vegetables, and cocoa. Liming demonstrations—to show the beneficial effect of lime on acid soils—were performed on an increasing scale, but most of the farmers were suspicious of the idea.[25]

In 1948, the governor approved a major experiment to resettle farmers from the overpopulated parts of the eastern provinces to underpopulated lands at Ejagbam in the Oban hills of the Calabar province. The settlers would care for oil palms, live in special housing, and follow instructions on hygiene. In 1949, the Agriculture Department described the experiment as a success and began to think of larger schemes to open new land for forest utilization, oil palm production, and farming.[26] Starting with Onitsha province in 1945, a major soil conservation project began, using experimental gullies, contour ridges, and trees.[27] There is little data to support the official conclusion that the resettlement scheme was popular or that erosion was successfully combated.

Thus, planning efforts in the agricultural sector did not change the export orientation. Most of the new technical projects and ideas were designed to improve export crops, increase cultivated acreage, interest young people in farming, and overcome some problems such as soil erosion, crop diseases, and land infertility. Yet, the broadening of the research goal was a step forward, and the new approaches to improving productivity were definitely positive steps, far beyond the previous ones limited to research on rotational fallow and mixed farming.[28] Results were not immediate, especially those that involved detailed investigations. There was nonetheless a weakness in the early years: for example, indigenous ideas for coping with agricultural problems were ignored because the officers and technocrats assumed a superior knowledge. Other difficulties included the lukewarm reception of fertilizer use and the failure to pay attention to farming techniques in the various investigations.

Little was accomplished by the Forestry Department, in spite of an elaborate plan to establish forest estates throughout the country, as well as to train Nigerians for higher job skills. More activities occurred in the north with tree planting in Katsina, the acquisition of new land for a reserve, the installation of a portable sawmill in Kaduna, the survey of twelve communal forest areas at Biu in Borno province, and the creation of a forest estate in Sokoto. There was little to report from either the eastern or western provinces, beyond the consolidation of previous research.[29] The failure to recruit forest workers was glaring, and several stations were closed temporarily because of lack of operating staff.[30] Furthermore, planning failed to change many people's perception that forest reserves were created partly to rob them of their land.[31]

With respect to research, which enjoyed a separate allocation, there were many difficulties in these early years, such as the scarcity of trained research personnel, selection of appropriate research goals and the methods to pursue them, and arranging travel for foreign experts who dominated the field.[32] Nevertheless, a good foundation was laid after 1946. To initiate and coordinate research projects, the West African Institute of Social and Economic Research was established in 1948 and attached to the new University College of Ibadan.[33] By 1950, it had begun major studies on Islamic law, an ethnographic survey of the north, and research on land and indigenous political institutions.[34]

The Colonial Office strengthened its research division by creating the Economic General Department of the Colonial Office (a modification of the earlier Economic Intelligence and Planning Department). This department sponsored analytic research based on data either available in Britain or gathered overseas by researchers. The interest in economic and social research encouraged both pseudo and genuine investigations that were sponsored by the government and the marketing boards.[35]

As a first major step in gathering useful data on some aspects of the country's economy and politics, research as an aspect of planning would play a vital role. By committing itself to research, the state assured the creation and survival of a good number of research institutions and introduced a culture of investigation by a few dedicated indigenous and foreign scholars who flourished in the 1950s and 1960s. There were some limitations: topics of investigations were too closely connected to the improvement of export crops; there were few or no discussions on the utilization of the final results of research; and the facilities for sustained research were poor.

The Ten-Year Plan included a few programs to stimulate local industries. Several government textile experts were recruited to train some Nigerians in modern weaving methods, surveys were conducted on local weaving techniques, textile exhibitions were organized, and there were demonstrations of weaving equipment.[36] Three Textile Centres were established in the west to train people in cloth production, although the major problem was that their graduates could not get wage-earning jobs. Textile officers demonstrated the use of looms to weavers in many locations, although little was achieved by doing so. An annual export quota of craft products to the value of £5,000 was approved in 1945, mainly for some varieties of mats.[37]

Almost everywhere, colonial officers compiled detailed information on local industries and promised people that the government would contribute to the promotion of their industries. No significant transformation of local industries occurred, but the decade proved the best so far in terms of official interest in local crafts and investigations of artisanal techniques.[38]

A more significant criticism is that the focus was restricted to rural, small-scale traditional industries or crafts, rather than to manufacturing. As the government stated in 1945, there was no plan to industrialize: "A great deal of its future must rest in agricultural development in its widest sense, and the improvement of village industries."[39] This was another way of emphasizing the colonial objective that the country existed for the production of raw materials. Such a policy failed to relate agricultural expansion to manufacturing or provide alternative work outlets to those who did not want to farm.

The expansion of the infrastructure focused mainly on roads, with a small fund for marine improvement. The marine projects were designed to improve and modernize services, open new inland waterways, and provide additional dredging and sand-pumping equipment to improve the Lagos port. Progress on roads included the construction of feeder roads in many parts of the country and the tarring of Trunk A and B roads to link major cities so that provinces would have better access to their neighbors. In reality, the country needed more roads than were built, the quality of construction was poor, and the motive was still to connect the administrative centers and ensure the transportation of raw materials to the ports. While the plan recognized the importance of the infrastructure, it set out to accomplish only the "minimum necessary for the general improvement of the country and its population"[40]—in other words, to move raw materials and connect administrative centers.

Water supplies became a national priority in social services, with a general expectation for piped water supplies. If the desire for an iron-roofed house was the greatest ambition of an individual in the 1940s, that of a community was to have pipe-borne water—or at least a well and electric lights.[41] The scheme that the most people would benefit from was that of safe water supplies, which would reduce the need to travel to streams and decrease the risk of infections from waterborne diseases like guinea worm. People cooperated readily in collecting materials for sinking wells and road clearing.

In addition to the measures outlined in the original plan, there were other local schemes concerned with water supplies. Two separate funds were allocated to water, one for urban areas with populations of over 5,000 and the other for small rural areas. More than 2,000 wells were sunk and twenty-two urban water schemes completed,[42] a good result judging by the provision in the Ten-Year Plan. The experience of the people was a different matter altogether. Projects were not successful in all cases. For example, 50 percent of the wells in Owo had no water at the end of the first dry season.[43] Where the program concentrated on wells, those who lived far away did not benefit because they had to travel. Above all, the facilities were too few to have a profound impact.

The next priority was electricity. The Ten-Year Plan provided for the installation of electricity in many towns as well as the expansion of existing facilities. An acute shortage of engineers, artisans, plants, and equipment limited progress. Reconnaissance investigations were conducted to determine how to generate electricity in suitable power station locations. The possibility of a hydroelectric dam at Benin was investigated.[44] In the north, a proposed dam was selected for the Shiroro George Hydroelectric Scheme. Other minor projects included electrical installation for new buildings and the extension of main lines in Jos.[45] In the east, power output increased, and new equipment was installed in Port Harcourt and Calabar. The Kwa Falls Hydroelectric Scheme was under consideration, and on December 24, 1949, the first streetlights in Enugu were switched on.

The improvement of towns and villages was considered along with social services.[46] Sanitation campaigns in the north sought to improve hygiene and environmental cleanliness. Most sanitation propaganda was futile because few people were willing to gather in public to listen to boring training classes.[47] Town and village reconstruction was equally slow: limited funding and a cautious response to new ideas impeded progress. In general, funding was too meager to meet the ambitious goal of remodeling many cities and villages.[48] Three Protestant missions were given grants to establish a Rural Training and Demonstration Centre.[49]

Grass planting by school children was encouraged in several towns, layouts were created for new towns such as in Ibadan, and market stalls, lorry parks, and new town halls were built in several places. Preliminary steps were also taken to establish a Town Planning Authority in a few towns. There were many small "improvement" projects such as revetment along roads and the construction of culverts, reading rooms, school dining sheds, community centers, and cattle markets.

There were many suggestions on village and market remodeling, model houses, and settlements, all in the desire to change the architecture of traditional houses and living styles. Few changes went as far as demolishing a whole village (as in the one case of Oporomu in Owerri province) or the relocation of an entire population from one place to another (as in the case of the Biliri Hill villages in Bauchi province, which were entirely evacuated to the plains).[50] In the north, a proposal to build model houses to replace the traditional circular huts was accepted in 1946, without considering people's preferences or the high cost of the model houses.[51]

The improvement of communications was part of infrastructural changes. Post offices were located in a number of places, and telegraph and telephone services were expanded, mainly in the south. The Gaskiya Corporation, a publishing house in the northern region, was funded. By 1950, the Corporation was producing four successful newspapers, one in English (*Nigerian Citizen*) and three in local languages (*Jakadiya, Mwanger ur Tiv,* and *Gaskiya Ta Fi Kwabo*). These newspapers were successful in spreading information and in popularizing literacy and reading. They remain part of the enduring legacy of the 1940s.

The Ten-Year Plan rightly noted that many communities were interested in education.[52] Education was divided into two schemes, general and technical, and a small fund was set aside to support two advisers for the Protestant and Roman Catholic schools. In 1948 the northern provinces received an additional sum to carry out a supplementary plan to provide more schools. Seven new secondary schools were founded in the west, fourteen in the east, and three in the Lagos Colony.[53] For most areas, the schools "proved to be the only tangible achievement which the people were able to ascribe to progress of the Development Plan."[54] The teacher training program in the proposed government Women and Men Centres hardly got off the ground. However, the missions were active in running training schools.

In the north, mass education was proposed in Ilorin province.[55] The push for mass literacy became widely popular with local authorities in many northern towns. The Kaduna Trade Centre, a technical training facility, expanded.[56] In the east, adult education classes began in 110 centers in Calabar province.[57] The reconstruction of the R. C. Mission Holy Family College at Abak began, in addition to a new Teacher's Training College.[58]

The technical education plan provided for the training of artisans and technicians. A new branch for technical education was created in the Education Department, with its newly built headquarters in Lagos. The Technical Institute in Lagos was expanded.

In 1947, the Inter-University Council (based in Britain) recommended the establishment of three regional colleges to operate as polytechnics. Staff recruitment and construction of major buildings began for these three centers, initially conceived as trade centers in Kaduna, Enugu, and Yaba. Except for Enugu, which only recruited its first set of students in 1950, the other two gained experience in recruitment and training of apprentices in the fundamentals of their crafts as well as practical training.[59] The centers acquired an instant reputation for training excellent craftsmen in carpentry and construction, electrical installation, and plumbing, and for providing careers for those who did not want to teach.

Centers for training primary school teachers were established in some provinces by the Native Authorities and several Christian missions with small grants from the development fund. The teaching profession was well regarded by the populace, thus assuring recruitment to these schools, despite inadequate facilities. Domestic Science Centres were provided in a few locations to train women in child care,[60] catering techniques, and sewing, in order to provide alternative forms of income.[61] The centers in those areas were the very first to give attention to women's vocational training. The general perception was that the beneficiaries had no opportunities to attend elementary or other schools and that their training provided no job skills for paid employment, but it might at least be useful in their household duties as mothers and wives. Unlike the technical training institutions, the domestic centers did not expand rapidly or grow in prestige.

Construction began on the University College of Ibadan. On November 17, 1948, the college was officially inaugurated and within a year it boasted 220 students and forty academic staff members.[62] Many of the elite grumbled that they wanted a university and not a college and that the attachment to London University was yet another case of subservience.

It is difficult to ignore the major changes in education in terms of more schools, increased enrollment, and the establishment of the first university. Indeed, the 1940s set the stage for the great expansion of the 1950s. Nevertheless, the government was slow in changing curricula in response to the demands for science, law, medicine, and other professions. The missions still exercised great control over schools, spending more money than the government and determining the quality of education. To the missions, religious education could not be compromised, and the core subjects in the elementary schools remained Bible study, English language, arithmetic, and writing.

Over 90 percent of the student population attended voluntary agency schools. Some of these schools were so bad that they failed to attract grants from either the government or development fund. The schools lacked any uniform standard, and space was so scarce in some places that it was a privilege to be in school. Facilities were unevenly distributed—the northern region, for instance, had so few schools that less than 13 percent of school-age children were in primary schools, 3 percent in secondary schools, and 20 percent in teacher training institutions.

Health care, the cornerstone of social services planning, had five components: leprosy control, malaria service, medical and health services, pathology research, and physiology research. This is quite broad, and progress on the first three was slow. By the early 1950s, new schools for the training of nurses and midwives at Aba and Ibadan were almost completed and students were soon admitted. The training of Nigerian dispensers and sanitary inspectors (to maintain environmental hygiene) was much better in three locations: Aba, Zaria, and a new one in Makurdi.

Four of the six projected leprosy settlements were completed at Oji River, Uzuakoli, Ossiomo, and Isoba. With 33,000 cases in treatment in 1950, filling the settlements with patients was easy. Many communities treated lepers as outcasts and were happy to get rid of them.[63] The same enthusiasm was not extended to the malaria control project because fever patients relied mainly on local medicines.[64]

The plan for medical and health services provided for improved hospital facilities, mass treatment of epidemic and endemic diseases by operating mobile epidemic units, and setting up rural health centers as an ancillary service to the hospitals. The plan also provided for staff training (nurses, midwives, pharmacists, and sanitary inspectors) and new specialist hospitals for maternity work, tuberculosis, and mental illness. Three medical units were established, two in the north and one in the south, that trained a limited number of personnel, vaccinated hundreds of people against smallpox, and treated many cases of yaws, scabies, and trypanosomiasis.[65] The first mental hospital opened in Abeokuta in 1947. Some hospitals were expanded to include maternity wards and six more hospitals were built. Each province was to have a midwife and nurse, a small maternity ward (four beds), and an ambulance service. The Preliminary Training School for nurses opened at Ibadan in April 1949.

The Adeoyo Hospital in Ibadan improved its efficiency and served as a temporary teaching hospital for the new University College. One medically equipped launch was provided for the waterside area in Ijebu province.

A leprosy control unit site was chosen for a proposed provincial leper home and segregation village in Plateau province. Progress continued on the construction of the Central Leprosy Unit at Oji River in Onitsha province, while several segregation villages and clinics were completed in Awgu and Nsukka divisions, all to maintain those already infected with leprosy. The Scottish Mission received a grant for the construction of a new hospital at the Itu Leper Colony in Calabar province where there was a large population of lepers.[66]

In the north, medical field units were opened in the Benue, Plateau, Sokoto, and Borno provinces. New health centers, maternity and child welfare centers, and dispensaries were opened in all the provinces, and the registration of births and death was introduced in Katsina.[67] In the east, additional female wards were added to the government hospital in Abakaliki. Work began on new hospitals at Bori in Rivers province and at Onitsha and Omigbo in Orlu division. A floating dispensary was provided for the riverine area in order for the limited service to get to as many hamlets as possible. New projects in the preliminary stage included the acquisition of land for a new hospital by the Lutheran mission and the building of a new maternity ward at St. Luke's Hospital in Anua.[68] Due to the scarcity of medical personnel and public health facilities, the majority of the population continued to rely on indigenous medicine. Yet, the demands for hospitals and dispensaries were many, an indication of the growing popularity of Western medicine.

Assessment and Limitations

In discussing the plan's implementation, I have focused on the accomplishments in the various schemes. Some projects received an enthusiastic response, as in the case of water supplies. Some became a symbol of national pride, like the University College of Ibadan and its teaching hospital. Some were dazzling in their impact, as in the case of electricity which attracted onlookers whenever it was first switched on.

These accomplishments occurred in the context of economic and social changes in the 1940s. While the implementation of the plan generated its own activities, other administrative routines moved forward as well. Agriculture and mining continued to sustain external trade. In the early 1940s, incomes rose through war-generated expenditures while the importation of consumer goods was restricted.

Prices of imported consumer goods increased. The price index of major imports increased from 100 in 1939, to 166 in 1942, to 275 in 1947. In Lagos alone, the cost of living index increased by 76 percent between 1939 and 1945.[69] After 1945, the increase in per capita income was continued through demobilization payments to soldiers and through increases in cash crop prices. By the late 1940s, the supply of consumer goods also increased. The volume of currency in circulation increased from £15.4 million in March 1945, to £24.5 million in June 1948, to £31 million in May 1949. In addition, the value of salaries and wages increased. The quantity of imported goods appreciably increased. For example, the imports of cotton piece goods increased from 81,828,187 square yards in 1946, to 104,076,711 square yards in 1947, to 125,893,936 in 1948. Total imports (excluding bullion and specie) increased in value after 1945.

Centralized marketing of cash crops was one of the most important changes of the 1940s. The price paid to the producer was less than that earned in the world market, and the balance went to a stabilization fund to reduce the amount of money in circulation and create a reserve. The increments to the cocoa stabilization fund reached £5.8 million in 1946–47 and £7 million in 1948 (there were similar schemes for oil seeds). The increment to the stabilization funds by the end of March 1949 was estimated at £14 million. Moreover, savings bank deposits steadily increased to an aggregate of approximately £2.5 million at the end of 1948.

The government expanded the revenue base through taxation. In 1946, income tax rates for individuals increased by 50 percent and in 1949 company taxes increased from 7s. 6d. to 9/- per pound. Import and export duty rates increased in 1948 and 1949. On March 31, 1948, the surplus revenue balance was £9 million after setting aside £750,000 for the Revenue Equalisation Fund (REF). The estimates for 1949–50 indicated a surplus of £843,000 after provisions had been made for the payment of £1.75 million to the REF and £700,000 to the Supplementary Sinking Fund.[70]

While the plan pumped some money into the economy, it was not the only impetus for change in the 1940s. The Native Authorities and other levels of government funded development-related projects in addition to those stated in the plan. Through self-help, many communities built feeder roads, halls, wells, and other improvements because they could not wait for government projects or because they thought that funding would never be available for them. Thus, voluntary development projects were in many instances a response by those who believed that they were left out or who thought that their chances of being included in a future plan would be enhanced if they provided evidence of their seriousness.

Created between 1947 and 1949, the production and marketing boards financed a number of schemes. By buying and selling the principal export crops (cocoa, groundnuts, oil palm products, and cotton), the boards were intended to stabilize producer prices, promote economic development, and encourage research. Due to the increase in world prices, the marketing boards quickly acquired large surpluses. In order to maintain Nigeria's position as the leading supplier of palm oil and kernel, the boards sponsored pioneer mills in the south to increase the amount of oil extracted from palm fruit as well as improve the quality of oil.[71] For example, they funded projects to improve production methods of oil, sponsored research on improved quality and production of major cash crops, awarded grants to cooperative societies and individuals, and financed road construction. A 1950 report on the activities of the boards concluded that their "combined contribution to progress of development in Nigeria [was] comparable in magnitude to that undertaken in the Plan and in the field of purely economic development probably exceed[ed] the provisions of the Ten-Year Plan."[72]

Although the plan virtually excluded the private sector, the projects on roads, electricity, and other infrastructure components were supposed to benefit all. In addition, small-scale assistance was offered to support some private projects. For instance, £25,424 was granted to the Church Missionary Society Training Centre at Owo, following the recommendation of the Western Area Development Committee. In 1946, the CMS proposed a Rural Training and Demonstration Centre near Asaba to teach agriculture. While the government was willing to encourage private development projects, it was always worried as to whether the scale was ambitious and whether it would have to finance them with huge public expenditures over a long period of time. Assistance to private organizations, like the church missions, was an exception, as long as they agreed to government supervision and control of expenditures from the development funds and provided there was no government department pursuing a similar project.[73] Guidelines were implemented to administer grants and ensure that the government retained control when it assisted private agencies. Thus, the plan made some generous grants to voluntary educational agencies for staff recruitment, equipment, and buildings.[74]

One external private company in particular benefited from the development funds throughout the colonies. The Colonial Development Corporation (CDC) was established in full cooperation with the Colonial Office under the Overseas Resources Development Act of 1948. It included several areas of responsibility: (1) to investigate, develop, and implement projects for developing colonial resources in animal, agricultural, and forestry products, fisheries, minerals, mining, and fertilizer production, (2) civil engineering and public works projects, and (3) manufacturing and processing projects, including the establishment of new local industries.

The CDC operated with public money but conducted its operations as a private concern; it considered only projects that were commercially sound and had some prospect of becoming self-sufficient. In 1948, a subsidiary company was formed, the Colonial Development Corporation (West Africa) Limited, with an office in Lagos. In 1949, the CDC established a depot for engineering and ancillary repair facilities in Lagos for mechanical plant and maintenance units,[75] as well as a fisheries and cold storage unit in 1950.[76] The CDC assisted with the training of the Nigerian staff for the Labour Department and the Land and Survey Department, in addition to participating in many joint projects with the government. The CDC was not a philanthropic agency: it collected money in return for all its services and was able to move its profits abroad.[77]

The combined activities of planning and other government activities were nonetheless too little to make a difference to the majority of the population. The low-income earners, city dwellers, and job seekers continued to voice their complaints. The 1940s was a decade of rising expectations, due mainly to promises made during the war and to expectations of expansion in the export trade after 1945. People's expectations were disappointed, however, in spite of the promise of the Ten-Year Plan, because of the scarcity of imports. The peasants were cheated by the marketing boards which withheld part of their proceeds. Economic expectations fueled labor union militancy, elites' complaints, and nationalists' demands for independence. The emerging politicians promised a better life with more money for peasants, better wages, industrialization, and control over foreign firms' activities.

The fortunate places that had been included in a proposal had something to look forward to. The problem, however, was that the slow rate of progress had turned such optimism into disillusion by 1948.[78] Many districts complained of neglect or of inattention to their demands; complaints that were so common that political officers included them in their reports. Consider this example from central Nigeria: the officer in charge of Benue noted the harsh criticisms of development in the media, but he was unable to defend the government because he believed that most of the people "have been but little affected so far by the development programme and have little conception of its meaning and relevance to them."[79]

Every place, large or small, desired visible change. The characteristics of a "developed" town in 1950 included good roads, a post office, pipe-borne water, and electricity.[80] Towns with influential citizens or knowledge of development funds were quick to realize that they had to struggle to gain attention for government projects.

Indeed, one negative outcome from the plan's very early years was that towns, villages, and regions began to compete with one another for scarce resources. Thus, planning intensified inter- and intraregional competition for development funds. In this atmosphere, major towns benefited the most, either because they were administrative centers or contained a substantial number of Europeans and Asians. For instance, in 1947 the west wanted more money for road construction, and it accused other regions of obtaining a larger share of development funds. Within the west itself, the Oyo province wanted to be on the list with the others in the provision for water supplies.[81]

In another case, residents of the main palm oil belt in the east complained that Benin province (which produced less palm oil) had been favored in the establishment of the West African Institute for Oil Palm Research. The government had to justify the institute's location by saying that Benin had more land and was more suitable for research.[82] At other times, there were demands for more money, as in the case of colliery housing in the east, for which a request for more funding was denied. The north wanted more money for the leprosy control scheme.[83] Both the north and east demanded money for social welfare services only enjoyed by the west, whereas the government wanted only a gradual growth in expenditures. The west had more Development Officers, and other regions complained about that. In addition, the east could not understand why the west had more agricultural projects.

The provincial development committee (PDC) meetings provided opportunities for wrangling among the districts, as each touted one proposal or another. The PDC chairperson became a political mediator, explaining why one area had a project and another did not, insisting that districts and chiefs should consider all the amenities in their province as collective property, and promising that better days were ahead for everyone.[84] When a district or town had received a project, it pressed for the scheme's immediate execution, since shortages of funds were always anticipated and could force abandonment of a project. Nonetheless, all districts and chiefs requested more money, beyond the funding limits in the estimates. Villages and small towns complained that they were neglected at the expense of the provincial headquarters.[85] Vested groups like the cooperative societies complained that they were not even mentioned in the Ten-Year Plan.[86] Ethnic associations also asked for more funds on behalf of their towns.[87]

There were specific practical problems relating to the plan's implementation that limited its effectiveness and impact as an instrument of change. The Ten-Year Plan failed to meet its budgeted commitments. In 1947, the Secretary to the Central Development Board (CDB) informed its members that actual expenditures fell short of estimated goals by £3.15 million and that it was unlikely to spend the anticipated amount of £4.9 million for the 1948–49 fiscal year.[88] By March 1949 the expenditures should have been £12 million, but this fell short by nearly £3.75 million, similar to the shortfall for the previous year. At the end of 1950, the plan provided for expenditures of £16.25 million, but the actual expenditures were £13.5 million.[89] Due to the heavy rising costs of the plan's implementation, development fell far short of its target by a greater margin than the figures and tables suggest. The plan was doomed to failure, as figures from the first three years attest, showing a marginal loss of £1 million per annum (table 4.1).[90]

Even if the plan had met its funding goals, difficulties existed in completing the proposed schemes. The plan used 1945 costs to arrive at its published estimates. Prices did not drop after the war, as some departments had expected, and the government had to seek an additional £35 million five years later.[91] The plan's authors had anticipated a number of difficulties. They expected that the shortage of resources would hamper the execution of some projects. One unproven prediction was that obtaining land might be difficult. Indeed, as early as 1944, measures were initiated to enact legislation on land use. This in itself was difficult because it raised people's suspicions as to the government's real intention. The government decided to give the Native Authorities a great deal of power in land matters and to make a distinction between interfering in land ownership and the method of land use. Also, the government was careful not to pay for the acquisition of land with the Colonial Development and Welfare Fund (CDWF) but was able to draw on a separate fund in the Land and Survey Department. In practice, obtaining land for most of the projects posed little or no problem.

The anticipated scarcity of laborers and materials proved to be correct. The 1940s saw a widespread shortage of capital goods and labor.[92] The government did not hide the labor shortage or its implications for planning. Workers in midlevel and subprofessional grades were in very short supply.[93] Less competent hands had to be recruited. While it is true that all provinces were excited about the plan as well as the possible new projects, they were very frustrated at the slow pace, even when some money was allocated to them.[94]

Shortage of iron and steel impeded building and engineering works. Inadequate plants, equipment, and materials also reduced the pace of construction of many building projects.[95] Due to such shortages, many projects did not start until 1949. Many parts of the northern provinces experienced these delays—people heard propaganda on development but saw very little progress, and they began to express doubts as to whether anything would ever be achieved. A year later, the same observation was repeated for the entire country.[96]

Almost everywhere, the general complaint was that plan implementation did not proceed on schedule. Among the reasons for this were the need to obtain approval from the Colonial Office in decision making, reliance on imported items, and scarcity of resources.[97] Another reason was the competing demands for time and money. The political demands, reforms, and changes of

Table 4.1. Expenditures for selected years (in £)

	1947–48 Expenditures			1948–49 Expenditures		
Projects	*CDWF*	*Recurrent Costs*	*Loans*	*CDWF*	*Recurrent Costs*	*Loans*
Agricultural development	46,299	17,481	—	61,364	10,219	—
Bamenda-Cross River/Calabar Resettlement Scheme	—	—	—	—	—	—
Building program	97,168	—	107,982	145,785	—	251,322
Development Officers	43,764	—	—	—	—	—
Education, general	11,914	—	238,550	24,177	48,952	403,675
Education, technical	34,368	23,209	—	62,226	27,315	—
Electricity development	31,895	—	14,514	108,020	—	28,930
Fisheries development	—	8,690	—	—	12,816	—
Forestry development	21,414	—	—	21,473	—	—
Gaskiya Corporation	24,767	5,002	—	19,533	2,500	—
Leprosy control	52,061	4,965	—	54,785	537	—
Marine development	—	2,650	560,954	—	14,483	539,065
Medical and health services	43,355	1,616	—	92,570	335	—
Mineral resources research	2,950	—	—	3,875	—	—
Nigeria Local Development Board	—	247	249,975	—	593	250,025
Oil Palm Research Station	41,015	12,096	—	61,454	14,919	—
Pathology research	113	—	—	—	—	—
Physiology research	1,300	—	—	840	—	—
Rice research	—	—	—	—	—	—
Road development	308,049	—	6,511	426,354	3,970	6,304
Rural Training and Demonstration Centre	—	—	—	2,189	8,505	—
Social welfare	—	28,255	—	46,082	—	—
Soil conservation	—	6,816	—	—	3,381	—
Telecommunications	23,603	—	—	59,571	—	—
Textile development	6,190	7,916	—	5,114	2,483	—
Town planning and village reconstruction	365	—	—	31,946	12,311	—
University College, Ibadan	20,991	1,481	—	—	—	—
Veterinary development	25,914	3,186	—	29,432	4,707	—
Water supplies, rural	100,919	3,139	—	188,004	3,136	—
Water supplies, urban	45,987	—	15,858	64,067	—	66,781
West Africa Institute of Trypanosomiasis Research	5,917	144	—	30,843	19,441	—
West African Pest Infestation Survey	3,035	—	—	8,666	—	—
Total	993,353	126,893	1,194,344	1,570,085	236,685	1,546,102

Source: Compiled from Nigeria, *Annual Report,* 1948–1950.

the period sometimes demanded more urgent attention than the implementation of the plan. When regional legislatures and administrations were created in the 1950s, the need to respond to political concerns became more urgent than the implementation of the plan. The Public Works Department report of 1948 explained that the slow rate of implementation was due to other projects taking priority.[98] Making similar complaints, the Land and Survey Department was forced to prioritize its projects throughout the country.[99]

The 1940s revealed the severe limitations on planning in a colonial context. No matter how sincere the colonial officers pretended to be, they faced overwhelming constraints. They could not change the economy's orientation beyond that established by the British. They had to function in the international system as part of the British Empire rather than as a distinct, sovereign territory. They could not initiate or develop multilateral relations unless these were approved by the Colonial Office.

We must remember that Lagos did not initiate the development plans. Rather the Colonial Office provided the guidelines and a portion of the funds and set the limitations by encouraging a cumbersome bureaucratic arrangement that involved the approval of development schemes and budgets. The bulk of development funding was spent on "bolstering the bureaucracy," instead of on needed welfare programs.[100]

There were aspects of the economy that also served as obstacles to rapid progress. One was the monetary conditions in which it operated. Although the Ten-Year Plan aimed at transferring funds from Britain to development projects in Nigeria, more money left the colony through other means, including the proceeds from the marketing boards' balances and a substantial proportion of public funds. There was little opportunity to mobilize domestic capital for development. The Nigerian currency lacked an independent value of its own; its fate and convertibility were tied to sterling, with restrictions even on how to spend foreign exchange.

In spite of Nigerians' reservations and the limitations of implementation, there was a commitment to the Ten-Year Plan beyond the 1940s. The majority of the population wanted one project or another, the intelligentsia was relentless in calling for change, and the state had to make concessions to a restless population.

CHAPTER FIVE

Midterm Reflections and Revisions, 1950–1955

> The Revised Development Plan is not an end in itself, it aims at no single goal since development is a continual process.
>
> *Annual Report on General Progress*, 1952

The changes in colonial planning—and indeed in the economy in general—during the 1950s are the least understood, partly because they are dismissed altogether or lumped with those of the immediate postwar years. Such changes as the shift toward economic rather than social programs, a new model of planning after 1955, a larger role for Nigerians in business and government (due to reforms in the business methods of foreign firms and the transfer of power by the British), and increasing regional polarization made the 1950s more eventful and definitely more important than the 1940s. In addition, this decade witnessed many significant changes in planning strategies.

After its first five years, the Ten-Year Plan was revised by slightly modifying its focus, reviewing costs and projects, and transferring many responsibilities to the new regional governments. In this chapter I will examine the impetus for the revision, the contents of the revised plan, and its implementation. The plan's time limit was never explained; the only justification was no doubt the promise of funding by the Colonial Office over a ten-year period. However, it was anticipated from the very beginning that the plan would have to be reviewed before it ran its course, by reexamining the schemes in light of experience and responding to demands and requests by Nigerians.[1]

In 1945, several departments' proposals indicated that they had not yet decided on many projects and policies. The Ten-Year Plan accommodated this tentativeness. In terms of its implementation, the plan was divided into two five-year cycles, with the objectives of the first better defined than those of the second. Funds from the Colonial Office were assured for the first five years, while it was difficult to estimate project costs over such a long period of time. Data were not available to make an educated projection to form the basis of long-term planning.

After the approval of the plan, many ideas were proposed by consultative committees and departments. There was pressure to crowd the new ideas into the document, although it was clear that the plan would become unmanageable.[2] Advocates of a plan review criticized the Ten-Year Plan for not allowing for occasional revision, "when progress [was] inclined to outrun the imagination."[3]

Due to major economic and political changes that called for a more comprehensive examination of the plan, however, the 1951 document was a revision, not a review. Economic concerns included inflation. Postwar planning was affected by the inflation of the costs of all essential imports. Moreover, inflation forced labor to demand more money, which inevitably led to higher wages. The 1945 estimates for the plan's projects bore little or no relation to their actual costs as the economic situation changed. For instance, building projects consumed more money than estimated.

By 1948, all departments were urging revisions of estimates because of increased costs. The sharp rise in the cost of materials and labor affected virtually all the principal projects. By 1950 the increase in estimated costs amounted to almost 60 percent. While some initially suggested recosting or reviewing, the government realized that this was not an appropriate avenue because by doing this "there could be no plan; the residual annual cost of development arising from a review and recosting would have been a strain upon the resources of Nigeria, which would have stultified further progress and resulted in retrenchment and the abandonment of services created, with all the attendant frustration, waste of energy and money that this would have involved."[4] A revision, on the other hand, allowed for a better assessment of the future, in addition to benefiting from the lessons of the past. The official position was that a useful revision would result "not in the scaling down of the original plan, but in an overall change in the general picture of development which to many may lack the grace of the more classical features originally drawn."[5]

At the same time, there was a substantial increase in government revenues because of the rise in commodity prices—the second unanticipated economic change. Increased revenues gave officers the confidence to call for greater spending if only to bring the plan within its original cost estimates, that is, by adding funds to offset inflation. The big problem, however, was that there was no assurance that the economy was capable of supporting recurrent liabilities arising from a program largely devoted to the provision of a social and physical infrastructure. The fear of an annual recurrent liability drove leading administrators to recommend a change in sectoral emphasis from the social to the economic, which would be self-financing.

Originally estimated at £4 million beginning in 1956, recurrent costs of social services were revised upward by £2 million in 1951. Faced with a high rate of taxation and without any assurance that more money would accrue from export products, leading officials suggested scaling down the plan's social programs. In the late 1940s the complaints about inadequate funding led to suggestions in favor of an approach that would disburse money on an annual basis to pay for a limited number of projects.

The economy fostered several negative tendencies, in spite of the plan. The rate of inflation and unemployment, particularly of women, was high. Migration to the towns occurred at an alarming rate. There were social problems like poverty in urban areas and deplorable living conditions in the mining centers of the Jos Plateau and Enugu. Available health care facilities were grossly inadequate. Leprosy and tuberculosis were on the rise.[6] A consensus of opinion existed, even among the most conservative officials, that the country was still poor. Official sources pointed increasingly to the economic marginalization of women, widespread malnutrition among all ages, and high prices of food. The crisis that would plague agriculture after independence had also begun, as young men and women abandoned farms and villages.[7] The limited revenue base of the country—excessive dependence on revenues from customs and excise and income taxes—served as another constraint.

The politics of decolonization also necessitated revision of the plan. The impact of regionalism on planning began in 1947, as a consequence of the Richards Constitution, which ended the centralization policy that had been in place since 1914. The post–1945 constitutional changes fostered a move toward a federal system. Senior colonial officials concluded that the differences between the Nigerian ethnic groups were substantial and that, as much as possible, each region should be allowed to manage its own affairs. The 1951 constitutional revision created three divisions, introduced an elected government, and provided for a federal form of government and for regional governments in the east, west, and north. The regional bodies could raise and appropriate funds and pass laws on education, health, agriculture, and local government. In 1952, Nigerians acquired responsibilities as leaders of regional businesses and politics. One of the three political parties dominated each region: the National Council of Nigerian Citizens in the east, the Northern People's Congress in the north, and the Action Group in the west.

The 1951 Constitution provided for the establishment of a central legislature, an executive with full legislative and executive powers, and a legislature and executive in each region with limited executive and legislative powers subject to the control of the central legislature and executive. In 1952, the regions began a ministerial administration. In addition, there was a far-reaching reorganization of local administration that transferred power and responsibility to the local level of government.

The increasing autonomy of the regions began to weaken the central development institutions and the mechanisms for plan implementation. The competition between the provinces (and later regions) for the benefits of planning and for resources began after 1946, as every province requested more projects and money. Economic disparities between the regions contributed to political rivalries and regional nationalism. Areas with profitable cash crops witnessed some changes, and their people demanded more welfare programs.

The Yoruba in the west, who benefited from cocoa wealth and a middleman position in the retail trade, looked forward to more economic power. The revenues from cocoa assured access to imported goods and Western education and spurred demands for better services. The Yoruba elite demanded a political arrangement that would ensure their leadership in the country, as well as economic prosperity.

In the eastern region where palm produce generated less money than cocoa and where fertile land was inadequate for its growing population, people migrated elsewhere and demanded more resources from the central government. To derive advantages from their migrations, the Igbo in the east desired a political system that would treat strangers with respect and equality. Northerners feared southern domination of the northern economy and bureaucracy. Slow development and scarcity of skilled labor aggravated this fear.

In 1947, the regions sought additional financial independence and power. As departments were regionalized, so too was the funding to run them. Certain aspects of the regionalized departments, such as research, funding for the colony of Lagos, and countrywide institutions, were supported through central government expenditures.[8] The regions demanded more money, on the grounds that certain activities could best be performed on a regional basis. In 1950, regional leaders began to express the opinion that a decentralized plan would bring more projects and money to their regions than a centralized one controlled by the Secretariat in Lagos. The minorities in central and southwestern Nigeria even pressed for separate regions and more power because of the need to attract more development funds for themselves, as well as because of a belief that the larger regions would always impede their growth.[9]

The 1951 Constitution favored a decentralized plan. By establishing a federal system with regional governments, and by creating powerful African majorities in local and legislative councils, the political changes rendered obsolete the plan's assumptions of a unitary system of government and of a political organization in which the decision-making process was dominated by colonial officers. The Ten-Year Plan was criticized for insufficiently considering the opinion of Nigerians. Previous consultative bodies (PDCs and DDCs) were no longer considered satisfactory, and the government accepted the criticism that "authority and representation more suited to modern ideas" should be involved in the planning process.

The final reason for plan revision was the Nigerians' repeated demands for development projects. The spate of demands created pressure on the government either to do more or to increase the rate of implementation. The overall assessment of the results of planning between 1946 and 1948 indicated that little had been accomplished. Even sympathetic officers concluded that there had been no observable effect on people's general welfare. Many Nigerians expressed disappointment and frustration at the complete lack of progress between 1948 and 1950. There were hundreds of demands for small projects such as parks and botanical gardens[10] and for larger projects like schools, hospitals, and roads.[11] Members of the vocal trade unions in Lagos focused on demands for better pay and for a voice in the planning process. Some unionists even recommended a social security system to cover medical bills, unemployment benefits, and so on.[12] The politicians wanted more of everything.

In making all these demands, Nigerians did not accept that there were not adequate funds. They believed that there were available staff or people who could be trained on short notice. In the short run, Nigeria could recruit staff from all parts of the world or, as one member of the Ondo PDC interestingly suggested, African Americans could be asked to return to their "home" country.[13] Some communities were even demanding the authority to establish schools for training personnel. Many requested that hundreds of Nigerians be sent to Europe for three years to receive training in every aspect of development. The belief that a quick transformation was possible made many people less sympathetic to the government's excuses.

What Was Wrong?

Recognizing the country's underdevelopment served to direct attention to criticisms of the plan and of society in general. The Colonial Office and the Nigerian government still made statements that repeated the ideas of the Ten-Year Plan or new ones that clarified its contents. The dominant official thinking, as before, was that the bedrock of development should be agriculture: only an increase in productivity would enhance living standards. This increase could be produced by a combination of many actions: improved production methods, land utilization and tenure reforms, fertilizer use, efficient local government administration involved in production, and improved soil fertility, to mention the leading ones. Secondary industries also had to be built gradually, by changing customary attitudes, creating a cadre of factory workers, and establishing a number of local industries.[14]

From the viewpoint of the administrative officers and representatives of the firms, the attitude and capacity of Nigerians constituted the most serious limitations to progress. On the one hand, the educated elite were criticized for paying too much attention to politics, contributing very little to economic progress and making too many unnecessary demands. Frank Samuel, managing director of the United Africa Company, expressed a common opinion when he criticized Nigeria and the rest of Africa for its "poverty of wealth, body and mind" and demeaned its educated elite:

> Strenuous attempts must be made to ensure that the educated Africans—and they are rapidly growing in number—have some appreciation of the need for great efforts to be made by the African peoples themselves. The understanding of simple economics is woefully lacking in even the best educated of them, and there is at the present time far too great a tendency to regard grants-in-aid as payments belonging to them as of right—and to demand them in ever-increasing measure. Were the educated classes to devote a tithe of the efforts which they at present devote to political agitation to the bettering of the social and economic condition of their countries, the outlook would be more cheerful than it appears at present.[15]

On the other hand, there was "the human problem of the African peasant,"[16] a class described as unimaginative, conservative, and unproductive. In the 1950s, leading economists argued that economic growth and entrepreneurship depended on personality and cultural factors and that most Africans, notably the peasants, were not concerned with achievements.[17] The Colonial Office suggested the use of force in changing their attitude. If force was not possible, other methods, such as inducement or massive transfer of peasants to sparsely populated places, had to be found to secure their cooperation and ensure the productive use of their labor. In pushing the blame on poor peasants, few officials noted that peasants continued to be active and productive, like their counterparts elsewhere in the continent, in spite of poverty and low technology.

Many Nigerians and even the colonial officers in the provinces were more critical, questioning many aspects of the plan and its philosophy. A number of alternative suggestions were made by several administrative officers (reflecting either their concern for the people or their closeness to the grass roots) and by frontline Nigerians in both politics and the press. Rather than blame the peasants, this group pointed to reasons such as shortages of funds and staff, instability in world prices, and the failure to promote research and new farming methods.[18]

Although some of the critics still held a condescending view of the peasants, they did not think that it would be an easy task to change peasants' lifestyles and production techniques. Some of their suggestions for changing the peasants were reviewed in detail. For instance, if the use of imported machines was encouraged, it would give rise to the use of many supervisors, thus reducing the income of peasants. If the government intervened directly by hiring labor, the peasants would regard themselves as employees entitled to rights that were not necessarily commensurate with their duties. If plantations were allowed, the peasants would become laborers exploited by a few entrepreneurs. Thus, the situation of the peasant had to be understood before any measures could be taken. There is no evidence, argued the critics, that the farmers had little food to eat (instead, they were well nourished), were lacking in ambition (they saved money to educate their children and build houses), or lazy (they worked most of the time).[19]

Among the critics' suggestions for improvement were increasing educational opportunities, transferring power at the local level to the educated elite, advancing loans to farmers, creating farm schools to teach modern methods, conducting more research on how to increase productivity, promoting cooperative farming, and giving more attention to economic rather than political problems.[20] On political versus economic problems, one officer remarked that without economic development there would be no political advancement.[21]

The Nigerian politicians and nationalists who pressured for a revision of the plan argued that industrialization was the key to rapid progress. Secondary industries should be established to employ more people and raise living standards. They disagreed with the official policy of emphasizing agriculture:

> To them, Nigeria would never develop without large-scale secondary industries. In making specific suggestions on industries, they wanted the development of local resources to build houses, manufacture cloths, distill spirits. The new local industries should be protected from competition from imports. Huge dams should be constructed for electricity supply, the Niger used to irrigate the north and many Nigerians to be sent for training abroad. It is small consolation to an African to have magnificent roads in his country when he cannot afford the vehicles to drive over them or the goods to fill those vehicles, to see fine hospitals which he knows he must enter largely due to his poor housing conditions and deficient diet, to have an excellent education when his ambitions for a good job and respectable standard of living thereafter cannot be satisfied. . . .

> The position of economic and social development programmes should be reversed, there should be a full scale drive and expenditure on both primary and secondary industries with reduced expenditure on social services and Nigeria must be visualised as a country with an economic balance between primary and secondary industries which inevitably entails the establishment of many factories. Industrialization will be a slow and no doubt at first a disappointing and painful process but it is necessary now for its importance to be realised and the foundations to be laid.[22]

A strategy of industrialization would provide jobs and the necessary goods as well as create an industrial aristocracy to replace the existing "professional and clerical aristocracy," which did not enhance the wealth of the country.[23] The owners of small-scale enterprises and aspiring industrialists argued that without industrialization and assistance to local entrepreneurs, the benefits of the plan would not last.

In the final analysis, the revision did not go far enough in incorporating the alternative suggestions. Indeed, the revision wasted the suggestions and retained the essential philosophy of the Ten-Year Plan. The revisionist ideas survived, however, and were repeated throughout most of the 1950s and 1960s. Since many of those who propounded the ideas later became influential in the management of the regions and later of the country, they were eventually able to impose their vision, except that the radicals among them either lacked sufficient clout or converted to a more gradualist, conservative approach.

The Fundamentals of Revision: Regionalism and Flexibility

Rather than the integration of the ideas of the critics or the views of the nationalists and socialists, the revision was marked by two technical issues: (1) to give more power to the regional governments and (2) to create a flexible plan to allow the regions to introduce their innovations to the projects without waiting for permission from the Lagos Secretariat or the Colonial Office. While central coordination and overall control was necessary, the regional legislatures were given the "fullest possible scope" for planning, in order to relate it to the country's needs.

In the budget session of the Legislative Council in 1949, the Financial Secretary informed the members of the necessity of revision. This was followed by instructions to regional authorities to undertake reviews to ensure that proper proportions were maintained between social services and economic development and to suggest the reorientation of the plan through the introduction of new schemes or modification of older ones.[24] Regional development committees (RDCs) emerged, replacing previous area development committees. The RDCs included large numbers of emerging elites and politicians.

For the first time, each region had a realistic idea of available funds. In February 1950 the central government decided that proportions of about 50, 25, and 25 percent would go to the northern, eastern, and western regions (including the Lagos Colony), respectively, of the balance of funds remaining for the Ten-Year Plan. In monetary terms this translated as £12 million for the north, £5.3 million for the east, and £5.8 million for the west.

In collating its proposals, each region considered previous projects and aimed for their continuation or completion. A big error in many cases was that new projects were substituted for the original ones without justification or assessment. The regions distributed projects by provinces, ensuring that those containing regional headquarters had at least one major scheme. By involving all the provinces, regional governments worked through the planning bureaucracy of the 1940s, notably the provincial development committees (PDCs) and the Development Officers, although the divisional development committees (DDCs) played a minimal role.[25] Thus, the regional governments only coordinated the recommendations of the PDCs, as was the case in the 1940s. At every committee level, the members lobbied for projects for their own areas. The new elite who were in power for the first time learned about securing resources for their constituencies.

All the regions displayed enthusiasm about their enlarged role, but none used its new power to develop a new philosophy or suggest a different direction. They accepted the Ten-Year Plan as a given and thought that they could use other avenues to implement their own ideas. The review process provided limited opportunities for innovations. The regions adhered to the instructions from Lagos and continued with the tradition of planning beyond their means.[26] The plans submitted by the regions exceeded the working budgetary ceilings by £2.6 million. The need to impose a limit to total expenditures led to an instruction for the western region, the one with the highest excess, to scale down its allocation. The central government proposed a total expenditure of £34.1 million for the revised plan, an amount it thought the country could absorb, because it lacked the physical ability to spend much more.[27]

The variations between allocations in the regional plans and those in the approved revised plan were small.[28] To make it "a Nigerian plan," Lagos provided for central services and projects that benefited the country as a whole. In implementation it also remained essentially a Nigerian plan: the central administration did not loosen its supervisory power, and it in turn reported progress to the Colonial Office. Lagos controlled and disbursed the funds. The Development Secretary visited the regional headquarters to participate in the modification of priorities and plan variations.

The government abandoned a rigid approach to planning: "The revised plan therefore contains its own shadow plan for the future and in the list of projects under several schemes this can be seen. The estimates for the revised plan are so arranged, in every case where this can be done, in such a way that complete freedom will be left to the Regions to choose those projects from time to time which can in fact be undertaken with the greatest efficiency and which command the highest priority."[29] Officials also believed that flexibility would allow for adaptation and improvisation:

> The objective is to obtain the maximum development from the money available and the ability to spend it, and if costs continue to rise the credit will rest with those whose efforts fall shortest of the ideal through their ability to adapt and improvise without waste and inefficiency. There are many to whom the sight of a hundred children at school is a greater inspiration than a building so permanent as to outlast its usefulness, and there is more time to wait for perfection than there is to waste upon the retardation of the developments which are necessary to bring Nigeria to its final greatness.[30]

The regions were free to adjust the speed of development "by setting out the estimates as a statement of financial and executive capacity to undertake a certain amount of work against an approved list of development projects."[31]

Financial Allocations

The sources of finance remained the same. The balance from the Colonial Development and Welfare Fund of £16.2 million was applied by the revised plan. Lagos also sought the approval of the Colonial Office to use unspent funds in the principal and supplementary grants, draw loans as before, and use Nigerian revenues to meet the balance of total expenditures.[32] The revised plan was thus financed from three principal sources (table 5.1). Tables 5.2 to 5.12 provide the details of allocations to sectors and regions.

The revised plan fell into two parts: (1) the acceleration of departmental activity where this involved the necessary foundation work and research upon which future development would rest and (2) specific schemes of development that were outside ordinary government activity. Both parts included projects in agriculture, education, forestry, medical services, communications, roads, textile development, water supplies, community development,

Table 5.1. Sources of financing for Revised Ten-Year Plan

CDWA grants	£16,212,584
Loan funds	£9,950,450
Nigerian revenue contribution	£8,020,607
Total	£34,183,641

Source: Nigeria, *Revised Plan.*

Table 5.2. Estimated expenditures, 1951–1956 (£)

Schemes	*1951–52*	*1952–53*	*1953–54*	*1954–55*	*1955–56*
Agriculture	9,190	8,770	8,910	8,910	9,510
Broadcasting	(100,000)	(100,000)	(153,762)	(100,000)	(71,095)
Building, staff, etc.	67,500	66,000	58,500	47,500	38,000
Community development	7,000	7,000	7,000	7,000	7,000
Development officers	14,864	14,864	14,864	14,864	15,864
Education, general	21,050	27,570	40,920	15,150	15,480
Education, technical	580,940	607,292	575,972	318,142	262,808
Electricity	500,000	—	—	—	—
Fisheries	19,460	17,860	18,040	18,250	18,380
Forestry	10,403	8,982	7,610	7,900	8,090
Geological survey	25,000	25,000	25,000	—	—
Leprosy control	16,136	15,353	15,588	15,879	16,064
Marine	156,590	457,360	458,605	260,350	162,695
Medical and health	192,193	174,064	134,518	140,390	137,709
Meteorology	22,640	—	—	—	—
Preliminary investigations	10,000	10,000	10,000	10,000	10,000
Roads	96,100	39,600	39,100	33,600	28,600
Rural Training Centre	25,588	17,769	9,356	8,873	8,134
Social welfare	41,605	42,933	43,982	8,873	8,134
Telecommunications	254,000	99,500	7,000	45,052	46,040
Textiles	17,780	17,340	17,610	—	—
Veterinary	32,318	34,950	15,574	17,860	18,090
Water supplies, rural	6,900	10,420	2,560	17,100	17,140
Water supplies, geological	7,680	7,975	8,173	2,560	2,560
Water supplies, urban	62,100	29,000	17,800	9,431	9,945
Major communication	2,000,000	—	—	14,300	12,800
Teaching Hospital	60,020	—	—	—	—
Fever and smallpox vaccine research	25,000	15,000	15,000	15,000	15,000
Research	45,858	32,002	31,794	32,314	15,304
Total	4,427,915	1,886,604	1,737,238	1,160,344	946,309

Notes: The grand total is £10,158,410; figures in parentheses are approximate.

Table 5.3. Estimated expenditures, Northern Region, 1951–1956 (£)

Schemes	*1951–52*	*1952–53*	*1953–54*	*1954–55*	*1955–56*
Agriculture	382,609	345,645	286,275	266,343	254,480
Building, staff, etc.	55,000	51,000	42,000	36,000	31,000
Development Officers	41,540	41,540	41,540	41,540	49,040
Education, general	190,690	204,910	365,810	181,820	160,610
Education, technical	159,700	167,780	177,050	107,020	103,290
Fisheries	5,390	5,640	5,790	5,570	5,800
Forestry	28,230	42,575	32,240	26,460	26,470
Leprosy control	(41,296)	(41,296)	(41,296)	(41,296)	(41,296)
Medical and health	(398,934)	(398,935)	(398,935)	(398,935)	(398,935)
Roads	481,000	387,000	368,000	360,000	249,000
Social welfare	3,297	2,984	3,478	3,127	3,631
Telecommunications	34,000	42,500	122,500	50,000	50,000
Textiles	11,356	10,230	10,470	10,700	10,910
Veterinary	37,956	33,454	26,196	26,152	26,166
Water supplies rural	442,000	490,000	532,000	537,000	471,000
Water supplies, urban	141,100	133,800	131,300	126,300	67,500
Industrial projects	(200,000)	(200,000)	(200,000)	(200,000)	(200,000)
Rice research	14,236	11,966	5,675	5,302	5,405
Total	2,668,334	2,611,254	2,790,555	2,425,565	2,155,033

Source: Nigeria, *Revised Plan.*
Notes: The grand total is £12,648,741; figures in parentheses are approximate.

veterinarian services, fisheries, and leprosy control, as well as housing construction by the Public Works Department.

Some of these were new projects or new arrangements of old ones. For instance, the Building Program for Development became a separate scheme involved in plants, vehicles, and staff only, whereas construction was included in individual schemes, thus showing a true total expenditure for each project. Performance needed strengthening in local industries like textiles.[33] By increasing miles of roads, communications would be improved. Although there was a general reduction in social services, the revised plan provided for the expansion of medical services and continued its emphasis on establishing water supplies in new areas.[34]

The revised plan recognized the need to budget for recurrent residual costs, to be paid for by the Nigerian revenues beginning in 1956. Schemes that would yield more revenue at the expense of the social were emphasized. While it remained a "Nigerian plan" in the sense that Lagos still gave final approval to the schemes and allocated the money, regionalization was extended to most spheres of the plan: every region was to receive its monetary share for projects,

Table 5.4. Estimated expenditures, Eastern Region, 1951–1956 (£)

Schemes	*1951–52*	*1952–53*	*1953–54*	*1954–55*	*1955–56*
Agriculture	118,525	120,030	136,205	117,615	108,340
Building, staff, etc.	21,900	21,900	17,900	13,900	13,900
Community Development	50,000	50,000	50,000	50,000	50,000
Development Officers	21,020	21,020	21,020	21,020	23,520
Education, general	140,870	175,500	171,000	80,000	164,000
Education, technical	135,280	138,029	105,059	74,245	85,630
Fisheries	4,070	4,360	4,540	4,730	4,990
Forestry	29,941	31,032	30,046	26,425	27,150
Leprosy control	(147,656)	(147,656)	(147,656)	(147,656)	(147,656)
Medical and health	(151,746)	(151,746)	(151,746)	(151,746)	(151,746)
Roads	141,600	126,100	124,600	123,600	104,100
Social welfare	15,606	14,360	—	—	—
Telecommunications	35,700	56,300	94,800	51,200	62,000
Veterinary	19,451	14,277	13,036	12,957	13,233
Water supplies, rural	50,400	37,800	42,800	40,400	28,600
Water supplies, urban	59,200	66,300	63,300	40,300	20,900
Rice research	13,950	6,745	7,630	5,875	5,325
Total	1,156,915	1,183,155	1,181,338	961,669	1,011,090

Source: Nigeria, *Revised Plan.*
Notes: The grand total is £5,494,167; figures in parantheses are approximate.

Table 5.5. Estimated expenditures, Western Region 1951–1956 (£)

Schemes	*1951–52*	*1952–53*	*1953–54*	*1954–55*	*1955–56*
Agriculture	205,063	177,703	158,478	166,183	163,523
Building, staff, etc.	33,600	35,100	28,600	21,600	19,100
Community development	40,000	40,000	40,000	40,000	40,000
Development Officers	16,916	16,916	16,916	16,916	18,416
Education, general	122,590	229,132	364,793	139,273	144,212
Education, technical	55,890	83,940	88,920	61,280	44,280
Fisheries	5,550	6,160	6,300	6,470	6,750
Forestry	25,248	24,573	25,636	26,705	27,772
Launch services	(10,000)	(10,000)	(10,000)	(10,000)	(10,000)
Leprosy control	(41,544)	(41,544)	(41,544)	(41,544)	(41,544)
Medical and health	(188,127)	(188,128)	(188,128)	(188,128)	(188,128)
Roads	119,800	108,500	106,700	95,200	44,800
Social welfare	12,327	12,458	12,328	12,777	13,160
Telecommunications	25,300	28,700	77,000	70,450	72,400
Textiles	10,230	9,090	9,270	9,440	9,640
Veterinary	27,209	25,069	26,794	20,767	16,051
Water supplies, rural	40,500	38,800	40,800	40,300	34,600
Water supplies, urban	110,200	163,900	192,200	148,200	108,500
Total	1,090,094	1,239,713	1,434,407	1,115,233	1,002,876

Source: Nigeria, *Revised Plan.*
Notes: The grand total is £5,882,323; figures in parentheses are approximate.

Table 5.6. Allocations in the Revised Ten-Year Plan (£)

Schemes	*North*	*East*	*West*	*Central*	*Total*
Agriculture	1,521,001	593,540	863,735	73,990	3,052,306
Broadcasting	—	—	—	524,857	524,857
Building, staff and plants	215,000	89,500	138,000	277,500	720,000
Community development	—	250,000	200,000	35,000	485,000
Development Officers	215,200	107,600	86,080	75,320	484,200
Education, general	1,103,840	731,370	1,000,000	120,170	2,955,380
Education, technical	714,840	538,243	334,310	2,345,154	3,932,547
Electricity	—	—	—	500,000	500,000
Fisheries	28,190	22,690	31,230	91,990	174,100
Forestry	155,975	144,594	129,934	42,985	473,488
Geological survey	—	—	—	75,000	75,000
Launch services	—	—	50,000	—	50,000
Leprosy control	206,480	738,280	207,720	79,020	1,231,500
Marine	—	—	—	1,495,600	1,495,600
Medical and health	1,994,674	758,730	940,639	778,793	4,472,836
Meteorology	—	—	—	22,640	22,640
Preliminary investigations	—	—	—	50,000	50,000
Roads	1,845,000	620,000	475,000	237,000	3,177,000
Rural Training Centre	—	—	—	69,720	69,720
Social welfare	16,517	29,996	63,050	219,613	329,146
Telecommunications	299,500	300,000	273,850	360,500	1,233,850
Textiles	53,666	—	47,670	88,680	190,016
Veterinary	149,924	72,954	115,890	117,082	455,850
Water supplies, rural	2,472,000	200,000	195,000	25,000	2,892,000
Water supplies, geological	—	—	—	43,204	43,204
Water supplies, urban	600,000	250,000	723,000	136,000	1,709,000
Major industrial projects, north	1,000,000	—	—	—	1,000,000
Extensions to communi-cations, Borno	—	—	—	2,000,000	2,000,000
Teaching Hospital	—	—	—	60,020	60,020
Yellow fever and smallpox vaccines	—	—	—	85,000	85,000
Research	42,584	39,525	—	157,272	239,381
Total	12,648,741	5,494,167	5,882,323	10158410	34183641

Source: Nigeria, *Revised Plan,* 12.

and the budgets of departments were decentralized. Regionalization extended to some other related development agencies, such as the production and loan boards.

The activities of the Nigerian Loan Development Board (NLDB) were suspended in 1949 to prepare for a regionalization policy that divided it into four boards, a board for each region and the Lagos Colony. On December 13, 1951, the most far-reaching step occurred with the enactment of a new ordinance, which replaced and repealed the sections of the 1949 Nigeria Groundnut Marketing Ordinance and the Nigeria Oil Palm Produce Marketing Ordinance under which the boards had hitherto functioned. This change consolidated the provisions on the functions and operations of all the Regional Production Development Boards (RPDBs). The new ordinance also authorized the Nigeria Cocoa Marketing Board's transfer of its development powers to the RPDBs. The new ordinance provided an opportunity to include declaratory provisions to broaden the boards' methods of fund allocations and their investment powers.[35] The funds of the marketing boards were apportioned in such a way that they had to allocate at least 22.5 percent of their surplus funds to development projects and another 7.5 percent to research. These funds went to support the projects carried out by the regional governments.

The core of the Ten-Year Plan revision addressed the problems of implementation, some of the changes in politics and economics highlighted above, and additional changes that the government wanted to make. Table 5.4 compares the allocations in the old and revised plans, which reflect the attention to "basic equipment"—services that the government believed would enhance production.

The Implementation of the Revised Plan

The revised plan did not aim at any ultimate goal or contain "within itself any sense of satisfaction that it will complete one single task for ever: its only objective [was] to forward many tasks by planned effort during five years at a greater speed than would otherwise be achieved by uncoordinated day to day routine."[36] The revised plan accepted many of the ideas, in addition to the achievements and responsibilities, of its parent. In general, the majority of the projects were continuations of previous ones. Thus, the criticisms of the earlier plan are valid here as well.

The agriculture projects assisted the expansion of services by setting up experimental and demonstration stations and livestock improvement and breeding centers, as well as by research and investigation so that farmers could benefit from improved agricultural knowledge. Research was conducted by

Table 5.7. Phases 1 and 2 of the Ten-Year Plan (in £ and by percentage)

	Ten Year Plan £49,468,266 (exclusive of loan charges)	*Revised Plan £34,183,641 (5 Years)*
Social services and Administration		
Development Officers	895,500	484,200
General education	6,032,340	2,955,380
Medical and health	10,438,837	5,849,356
Gaskiya Corporation	152,350	—
Social welfare	384,000	329,146
Statistics	100,000	—
Building, staff, and plant	821,000	720,000
Total	18,824,027	10,338,082
	(38%)	(30.3%)
Basic equipment		
Water supplies	8,062,000	4,644,204
Roads	7,046,300	3,177,000
Electricity	1,544,200	500,000
Telecommunications	820,000	1,233,850
Marine	3,517,940	1,495,600
Technical education	1,115,453	3,932,547
Community development	332,000	485,000
Rural Training Centre	—	69,720
Total	22,437,893	15,537,931
Percent	(45.3%)	(45.4%)
Productive services and revenue earning projects		
Remainder of plan	8,206,346	8,307,638
Percent	(16.7%)	(24.3%)

Source: Nigeria, *Revised Plan,* 4.

the West African Institute for Oil Palm Research, the West African Cocoa Research Institute, and the Agriculture Department. The problems of export crops were the core of most research work, although there were smaller projects on food crops.[37] More trained staff were recruited than ever before.

Research on improved methods focused on the use of tractors (with supplies to farmers organized by a small number of tractor units in the three regions), irrigation work, rice cultivation, soil improvement, farm settlements, and mixed farming. Information on the nature of agricultural problems was more available than previously. Output per unit of labor and land was low; obtaining access to land was increasingly difficult; the implements and tech-

Table 5.8. Allocations by sources of revenue (£)

Schemes	*Total allocation*	*CDWA grant*	*Nigeria revenue*
Agriculture	3,052,306	2,289,230 (75%)	736,076
Broadcasting	524,857	190,000[a]	334,857
Building, staff	720,000	540,000 (75%)	180,000
Community development	485,000	—	485,000
Development Officers	484,200	484,200 (100%)	—
Education, general	2,955,380	2,216,283 (75%)	739,097
Education, technical	2,351,273	1,763,455 (75%)	587,818
Education, technical[b]	1,581,274	500,000[a]	1,081,274
Fisheries	174,100	130,575 (75%)	43,525
Forestry	473,488	355,116 (75%)	118,372
Geological survey	75,000	75,000[c] (100%)	—
Launch services	50,000	—	50,000
Leprosy control	1,231,500	923,625 (75%)	307,875
Marine (staff)	165,000	—	165,000
Medical and health	4,472,836	3,354,627 (75%)	1,118,209
Meteorology	22,640	22,640[c] (100%)	—
Preliminary investigation	50,000	—	50,000
Rural Training Centre	69,720	52,290 (75%)	17,430
Social welfare	329,146	—	329,146
Textiles	190,016	142,512 (75%)	47,504
Veterinary	455,850	455,850 (100%)	—
Water supplies, rural	2,892,000	2,641,680 (90%)	293,524
Water supplies, geological	43,204		
Industries, north	1,000,000	—	1,000,000
Teaching Hospital	60,020	—	60,020
Yellow fever and smallpox vaccines	85,000	—	85,000
Research	239,381	75,501[b]	163,880
Total	24,233,191	16,212,584	8,020,607

Source: Nigeria, *Revised Plan,* 13.
[a]In respect of capital costs.
[b]Nigerian College of Arts, Science, and Technology.
[c]Completion of old schemes.

niques of cultivation had changed little from those at the beginning of the century; and the peasants were overworked. The colonial changes in the land tenure system encouraged individual ownership, promoting the emergence of landlordism in those with the money and power. Planning failed to resolve ownership problems such as unused land, uneconomic holdings, or ways to prevent peasants from pawning their limited land assets for small credit.

The 1950s began to yield evidence on the success and failure of some of the projects begun in the 1940s. In most cases, the government stubbornly pursued its programs, even in cases where people expressed doubts. Productivity had to be enhanced through the application of fertilizers, irrigation, mechanization, farm resettlements, and soil conservation. The majority of the farmers continued to express doubts on fertilizer use,[38] but the Agriculture Department was relentless in convincing them of its great potential through demonstrations and announcements of great results.

Irrigation was more common in the north, receiving some praise in the dry season but condemnation in places where the people thought that their supply of water was affected.[39] Mechanical cultivation of swampland in parts of the north proved profitable by allowing rice cultivation in large areas of fertile land. Upland cultivation was a different story: the cost of adequate supervision and maintenance made it difficult to perform these operations economically. In 1953, the Agriculture Department had to close down a number of tractor unit farms in the north (at Amoyo, Muna, Kafinsoli, and Maru) and the remaining ones were closely supervised to obtain accurate information about operation costs.[40]

Everywhere people complained that neither tractors nor any other machine could perform certain operations like weeding, and the cost of hand labor was high. Moreover, in cases where modern machines were useful, their numbers were too small to meet demands and make a difference. The government owned virtually all the equipment, and it had to address distribution and repair problems.

Soil conservation work was generally on a small scale. Until 1955, its impact was marginal and most people were unimpressed either by the idea or the result.[41] The Land Settlement Scheme was retained, and official reports were usually positive. For instance, in 1953 the analysis of the Kontagora Resettlement Scheme indicated that "in general, the settlers appeared to be thriving. New bicycles were in evidence in some of the hamlets, and there was a growing demand for a school and for adult literacy classes."[42] The opinion of the survivors of the resettlement projects is contrary: their dream of cheap income and quick profits did not materialize. The settlers were right: the decade witnessed the failure of many large projects. Kontagora turned out to be a colossal failure, and the resettlement project and plantation were eventually abandoned.[43] Kontagora's failure convinced planners that small-scale holdings were best for the country.

The farm schools established in the 1940s, like those of Oyo and Ogbomoso, were unsuccessful; after 1951, a fresh beginning was made to reorganize them. Some expressed reservations about the oil mills—the hope for an expected revolution in palm oil production. While the oil mills added to the

Table 5.9. Schemes scheduled for loans fund allocations (£)

Electricity	500,000
Marine (excluding staff)	1,330,600
Telecommunications	1,233,850
Water supplies, urban	1,709,000
Extension to communications in Borno	2,000,000
Roads	3,177,000
Total	9,950,450

Source: Nigeria, *Revised Plan,* 13.

Table 5.10. Annual expenditures of C. D. and W. F. grants (£)

Schemes	*1951–52*	*1952–53*	*1953–54*	*1954–55*	*1955–56*
Agriculture	536,540	489,110	442,402	410,288	401,890
Broadcasting	(100,000)	(90,000)	—	—	—
Building, staff	133,500	130,500	110,250	89,250	76,500
Develop. Officers	94,430	94,340	94,340	94,340	106,840
Education, general	356,350	477,732	706,893	312,082	363,226
Education, technical	395,675	427,862	389,235	281,642	269,041
Education[a]	(200,000)	(200,000)	(100,000)	—	—
Fisheries	25,853	25,515	26,002	26,265	26,940
Forestry	70,367	80,371	71,649	65,617	67,112
Geological survey	25,000	25,000	25,000	—	—
Leprosy control	(184,974)	(184,563)	(184,563)	(184,781)	(184,920)
Medical and health	698,250	684,656	654,995	659,338	657,388
Meteorology	22,640	—	—	—	—
Rural Training Centre	19,191	13,327	7,017	6,655	6,100
Textiles	29,525	27,495	28,012	28,500	28,980
Veterinary	116,934	107,750	81,600	76,976	72,590
Water supplies, rural	492,732	526,495	563,699	566,720	492,034
Research	23,501	13,000	13,000	13,000	13,000
Total	3,525,372	3,597,540	3,498,657	2,824,454	2,766,561

Source: Nigeria, *Revised Plan,* 13.
Notes: The grand total is £16,212,584; figures in parentheses are approximate.
[a]Nigerian College of Arts, Science, and Technology.

quality of oil, their operators began to complain that the mills were running at a loss because of the irregular supply of palm fruit. The oil mills also had to compete with the traditional manual system and the hand presses.

During the 1950s, the press expressed great worry about rising food prices and emphasized the need to use planning to correct this. While the government recognized an inflationary pressure it refused to panic, arguing that the country was still able to feed itself.[44]

In the western region, the new scheme was group farming, an official

Table 5.11 Estimated total expenditures 1951–1956

Schemes	*1951–52*	*1952–53*	*1953–54*	*1954–55*	*1955–56*	*Total*
Agriculture	715,387	652,147	589,868	559,051	535,853	3,052,306
Broadcasting	(100,000)	(100,000)	(153,762)	(100,000)	(71,095)	524,857
Building, staff, etc.	178,000	174,000	147,000	119,000	102,000	720,000
Community development	97,000	97,000	97,000	97,000	97,000	485,000
Development Officers	94,340	94,340	94,340	94,340	106,840	484,200
Education, general	475,200	637,112	942,523	416,243	484,302	2,955,380
Education, technical	931,810	997,041	947,001	560,687	496,008	3,932,547
Electricity	500,000	—	—	—	—	500,000
Fisheries	34,470	34,020	34,670	35,020	35,920	174,100
Forestry	93,822	107,162	95,532	87,490	89,482	473,488
Geological survey	25,000	25,000	25,000	—	—	75,000
Launch services	(10,000)	(10,000)	(10,000)	(10,000)	(10,000)	50,000
Leprosy control	(246,632)	(245,849)	(246,084)	(246,375)	(246,560)	1,231,500
Marine	156,590	457,360	458,605	260,350	162,695	1,495,600
Medical and health	931,000	912,873	873,327	879,118	876,518	4,472,836
Meteorology	22,640	—	—	—	—	22,640
Preliminary investigations	10,000	10,000	10,000	10,000	10,000	50,000
Roads	838,5002	661,200	638,400	612,400	426,500	3,177,000
Rural Training Centre	25,588	17,769	9,356	8,873	8,134	69,720
Social welfare	72,845	72,745	59,798	60,966	62,792	329,146
Telecommunications	349,000	227,000	310,300	171,650	184,900	1,233,850
Textiles	39,366	36,660	37,350	38,000	38,640	190,016
Veterinary	116,934	107,750	81,600	76,976	72,590	455,850
Water supplies, rural	539,889	577,020	618,160	620,260	536,760	2,892,000
Water supplies, geological	7,680	7,975	8,173	9,431	9,945	43,204
Water supplies, urban	372,600	393,000	404,600	329,100	209,700	1,709,000
Industrial, north	(200,000)	(200,000)	(200,000)	(200,000)	(200,000)	1,000,000
Extension to major communications	2,000,000	—	—	—	—	2,000,000
Teaching Hospital	60,020	—	—	—	—	60,020
Yellow fever and small pox vaccines	25,000	15,000	15,000	15,000	15,000	85,000
Total Dev. and Welfare	9,269224	6,870,023	7,098,449	5,617,330	5,089,234	33,944,220
Research	74,044	50,713	45,099	43,491	26,034	239,381
Overall total	9,343,268	6,920,736	7,143,548	5,660,821	5,115,268	—
						34,183,641

Source: Nigeria, *Revised Plan.*

Notes: Figures in parentheses are approximate; the total for 1951–52 includes £2,500,000 capital payments.

attempt to overcome the limitations of the land tenure system. In a group farm a family held the usufruct over a number of scattered irregular plots with some permanency. To mechanize, conserve soil, and have large farms, the government wanted "unified control" of land. Thus, the concept of a group farm was to prompt farmers to pool their land and to plant it on a planned basis. A group farm was defined as "an area of land in which the existing farmers have pooled their individual rights for the purpose of the orderly planning and efficient management of the area."[45]

The most common motivation for forming a group farm was the desire for mechanization. By 1954, seven such farms had been established in the southwest. More group farms were demanded because farmers thought that it would give them easy access to the government's tractors, fertilizer, seeds, and technical advice, as well as some protection against crop failure and falling prices. Initial success was reported with regard to increased yields. The problems, however, were many, some of which were related to the difficulty of collective management, leadership, and profit sharing. Many of the collaborators were dissatisfied because of a legitimate worry that they were not deriving benefits from group farming.[46]

All levels of government embarked on the development of Nigeria's fish resources. The objective was to increase the supply of protein by encouraging fishing from canoes and small motorboats at sea and by breeding fish in ponds. In 1951 and 1952, demonstrations of improved methods and new devices aroused many fishermen's interests.[47] Mechanized fishing by motorboats was unsuccessful everywhere. In the hope that money could be made from ponds and reservoirs, many communities and government agencies established ponds for fish, but only a few harvested anything on a profitable scale.[48]

Sleeping sickness and the propensity of many people to use animals only for ceremonial purposes continued to foil livestock industry development in the south.[49] Enthusiasm for the livestock industry was low, but action continued all the same. First, the central government sponsored research on rinderpest, and all the regions were expected to maintain their immunization centers. Second, funds set aside for livestock had to be utilized. The funds were spent on studying major animal diseases, the potential stock-carrying capacity of some areas, and the settlement of nomadic Fulani and their herds, as well as surveying cattle routes. The industry had always been successful in the north. As in the 1940s, the problem was how to apply the new knowledge and spread valuable information among the nomads. But to the few nomads willing to listen, it was less an informative dialogue than a series of instructions on how they should reject their traditional nomadic lifestyles in preference for becoming sedentary.[50]

Most communities were involved in self-help projects, allocated land for

Table 5.12. Overall development, 1950–1956 (in £ million)

Activities	1950–51	1951–52	1952–53	1953–54	1954–55	1955–56	Total[a]
Ten Year Plan	5.894	—	—	—	—	—	5.894
Revised Plan[b]	—	9.343	6.921	7.144	5.661	5.115	34.184
							40.078
Public Works[c]	1.968	1.500	1.500	1.500	1.500	1.500	9.468
Loan Program							
Accepted							
Capital of colliery	0.250	—	—	—	—	—	0.250
Apapa wharf extension	0.100	0.500	0.600	0.600	0.600	0.600	3.000
Coal and lignites	0.094	—	—	—	—	—	0.094
Niger Ag. Project	0.100	0.100	—	—	—	—	0.200
Electricity development	0.300	—	—	—	—	—	0.300
Railway development	0.500	1.000	1.000	0.750	—	—	3.250
							7.094
Projected	—	—	—	1.000	—	—	1.000
Electricity, capital[d]	—	—	1.200	1.000	—	—	2.200
Railway Corporation	—	—	—	1.000	—	—	1.000
Ports trust							
Cameroons Development Corporation[e]	0.500	—	—	—	—	—	0.500
							4.700
Cameroons Development Corporation[e]	0.100	0.100	0.100	0.100	0.100	0.100	0.600
Regional development boards (loans)[f]	0.100	0.100	0.100	0.100	0.100	0.100	0.600
Lagos Executive Development Board[g]							
Apapa Land Development	0.100	0.443	0.433	0.444	—	—	1.430
Slum clearance and housing	—	0.549	0.213	0.213	0.213	0.213	1.401
							2.831
							65.371

Source: Nigeria, *Revised Plan,* 143.

[a]Annual layout of figures was given at an even rate where no fixed program of annual expenditures was known.

[b]The Revised Plan contained complementary expenditures (in £ million) as follows: Public Work Extraordinary, £5.303; Railway development, £2.0; and Electricity development, £0.5.

[c]Public Works Extraordinary—inclusive of regional expenditures—at estimated average rate.

(*Table continues*)

Table 5.12. *(Continued)*

[d]It was proposed to find additional capital of about £3 million for the Electricity Corporation from Nigerian sources.

[e]This shows a nominal figure for contribution to development external to its own commercial operations only.

[f]This provision includes unspent balances of the original capital together with estimated returns to a revolving fund from loans issued.

[g]Lagos Executive Development Board schemes were financed as follows: (1) £1.25 loan from Colonial Development Corporation (guaranteed by government) and £0.18 from revenues of the Board; (2) £0.75 loan from government and £0.651 from revenues of the Board; and (3) in addition, and not shown in this figure, is ten-year "accommodation" loan by the government to tide over nonrevenue earning projects.

development purposes, and invited the government to acquire land free as long as it utilized it. Self-help, or what official documents call community development, became perhaps the most successful aspect of planning. Although community planning received no substantial allocation, the commitment to change spurred many villages and small towns to embark upon self-help projects. From the government's viewpoint, self-help was a cheap and rapid means of development and of stimulating mental and physical activities in the rural areas.[51]

Community projects were active in building new roads, bridges, village halls, markets, and drainage systems. Small "development grants" were available to many communities to assist them in completing small-scale projects on markets, adult literacy, post offices, streets, culverts, leprosy segregation, and youth clubs. Such grants encouraged self-help in rural areas and constituted about one-third of the value of the local contribution.

In all the regions, the Native Authorities cooperated with communities to build feeder roads, drainage facilities, maternity centers, palaces, dispensaries, and community centers. By and large, most communities implemented their projects by trial and error, without technical supervision or sophisticated techniques. What communities lacked in technical skill, they compensated for in enthusiasm and devotion.

There were some other minor activities at the community level. In the east, the Man O'War Bay Scheme was introduced as an experiment in education for citizenship, providing youth with a short training course to give them an idea of what could be achieved through leadership and initiatives. The Rural Training Centre, opened at Asaba in March 1950, expanded its poultry and ponds and admitted more students. A so-called "campaign against village backwardness" operated through the Young Farmers' Clubs in some provinces. The clubs arranged student visits to farms and government offices. A 1952 official report concluded that the clubs were "taking shape as a coherent movement to help the young farmer."[52] There was no evidence for this glowing report; neither was there any "coherent movement" nor a sustained interest in farming. The opportunity to leave the house and travel was the real motive of the young people involved.

In a few places female social workers held classes in the villages to teach women better homecraft and child care. While social workers filed positive reports, there is little indication that their work had a measurable impact. The formation of village betterment committees was sponsored as a forum for the elders to discuss village improvement, but these efforts also met with little success.[53]

Tensions grew over the allocation of grants to the communities. Many people complained either of neglect in preference for their neighbors or of inadequate funding. Ethnic associations, operating mainly from towns as progressive unions, generated countless petitions requesting money. Communities and local authorities quarreled over the type of assistance to be provided.

In the south, local authorities were generally unwilling after 1954 to support the construction of schools because such funding demands were too large. Grants for roads created problems, too, because the communities wanted local authorities to pay and maintain roads after their construction. In cases where roads were not maintained, they quickly fell into disrepair and disuse. As the Native Authorities collected market rents in most places, many communities began to wonder whether they should use their limited funds to build markets that in turn benefited the government. Some communities complained of betrayal by the government: having done their own share through self-help, the expected grant failed to materialize.

The revised plan divided education into three parts: general, technical, and the Nigerian College of Arts, Science, and Technology. Funds for general education were spent largely on expanding secondary education and teacher training. There was a small expansion in technical education, mainly in new staff and buildings.[54] Everywhere people talked about expansion and mass education, although a few were beginning to wonder if quality would not be sacrificed in the process. Grants were provided to voluntary agencies to assist in the administration of secondary schools and Teacher Training Centres.

In 1952, the Nigerian College of Arts, Science, and Technology was established at Ibadan, Enugu, and Zaria, providing advanced education to those who wanted a university education or work in intermediate capacities. The University College of Ibadan grew, receiving a grant of over £3 million from the Colonial Development and Welfare Fund (CDWF), the Nigerian government, and the marketing boards. Buildings were completed in order to extend school facilities in all the regions. Press and nationalist criticism of the University College was so fierce that the first principal admitted in 1952 that the college did not enjoy maximum public confidence.[55] Nigerian critics claimed that the college discriminated by race in appointments and salaries in favor of foreign teachers. It had a strict standard of prior education and admission, allegedly to frustrate Nigerians, and pursued a narrow curriculum, without courses in education, law, or engineering.[56]

The provision of medical amenities was still a top priority for communities. Existing facilities were expanded by adding staff and buildings, in addition to providing a few additional hospitals in several locations. A mobile X-ray unit to test for tuberculosis was added to the medical field units. Training institutions were expanded in all the regions, while voluntary agencies received financial support to run their hospitals and dispensaries. The central government took responsibility for the mental hospital at Abeokuta, and proposed expanding it from 200 to 500 beds; the government also took responsibility for the Malaria Service, which investigated drugs to combat fever.

In the north, new additions were constructed at hospitals at different locations. Two new rural health centers were completed, in addition to expansions of four training institutions in Kano and Zaria. Voluntary agencies received support. Activities in the other regions were similar to those in the north.[57] All medical facilities were grossly inadequate, training was slow in all fields, and many areas were not covered by any modern facility.

A Leprosy Control Service, 75 percent financed by the CDWF, coordinated all antileprosy work in the country, whether it was operated by voluntary bodies or by the government. The Service was operated on a provincial basis, with the aim of establishing a leprosarium in each province. Local governments and communities established leprosy segregation villages supervised by staff from the provincial leprosarium. By 1953, only four provinces lacked such institutions. With over 11,000 patients, the facilities were well used. With the evidence that leprosy was treatable, public attitudes toward lepers began to change and the patients themselves gained some self-respect.[58] Stereotypes and prejudice were hard to counter but a strong foundation was laid to deal with this disease.

Social welfare activities included a limited amount of support for youth clubs in selected locations like Zaria in the north and Calabar in the east (but none in the west). The formation of nurseries and boys' and girls' clubs was encouraged.[59] The juvenile courts and remand homes in Lagos and Calabar received limited funding.[60] While in the north, a reformatory was built at Bungudu in Sokoto province, and a number of so-called destitutes and vagrants were repatriated, these services were too few to make any meaningful impact. Moreover, by confusing the remand homes with prisons, the public distanced itself from them.[61]

Road construction continued the course of previous programs. The central government retained the responsibility for the Trunk A roads. The lapses of the past began to surface. The majority of the previous roads, built for lower traffic levels, had become unsuitable and in some cases unsafe for modern vehicles by the 1950s. The roads needed to be strengthened and bridges modernized. All the regions were active in road construction and maintenance, because roads were the most desired physical development projects.[62]

In the field of telecommunications, there were some small-scale projects, such as the installation of the Lagos Automatic Exchange (for telephone service), radio telephone sets, teleprinters in regional headquarters, and many trunk roads. Telecommunications progress was not as rapid as that of road construction. The goal was limited to linking the important commercial and administrative centers. Radio services improved with the recruitment of more staff, assistance from the British Broadcasting Corporation (BBC), and installation of new equipment.

The building for the telecommunications headquarters in Lagos was completed in 1953. News was broadcast in English, Hausa, Yoruba, and Igbo. The radio-diffusion stations in each region were grouped around the main regional station as satellites, originating a small amount of local daily programming. Provisions for modern shortwave transmitters at Lagos, Kaduna, and Enugu served not only the primary regional audiences but also, under favorable conditions, foreigners living in any part of the country. Broadcasting progressed, and public reaction was favorable: listening to the radio was a sign of good living and enlightenment. All levels of government, too, were happy to have an effective way to reach the public. The trouble, however, was that broadcasting was used as a propaganda machine to sell the views of the government and in the regions to discredit opposition groups.

Work continued, for the most part, on port improvements and a few new canals. The notable projects of the 1950s included the further dredging of the Lagos harbor, Escavos bar, Burutu channel, and the Bonny River and bar. Navigational aids were also improved with the acquisition of new equipment and instruments.[63]

Many areas began to explore the potential of pottery as a local industry. In most cases, those who were optimistic became disillusioned, as few were able to make a living as potters. The interest of the government, focused more in textiles,[64] planned to develop a "peasant textile industry" by providing instruction in new methods of handloom weaving, spinning, and dyeing. Seven centers operated in areas where weaving was a traditional craft. Supervised by foreign technicians, trainees were taught to use the broadloom and bicycle spinning wheel, as well as methods of vat dyeing with synthetic dyes. Simple equipment, fiber, and a few other necessities were supplied to the trainees. In the revised plan, more emphasis was placed on the creation of skilled operatives and overseers to work in new power-loom factories. A mechanical training center was established in Lagos, and the dye laboratory was moved from Aba to Lagos to enable coordination with other relevant units. Over a hundred trainees graduated every year, and over 500,000 yards of cloth were produced in the centers.[65]

What the graduates of the centers would do to make a living, however, was still a source of concern. In the north, the Native Authorities absorbed most of them into their enterprises, which satisfied these workers because they received salaries. In the west, they were supposed to form cooperative societies, while the eastern regions encouraged them to go into private business; neither alternative ensured a regular income. Moreover, the market for finished products was unpredictable. Many had hoped that they would be able to continue to depend on the government to buy their products, but this was not the case.

Geological surveys and drilling for diamonds and clay were conducted in the east at the Nkalagu limestones.[66] A drilling program to determine the extent and quality of the iron ore of the Agbaja Plateau, north of Lokoja, began in May 1952, with encouraging results. Clay deposits were found in the coastal area between Badagry and Warri. Other major investigations were on lignites in Ogwashi-Asaba in Benin province and phosphates at Abeokuta.

The plan for water supplies was half completed.[67] Rural water supplies were extended in the north to twenty-seven new locations. In the east, 361 new water points were added, comprising 210 wells and 160 catchment springs. In the west, almost 200 new wells were sunk. Urban water supplies included the provision of water to new areas in Lagos, as well as extension works and new projects in many towns. Most of the towns that benefited were administrative centers.

Finally, while most building projects progressed on schedule, a cement shortage hampered some of them. The central government handed full executive control of building programs to the regions but retained the power to prepare architectural and engineering designs. The prefabricated buildings of the 1940s gave way to permanent ones.

Conclusion

By transferring power to the regions, Lagos successfully sold the idea of planning. One of the first things that the regional governments used their new power for was to initiate autonomous development plans from the mid-1950s onward. Before 1956, while the revised plan forced planning onto the agenda of the new regional governments, it limited their ability to innovate by insisting that they stay within the major schemes in the Ten-Year Plan. The federal and regional governments also expanded economic activities through the use of such boards as the loans and production boards to advance loans to individuals and government agencies and to promote research. The strategy was to plan for additional capital investment with a quick economic return sufficient to meet service charges on loans or those projects that could attract external aid. Those from which external aid was expected were five key projects that became prominent during the decade. The regional development boards, decentralized in 1949, awarded grants and loans to individuals, the Native Authorities, cooperative societies, and some individuals. The most active of the boards were the regional production development boards, founded in 1949 to plan and disburse development funds for "the benefit and prosperity of the producers and the areas of production." In 1951, the regional production development boards had a total of over £7 million for this purpose.

The awareness of the need for development had become more widespread than in the forties. The planning process was one reason, as ideas about it spread and proposals and schemes were created and executed. The Nigerian politicians did a great deal by way of promises and raising the expectations of the masses as to what the end of colonial rule might bring. The 1950s was a decade in which community leaders complained and demanded one thing or another for their own locale.

Moreover, the revised plan was haunted by the old problems of the 1940s. In 1952, there was an increase in salaries and wages that led to high expenditures. Both recurrent and capital costs also increased. The government's reaction was to delay construction and recruitment. This produced savings in order to keep to the financial limits of the plan without having to resort to extensive elimination of projects. Yet another problem was that the actual expenditures were lower than the estimated expenditures, thus affecting financial allocations for specific projects. Personal emoluments were high, thus reducing the amount of money that could be committed to the physical infrastructure. In the regions, a number of politicians began to complain that civil servants connected with planning derived unnecessary benefits from development funds, did little work, and were incapable of "developing anything at all."[68]

The shortage of materials and equipment hampered progress until the end of 1952. It was difficult to recruit staff for new projects. While the number of skilled people increased somewhat in the 1950s, acute shortages persisted. The increased spending by the regions and boards, the reform of local governments, and the transfer of power that began during the fifties were among the most important reasons for the shortages. Some areas had money but lacked personnel to organize projects. A few medical centers were completed without the staff to operate them. There was money to provide water in some provinces but no engineers to design and supervise the projects. One worried Resident described the plan as unrealistic and depressingly concluded: "There was too much talk about development and, as a result, in spite of all that had been done, there was an increasing sense of disappointment and frustration. What was needed was to get on and finish a few jobs and then only to consider, in the light of practical realities, what further projects could be tackled. Talk of 'the Plan' should stop and the present proposals should be regarded only as a 'Projects Register.' "[69] The "talk of the plan," that is, the Ten-Year Plan, stopped sooner than the Resident and others had expected.

CHAPTER SIX

"An Integrated Development Programme," 1955–1960

> The Federal Government's object in preparing this Programme is to promote the economic development of Nigeria to the fullest possible extent. There is no simple or single formula for success in achieving this aim, other than an endeavour to preserve a reasonable balance between all sectors of governmental activity so that development may advance on a broad front and provide a climate which will foster and encourage the productivity of the individual, which, in the last analysis is a true index of economic progress.
>
> *The Economic Programme of the Government of the Federation of Nigeria,* 1956

The Ten-Year Plan was terminated one year early on March 31, 1955. The newly established federal government announced that it had completed the programs in the Ten-Year Plan.[1] The second colonial plan, 1955–60, accommodated the uncompleted projects and carried forward the outstanding grants of the previous plan. Why did the colonial government decide to formulate yet another plan on the eve of its departure?

There are at least three important answers to this question. First, the Colonial Office decided to extend the life of the Colonial Development and Welfare Act (CDWA) beyond 1956. Funding was promised and as usual the colonies were requested to submit proposals covering the program's additional years. Second, the emergence of a federal system of government and the introduction of a new Constitution on October 1, 1954, affected the distribution of power and responsibility between the regions and the center to such an extent that it became necessary to examine the entire planning document. Third, the move was influenced by the new thinking on the concepts and methods of planning that followed a powerful commissioned report in 1954 made by a committee of the International Bank for Reconstruction and Development

(IBRD), which made far-reaching suggestions on the economic development of the country.[2] I will examine these last two reasons in some detail because they had the most critical impact on planning.

The New Constitution and Regionalism

The introduction of the new Constitution in October 1954 ended the government's sphere of responsibility as outlined in the revised plan of 1951–56.[3] For three reasons, however, the federal government was not in a position to embark immediately on another comprehensive plan. First, the recommendations of the recently submitted IBRD report needed study. As I point out later, the IBRD's report was crucial in guiding economic planning for the rest of the decade. Second, the federal government needed time to consider the financial implications of the new Constitution in order to establish the resources available for develpment allocation. Third, the federal government still needed to liaise with the Secretary of State in London about its proposals and funding from the extended Colonial Development and Welfare Fund (CDWF). Not until 1955 was legislation passed and the amount of the expected funds from the Colonial Office become known.

The political basis of the Ten-Year Plan was shattered by the constitutional changes of the 1950s. Originally, the central government held power over all spheres and was committed to a single development plan for the country. The 1951 MacPherson constitutional revisions retained the dominant role of the central government although they did allocate projects and funds to the regional level. Following these changes, increased regionalization led to the devolution of many responsibilities to the regional governments. Nigerian politicians who sought more power for their regions at the expense of the federal government expressed dissatisfaction with the MacPherson revisions.

Regional competition and conflicts had become so intense that by 1953 the north passed a motion that all regions be given complete legislative and executive autonomy with respect to all matters except defense, external affairs, customs, and the West African research institutions.[4] This was in response to the decision of the other regions to progress toward self-government at a faster pace than the north desired. Incidents in 1953, a year of turbulence, included a riot in Kano between rival northern and southern political parties, an aborted conference by the regions in London, threats of secession, and quarrels over federal assets, jurisdiction, and patronage.

The eastern and western regions were granted self-government beginning in 1956 and the north in 1959. The transfer of power affected most spheres of government activities, except the police, internal security, and some key services. The political atmosphere was conducive neither to economic cooperation nor to joint planning.

The 1954 Constitution established a federal system, with regional governments in the eastern, northern, and western regions. The regions were granted fiscal and spending powers; thus, the political power structure became highly decentralized and differentiated. Each region cherished its power and autonomy: areas in which the regions could exercise authority free of federal intervention were enumerated, and the judiciary and fiscal systems were reorganized. The revenue allocations to the regions were based on a principle of "derivation" (the return of revenue to its region of origin), and residual powers were vested in the regions. Most influential with respect to planning was the reorganization of the limits of responsibility, which confined the federal government to the following areas: countrywide communications (roads, postal services, telecommunications, ports and inland waterways, civil aviation, and railways), higher education and research, public services and utilities in the federal territory of Lagos, loans to statutory corporations, and the maintenance of security.[5]

The regional governments were responsible for their economies, a fact recognized by the IBRD's report, which recommended that each region should use its power to formulate a suitable plan. As power shifted to the regions, they were able to formulate and implement many new economic policies and initiate changes along lines other than those of the federal government.

The IBRD Committee

Whereas the intellectual ideas for the Ten-Year Plan and its revision were supplied by colonial officers both in Nigeria and abroad, the ideas of the 1955–60 revision originated externally: the brains (the IBRD) were based in the United States. Through the Colonial Office, the Nigerian government had invited the IBRD to "assess the internal and external resources, natural, human and financial, available for future economic development; to study the possibilities for development in the major sectors of the economy, and make recommendations for practical steps to be taken, including the timing and co-ordination of developmental activities."[6] A committee from the IBRD investigated the country in late 1953. Its members included a diverse group of fifteen economists, agricultural economists, mineral resources experts, and people involved in industry, transportation, social services, and commerce; they had little or no firsthand acquaintance with Africa.[7]

Published a year later,[8] the IBRD's recommendations matched the Nigerian plan for 1955–60 with only a few exceptions. While it is not necessary to discuss the committee's recommendations, its reasoning deserves attention, because it constituted both the intellectual framework for, and the philosophy of, the plan. The colonial state ended its career with the implementation of the bank's recommended program—stubborn till the very end in its refusal to listen to indigenous voices or to succumb to the pressure of the radical factions, who were lobbying for a socialist alternative to planning. So crucial was the IBRD's report that the major contribution of the government to planning was to implement its recommendations.

The IBRD's report was predicated on several assumptions about Nigerian society, the nature of change, and economic growth. Since the colonial government did not criticize these comments, we can conclude that its leading officers either agreed or identified with them. The committee came up with a working definition of development: a rise in living standards, improved health care, schools, housing, abundant food, "and the opportunity to participate in the cultural and spiritual life of the community."[9] This was more precise than the preamble to the Ten-Year Plan. To a large extent, the definition captured many essential desires of ordinary Nigerians in the 1950s.

There were, however, some differences between the IBRD and Nigerian critics. First, to Nigerians, development entailed increased individual wealth. To many people, the country's wealth meant nothing if its individuals were poor: planning must find a way of enriching all.[10] Second, development should facilitate assimilation to Western culture, although the Islamic intelligentsia did not share this viewpoint. Cars, radios, education, travel to Britain, and so on, must be readily available as rewards of planning.[11] These desires had risen from the interactions with colonial rule and were part of the consequences of change and westernization. Third, development must be rapid, attained within a generation, if possible. The IBRD and the government saw development as a slow process, but many Nigerians believed that ten years was too long to wait.[12]

Fourth, planning must include empowerment: the British must transfer power to Nigerians who could then impose their own vision. In other words, the "political kingdom" that Nigerians would preside over was a nonnegotiable prerequisite to planning. In planning, the IBRD and the colonial state did not consider Nigeria's sovereignty. Finally, how to assess the progress of development was an issue. To the committee, the value of all goods and services produced in the country (GDP) was a key indicator of development. Growth had to be calculated on the basis of per capita income and other quantifiable factors. In contrast, radical Nigerians stressed the need for a structural transformation of society and its social and economic institutions in order to bring about the elimination of poverty, a transfer of economic and political power to the masses, full employment with sufficient income, free education and medical services, and the removal of imperialist domination and exploitation.[13] Many others, less informed about the concept of the GDP and per capita income, focused on better lifestyles: availability of schools, food, hospitals, jobs, money, and good housing.

In the IBRD committee's view, the Nigerian economy had undergone substantial changes since 1940, with a higher productive capacity than before, but there was no assurance that the pace of change could be maintained unless adequate institutional and financial bases were established.[14] This is correct to some extent. There had been changes in the economy and limited growth and expansion, but the impact on people's lives was exaggerated; individuals were not better off than before.

The IBRD's report identified many impediments to development, many of which had been stated in the 1940s. Out of all these, the report stressed resource management and tradition's negative impact. Committee members found that economic growth was "far in excess of the rate at which the new financial resources could be absorbed and put to use for the lasting benefit of the country."[15] It was difficult to expand operations "to the level, and in the direction, of greatest use as an integral part of a growing economy" because of a shortage of labor and equipment, lack of basic information, and insufficient preparation and planning.

The main social obstacle to development was seen as an excessive reliance on the government:

> The need for self-help is not understood by the African businessman who looks to the government, and the government alone, for financial assistance in the expansion of his business instead of joining with others in a partnership or other form of common enterprise. It is not understood by rural communities and their leaders who demand school and hospital facilities but are not ready to pay for them by increased tax assessments. It is not understood by those who deplore graft and corruption in the hospitals, in the produce inspection service, in the railway and in private business, yet are unwilling to take effective action against these abuses.[16]

The committee blundered by denying Nigerians the appreciation of self-help. Most communities' feeder roads, public incinerators, and halls derived from self-help. At the root of corruption was resource scarcity and the conception that public service was an opportunity for graft. In terms of taxation, the trouble in the mid-1950s was not a failure to pay but the inability of the government to justify the collections and convince the populace that higher taxes were necessary.

According to the IBRD committee, many other things were flawed in

Nigerian society. Regionalism and political decentralization promoted antagonisms that deterred development. Greater national unity and individual initiative were necessary for successful development. The IBRD committee did not blame the colonial government for the interregional tensions. After all, the creation of a federal system was undertaken and manipulated by the colonial power. The committee also failed to recognize Nigerians' loyalty and morality, referring to their apparent disregard for personal rights and private property and their flouting of contractual obligations. Many of these were results of an unfamiliar urban lifestyle and the craze for money and goods.

The categorization of tradition as a liability reflected the committee's unstated belief that progress equals westernization. Further penetration of Western influence was considered both a condition for and evidence of development. Consequently, non-Western institutions were either criticized or misunderstood and in doing so they chose to concentrate only on negative aspects of indigenous culture. Positive attributes that could have been considered in the recommendation process were neglected. Committee members noted, for instance, that Nigerians had strong loyalties to their families, clans, and local unions, which encouraged the formation of cooperatives, savings and thrift clubs, and community self-help projects. How this cultural aspect influenced planning by stimulating mass participation and the formation of cooperative societies was ignored. Instead, many government measures encouraged individuals to compete rather than unite, and the colonial officers were not educated about the "loyalties" of the people.

Whereas the officers connected with promotion of agriculture had complained of people's apathy and the difficulty of teaching them anything, the committee noted one important cultural dimension in the learning process: Nigerians respected elders, *mallams* (Islamic learned men), and schoolteachers. But the committee and government disregarded these "traditional" authorities and their teaching methods. Instead, the government maintained a policy of using Western educated officers who related to the farmers from a position of authority.

On the whole, indigenous culture was unsystematically investigated. Echoing a widely held view among economists and experts on change, the committee felt that African chauvinistic culture constituted a severe obstacle rather than an aid to its future.[17] The very problem it was trying to solve was partly defined by culture. The continuity of indigenous institutions, in spite of the colonial changes, was yet another component of the way Nigerians defined progress and assessed every scheme and policy.

The committee commended the use of the marketing boards to keep reserves by regulating domestic prices, a blatant excuse for the exploitation of peasants who produced the bulk of the country's wealth. While the committee advocated external borrowing, it failed to address how existing large foreign reserves should be spent on development planning. It also noted that reserves were available, close to £200 million, but its ideas about spending this money benefited the colonists with a policy of wealth transfer to Britain, reliance on external loans, and expenditures that favored urban dwellers and foreign firms.

In addition, the shortage of workers with technical skills affected every branch of government. The committee believed that ultimately education would correct this lapse but that foreigners should be recruited in the short-run to fill the hundreds of vacant positions, somehow without jeopardizing the chances of qualified Nigerians. It also inadequately addressed the growing tensions between Nigerians and foreigners, arguing that Nigeria's citizens were tolerant of foreigners. There was no settler factor in the country, as in other British colonies in East Africa; nevertheless, the nationalism of the 1950s provoked hostility toward foreigners. The southern elite tended to interpret the committee's generosity to outsiders as a deliberate measure to block southerners from moving to the north to fill vacant positions.[18]

According to the report, the business community lacked a tradition of "sound business practices" and managerial experience. The committee believed that Nigerians should build many small firms, risking all their capital, in addition to spending their energies. True, the industrial sector was weak, but Nigerians could not take all the blame for this. The colonial economy had focused on import and export, a leading economic growth area where those who wanted to succeed could do so. The industrial sector was new, both to the state and the people. In its very slow beginning, those who were to derive immediate benefits were non-Nigerians.

The committee also commented that the lack of knowledge of the country's natural resources made it difficult and in some cases impossible to assess the potential for development. It called for research into soil fertility, crop varieties and yields, livestock, water resources, and local materials for industries. Although more was needed, some research had begun in 1954, but the main problem that the committee neglected was how to translate research findings into practical applications and how to focus on aspects that were not concerned with the promotion of exports.

To the committee, private investment was an inadequate means to sustain rapid development. Basing most of its recommendations on state intervention, the committee did not deviate from the earlier strategy of using public funds to promote private enterprises: the government should boost economic growth by providing roads and schools, supplement the financial resources of the private sector, and adopt policies to permit the functioning of private initiative and private capital accumulation.[19] As foreigners dominated the leading sectors of the economy, such a strategy would go a long way in consolidating itself. The ultimate success would therefore depend on individual initiatives and the enterprise of ordinary Nigerians. This "initiative" had never been lacking, as the committee tended to suggest, but there was little in the report about encouraging it.

The committee rightly noted that much private investment was small-scale, consisting of a "multitude of purchases of sewing machines and bicycles, lorries and cars and improvements to private buildings."[20] It made no specific recommendation on altering the level of investment, other than restating the view of the 1940s that public investment would generate expansion in the private sector.

In reality, the determinant of private investment was the volume of externally financed investments. In the early 1950s, such foreign capital had financed 12–25 percent of the total of private fixed investments. This was, however, misleading because a large proportion of reinvestment of earnings by foreign companies took place. Without stating how a substantial sum of money could be attracted, the committee proposed greater foreign investments to counteract the scarcity of capital and lack of managerial experience in manufacturing processes. It warned that development would only occur if foreign capital was attracted. This view reflected the premium placed on investment as the determinant of development and so-called inevitability of foreign trade. Such an attitude limited indigenous initiatives on domestic solutions and increased dependence on external markets and economies.

The "nationalist" mood of the 1950s was contrary to the committee's attitude. While many realized that Nigeria could not isolate itself, they still demanded the expropriation of foreign enterprises. Radicals believed that the country must be entirely free from exploitation by foreigners. Even the most conservative politicians wanted to limit both the power of foreign firms and their numbers, with a maximum of 49 percent foreign control of capital. The committee dismissed the call for control of foreign investments as confusing, stating that Nigeria needed the investments; it called for a package of incentives to attract foreign capital. Moreover, the federal and regional governments should accord foreign investors the same treatment as citizens, "neither discriminating against them nor granting them special privileges."[21] In addition, they should be assured of transferability of profits and repatriation of capital. In return these investors should provide training for Nigerians and allow a reasonable provision for the participation of local capital. By assigning a large role to foreign investments, the committee rationalized existing business relations in the country and encouraged the colonial government to strengthen its policies, thereby ensuring the continuity of the pattern of external trade after independence. Local entrepreneurs' demands for measures to enhance their access to capital and markets were neglected.

Based on their premises and recommendations for change, the committee expected an aggregate income expansion of 15–20 percent or an average of 3 percent per annum, a rate that was considered to be above that of the population growth. The country needed a five-year period to build a strong "institutional groundwork," laying a foundation for accelerated economic growth in the 1960s. An increase in the volume of public activity in all sectors would strengthen the machinery of government to support and sustain economic growth.

Capital and recurrent expenditures had to be increased. The committee recommended an increase in government expenditures from a level of £51 million in 1952–53 to £97 million in 1959–60, in addition to expenditures of £6 million per year by statutory corporations. It expected gross domestic investment, both private and public, to increase from 8 percent of the GDP in 1952 to 11–12 percent (from £90 million to £100 million) by 1960. The committee calculated that such an increase was sufficient to raise the rate of income growth above the 3 percent rate and assure a rapid economic expansion in the 1960s.

To finance the recommendations, all government authorities required £415 million that they should be able to raise through normal revenues, reserves of public funds, borrowing at home and abroad, and grants from the Colonial Office. The committee also strongly recommended a substantial increase in taxes supplemented by borrowing from the marketing boards and the London capital market.

The committee called for new government development institutions and considered how to minimize the federal administration's burden and attain the transition to self-government. It believed an Economic Secretariat, independent of other departments, was necessary to provide the federal cabinet (the Council of Ministers) with extensive information and proposals on economic policy and public investment programs. The regions should duplicate the federal organization, and a National Economic Council could be established for the representatives of the regional and federal governments. The Economic Secretariat would serve the Economic Council in at least two major ways: (1) gather, analyze, and evaluate information regarding the development potential of the country as a whole, estimate the financial requirements of development projects and programs, and, generally, prepare such studies and documentation as might be required by the economic committee of the Council of Ministers, including an appraisal of the economic situation for use in the preparation of the annual budgetary estimates, and (2) review departmental estimates of federal development expenditures in light of the priority needs of the country laid down in the development program, as agreed upon from time to time, and report thereon to the economic committee of the Council of Ministers before action by the committee.

The Economic Secretariat should have a large professional staff with a competent economist as director but would actually be headed by a powerful Secretary who doubled as the Secretary for the Council of Ministers. In addition, the Council of Ministers would establish small economic committees to advise on specific policies. The advantage of this arrangement was that it would encourage top bureaucrats and politicians to discuss proposals and make final decisions. The disadvantage was that planning would be a strictly technical affair dominated by those with the advantages of power and education.

The Nigerianization program notwithstanding, the committee called for a vigorous recruitment of not less than 2,000 foreign personnel. It recommended a Nigerian recruiting office in London. Overseas personnel should be attracted with incentives such as high salaries, emoluments, and for those who wished, the opportunities to engage in research or special investigations. While this recommendation would mean immediate availability of workers, it was costly. In reality, a large part of development expenditures went toward travel fares, salaries, and other emoluments.

The IBRD's report proposed strengthening some older agencies and creating a new one to organize development efforts. The new state bank, the nucleus of the future central bank, would issue currency, accept deposits from banks, regulate their operations, buy and sell government securities, and be the principal depository for government funds. In addition, statutory corporations, originally funded by the government but operated on a commercial basis, should be developed as autonomous bodies to run operations outside the normal administrative functions of government—the railway, port installations, power plants, and the coal mines. All the marketing and production boards should participate in development by encouraging investments in agricultural and industrial projects and by paying for part of the cost of education, infrastructure, and social services. The committee, however, wanted the marketing boards to stop financing development and research projects and instead use their reserves largely to advance long-term loans to the government.

The Nigerian government accepted virtually all the committee's proposals. The report, entitled "An Integrated Development Programme," became the core of the *Economic Programme of the Government of the Federation of Nigeria, 1955–60,* the plan for the country until 1962. In many instances, the recommendations of the committee were used verbatim or simply paraphrased, and many of the points were merely elaborated upon.

The federal government believed that the committee had managed to correct some of the shortcomings of the previous Ten-Year Plan, especially three major ones. First, the Economic Programme required a more thorough assessment of available resources to support planning. The shortage of materials, plants, and personnel still existed. In the late 1950s, the limited number of architects, surveyors, and engineers hindered the rate of progress. Therefore, the training of Nigerians and recruiting workers from abroad was accelerated.

Second, development plan formulation under the Ten-Year Plan had been too rigid. While recognizing that planning and flexibility were mutually antagonistic, the solution was to eliminate detailed planning. Consequently, the federal government plan allocated the funds necessary to meet the requirements of the different sectors, "leaving the details to be filled in year-by-year concurrently with normal budgetary procedure."[22]

The Economic Programme was divided into two parts: an overview of projected development between 1956 and 1960 and a detailed statement of the projects on which expenditures could be incurred. Minor projects involving expenditures of less than £25,000 or additional recurrent expenditures of no more than £50,000 per annum were excluded from the plan. However, such projects did fall under a broad rubric of "other public work" for which a fund of £3 million was allocated. In the context of a five-year framework, planning became an annual exercise. The drawback to this approach was that planning turned into more or less the normal, year-by-year activities of the government, and flexibility became an excuse for failure, lack of commitment, or abandonment of a project.

Third, the impact of wage increases on planning needed consideration. Before the program was enacted, there had been a general increase in salaries and wages. To incorporate this, block provisions were made to cover increases in the program's cost. The increases touched on virtually all the recurrent expenditures, and a sum of almost £8 million was added to meet labor costs.

Nigerians' reactions to many of the committee's recommendations and to the subsequent five-year program was similar to the points already made with respect to the previous plan. There was, however, no expression of radical nationalism to fight the recommendations by the IBRD. This can be explained by the fact that Nigerian politicians controlled the regions and had the opportunity to formulate their own alternative plans, spending regional resources as they deemed necessary. The new power holders were products of Western formal education, and many were assimilated to Western culture and believed in free enterprise, as did the colonial officers. Like the colonial state, the Nigerian power elite was itself criticized for its failure to fulfill people's expectations. In the words of one such critic: "When so-called 'nationalists' are out of office, they emit sparks of fiery speeches—even r-r-revolutionary ones. But let them put on the *toga virilis* of office, they change their attitude, and as long as they have their own three decent meals a day, the world is moving perfectly in its axis."[23]

Most of the other comments were similar to those made in previous years. Nigerians must direct planning, since the British acted in their own self-interest in an atmosphere devoid of freedom for the Nigerians and greatly controlled by foreign enterprises.[24] Few new suggestions surfaced, just the reiteration of the previous ones of making capital available to Nigerians, decolonization, industrialization, nationalization of foreign enterprises, and unity of all progressive Nigerians so that they would be able to combine resources and aggressively face alien competition. There were some new ideas on the role of the state and foreign investments.

The experience of regional administrations had convinced the powerful elite of the importance both of power and the state. The state, some argued, must in fact become more interventionist in the economy than the British had been. These critics believed that foreign investment was detrimental in the long run but desirable in the short run in order to attract capital and skill. Men like Obafemi Awolowo, Kingsley O. Mbadiwe, and other leaders of the major political parties, who had previously called for rapid nationalization, began to talk in terms of a partnership and to call some foreign investors their "friends from other countries."[25] In 1960 Chief Festus Okotie-Eboh, the Finance Minister, warned his colleagues not to frighten off investors with any "irresponsible" talk of nationalization.[26] To be sure, socialism was alive, but there was an increasing awareness that foreign investments should be accepted.

One other point should be made to explain the lack of enthusiasm in responding to the final colonial plan. The 1950s provided educated Nigerians with their best opportunity so far: they had access to power and their business interests flourished. The regional governments allowed politicians to build more influence and gain access to public funds. Many used their newly acquired power to divert resources to themselves and members of their network, through the award of agent licenses to buy produce, of sinecure positions, contracts, and state patronage. The British promise of power transfer was satisfactory enough. Those with higher education benefited from the policy of recruitment and rapid promotions for Nigerians. Economic reforms benefited the entrepreneurs who linked up with the regional governments for resources and who derived capital from the new indigenous banks and the loans boards.

In the 1950s, foreign firms began to move into manufacturing and to modify their business practices in the face of both the nationalist attack and the expansion in export trade. They reorganized their businesses by moving into sectors that required more capital and skilled labor in order to minimize competition with Nigerians. Started on a small scale, manufacturing concerns included such goods as drinks, food, construction materials, and textiles, all of which could be sold at affordable prices and yet offered substantial profits. For the same reason, and to benefit from generous tax breaks and protective tariffs, they also began import-substitution industries (for example, cement, beer, footwear, utensils, furniture). The Nigerian entrepreneurs entered the retail sector that had been abandoned by foreign firms and strengthened their involvement in ancillary services and foreign trade.

The Scope of the Economic Programme

In 1955, the federal legislature approved an interim plan, based on the recommendations of the IBRD's committee. Known as the Interim Development Plan (IDP), it projected expenditures of almost £19.8 million (exclusive of railway funds) on projects to begin in the 1955–56 fiscal year. Many of the IDP projects could not be completed within a year, so the 1955–56 period was devoted mainly to preparatory work that did not involve very heavy expenditures.

In June 1955, the economic committee of the Council of Ministers recommended a five-year period of economic planning, 1955 to 1960, entitled the "Economic Programme." The name was changed to avoid confusion with the previous Ten-Year Plan. The economic committee examined proposals by various departments and statutory organizations and submitted them to the Council of Ministers for approval. The permanent Secretaries, board managers, and senior bureaucrats became the principal initiators of development projects at the federal level. Discussions about mass participation in the 1940s had given way to elitism; even a suggestion to involve local governments was dismissed as unnecessary.[27]

The Economic Programme was drafted "on broad lines, the keynote being flexibility."[28] The federal government instructed all ministries to state the programs to be implemented for each year and to prepare projects without adhering to any rigid definition as long as each involved total capital expenditures of not less than £25,000 (not necessarily in one year), the final annual recurrent cost amounted to not less than £50,000,[29] or its economic, political, or social significance would be so great that, despite falling outside the two latter guidelines, the published Economic Programme would be incomplete without it (for example, research projects).[30]

The program also widened the scope of planning to include for the first time expenditures on customs, security, and administration. The capital requirements[31] of statutory bodies responsible to the federal government (including research institutes, higher education organizations, and public utility corporations) were included in financial planning. The program intended to strengthen the economy by promoting research in new methods for increased productivity, spending on energy to stimulate the growth of industries, expanding higher education to produce educated workers, providing social services and infrastructure in Lagos (the country's major port and commercial center), improving security and order (defense, police, prisons, and customs services), increasing the revenue base, and improving the communications system. In these areas the baseline was to promote trade within the country as well as between it and the outside world.

This new program contained more policy statements than the previous one, was more elaborate, better coordinated the sectors, set its target in terms of growth rate, and defined its priorities in a more refined manner. However, it also had problems. There was a preoccupation with the GDP because capital was held more important than the human factor in the development process. The program assumed the age-old colonial objectives and sought to achieve growth within the colonial system. It continued to advance the interests of the state and foreign business. Moreover, urban areas were favored over rural areas, especially in the location of new housing amenities and industrial estates.

The Finances of the Economic Programme

The financial requirements of the 1955–60 program were the best conceived since 1940. Revenues and expenditures were discussed and approved long beforehand, and the overall extent of commitments was more clear (table 6.1).

The plan distinguished between recurrent and capital costs and outlined the problems of both. Recurrent revenues would be relied on yearly even if the prices of export crops—the main source of wealth—fell. Nonrecurrent revenues comprised a variety of periodic payments and excess money from exports, when world prices rose above the minimum level. Recurrent expenditures included the annual commitments for established services and charges. The nonrecurrent expenditures were of a capital nature that could be controlled, depending on available resources. The program ensured that recurrent expenditures did not expand to a level above that of recurrent revenues. The program was careful to calculate the recurrent expenditure commitments involved in its priority projects and how to maintain the current level of existing services. In 1955 it was estimated that the impact of additional costs would increase recurrent expenditures from £22.3 million to £37.5 million by 1959–60. Recurrent revenues were expected to increase through proceeds from exports and without the need for additional taxation or increased

Table 6.1. Financial summary, 1956–1960

	Total of capital requirement £
Capital expenditures, loans	
Building Society	500,000
Cameroons Development Corp.	1,000,000
Electricity Corp. of Nigeria	7,170,000
Industry	800,000
Lagos town planning	3,260,000
Nigerian Coal Corporation	400,000
Nigerian Ports Authority	2,638,000
Nigeria Railway Corporation	10,020,000
West African Airways Corporation	280,000
Total	26,068,000
Capital expenditures on government account	
Broadcasting	400,000
Building Research Institute	80,000
Central Records Office	51,000
Civil Aviation	1,400,000
Customs and excise	135,000
Defense	2,701,000
Education, general	1,766,000
Education, higher	1,401,000
Geological survey and mining	42,000
Government Press	350,000
Hotels	40,000
Industry	515,000
Lagos town planning	1,050,000
Medical and health	2,591,000
Meteorology	76,000
Natural resources research	1,442,000
Police	1,000,000
Ports and inland waterways	10,214,000
Post and Telegraph services	12,890,000
Prisons	500,000
Public works, highways and bridges	13,633,000
Other public works (including works costing less than £25,000 each)	5,339,000
Social welfare	52,000
State bank	350,000
Survey	250,000
Total	58,268,000

	Total of capital requirement £
Capital Expenditures	
Loans (total)	26,068,000
Government account (total)	58,268,000
Grand total	84,336,000
Margin for increased cost	7,000,000
Total, capital expenditures	91,336,000
Consequential Commitments after 1959–60	
Loan Expenditures	
Electricity Corp. of Nigeria	1,500,000
Lagos town planning	450,000
Nigerian Railway Corporation	9,480,000
Total	11,430,000
Resultant Additional	
Recurrent Expenditures	*£ Per annum*
Broadcasting	232,000
Building Research Institute	15,000
Central Records Office	10,000
Civil aviation	50,000
Customs and excise	9,000
Defense	437,000
Education, general	300,000
Education, higher	311,000
Geological survey and mining	6,000
Industry	25,000
Medical and health	271,000
Meteorology	5,000
Natural resources research	312,000
Police	225,000
Post and Telegraph services	1,501,000
Public works, highways and bridges	325,000
Other public works	75,000
Social welfare	5,000
State bank	45,000
Survey	30,000
Total (per annum)	4,189,000

Source: Nigeria, *Progress Reports.*

charges for government services, from £29 million to £35 million by 1959–60. Thus, a projected shortfall of £2.5 million existed between recurrent expenditures and revenues for 1959–60.

An additional source of money was anticipated from the Post and Telegraph services. The P&T needed improvement so that they could increase their charges and raise revenues, or else the government might need to increase taxation. The wisdom in 1955–56 was that the country should set a limit on the pace of any development that called for increased expenditures in order to avoid a heavy tax burden.

For the first time since 1940, all the capital expenditures of the plan were grouped under one source, the Development Fund. One clear advantage was that the level of allocation was a known quantity. All available resources to finance capital expenditures were mobilized, and there was a separation between recurrent and capital commitments. The Development Fund was financed from previous balances, contributions from revenue surpluses, and the proceeds of receipts of a special or nonrecurrent nature in the form of loans, grants, and so on, both internal and external. In addition to meeting the program commitments, the Development Fund would also finance the completion of projects initiated before 1955 and oversee the accounting of expenditures incurred in 1955 before the program took effect. Other funds were merged and their balances transferred to the Development Fund.

A sum of £5.5 million was required to complete the capital projects not included in the program and another £21.5 million would be written off for expenditures during 1955. The sources of the Development Fund were varied (table 6.2). Compared to previous allocations, this was a lot of money from more diverse sources, reflecting the changes both in the direction of the economy and in concepts of development. The first source of general revenue balance was an accumulated surplus of revenue over "above-the-line" expenditures (or revenue over expenditure charged to a head of the annual estimates). As of March 31, 1956, the general revenue balance was estimated at £33.5 million, although only a sum of £7 million was available to the Development Fund. An additional £11.8 million, from the accumulated funds of the federal government, was added to the Development Fund.

The second source, contributions from annual revenues, was a form of nonrecurrent revenues: £2.5 million, calculated as a cost of a minimum capital works program, was paid to the Development Fund. Estimations in 1956 indicated that a total of £23 million should have been contributed by 1960. The Colonial Development and Welfare Fund was to contribute £4.1 million through territorial allocations to the Nigerian government by the Colonial Office. The rest of the Development Fund consisted of internal and external

Table 6.2. Sources of Development Fund (in £ million)

	Total available	*Total to finance plan*
General revenue balance and other funds	40.3	13.3
Contribution from annual revenue	23.0	23.0
Internal loans	21.3	21.3
CDWF	4.15	4.15
External loans	30.0	30.0

Source: Nigeria, *Economic Programme*, 6.

loans. The target was to raise an internal loan of £10 million, drawing from the reserves of public corporations and bodies such as the West African Currency Board. As stated earlier, a state bank would also be established, in part to facilitate raising internal loans. Another £11.3 million was raised before 1954 from the commodity marketing boards that undertook to lend the federal government £14 million. The resumed conference on the Nigerian Constitution decided that the loan commitment would be accepted by the regional marketing boards. Of the £14 million, a bulk sum of £11.3 million was available by 1956 and was redirected to finance the Economic Programme. Floating loans internally and applying the savings of individuals and corporate bodies for development became one of the major innovations in the late 1950s.

External loans were, however, more substantial. Memoranda from the federal government to the various ministries stressed the relevance of external loans, while warning that such money must be committed to the provision of capital works and basic services to "make a more direct contribution to the expansion of the Territory's resources."[32] Thus, insofar as external loans were concerned, the program served more as a consolidation of the advances already made than an expansion. The Constitution allowed the federal government to raise loans for itself and the regional governments. In 1956, the level of public debt was almost £20 million, but the goal was to raise £65–70 million by 1960, while meeting the obligations of previous loans. In effect, an annual sum of £4–5 million had to be committed to servicing the debt.

The colonial officers were most agitated not by debt servicing or the nature of expenditures but how to raise money. Nigerian politicians and the rest of the Commonwealth considered the London money market as the "most fruitful source of finance."[33] In 1956 they were very uncertain as to whether the £30 million expected from the market would in fact be forthcoming. The London market was so competitive that the British government had to maintain control of capital issues to curb internal inflation and meet the competing claims of all the members of the sterling area. Furthermore, there was no assurance whatsoever that Nigeria would have access to this market.

There were other great difficulties in obtaining external loans, besides the competitiveness of the market. The Secretary of State had to support the application and serve as guarantor. The amount of money that the country could raise in an open market was dependent on the extent to which investors wanted to spend their money in overseas government securities, the rate of interest, the ability of the country to repay interest and principal, and the prospects of political stability and economic growth. There were doubts that Nigeria would be able to justify the loans. The anticipated solution to failure to generate external loans was to scale down the projects.

The Individual Projects in the Economic Programme

Table 6.3 outlines the financial allocations to all the projects. The highlights of the 1956–60 plan included the establishment of a statutory broadcasting corporation, a building research institute at Zaria,[34] a Building Society to finance private housing in Lagos and other cities with housing shortages, and a central record office at Ibadan to collect and store public records. The civil aviation sector would be further developed by providing new aerodromes and improving existing runways, terminal buildings, and operation lighting to facilitate night landings, as well as updated telecommunications equipment. The expansion of customs services at Kano Airport and in the eastern frontier would prevent smuggling in the Cameroon border area, and at Port Harcourt a waterguard unit would be established for the same purpose. Defense initiatives included maintaining the military forces, providing more accommodations, offices, and a command headquarters in Lagos,[35] training more officers, and establishing a Nigerian Naval Force (table 6.4).

A sum of £1.7 million was allocated to general education in Lagos to build over nine hundred classrooms, meet the cost incurred by the abolition of school fees, repair and rebuild unsafe primary schools, acquire land for new schools, and expand secondary schools. The federal government assumed primary responsibility for the finances of the University College of Ibadan, the University College Teaching Hospital, and the Nigerian College of Arts, Science, and Technology. The goals for the University College were to provide housing for students, strengthen the agriculture faculty, expand the department of social studies and the study of African and modern languages, extend the chemistry laboratory, build a zoological museum and a botanical garden, and buy books for the library. In the case of the Nigerian College of Arts,

Table 6.3. Funding for approved schemes, 1955–1960 (£)

Projects	*Estimated costs*	*Expenditures*
Aviation	2,410,050	1,176,040
Broadcasting	1,563,090	463,090
Building research	82,050	68,210
Building Society	500,000	304,000
Colonial Development Corp.	258,000	258,000
Customs and excise	372,660	110,580
Defense, Army	6,243,660	2,506,580
Defense, Navy	1,300,000	266,210
Education, general	3,679,910	1,957,400
Education, higher	3,847,710	2,922,520
Education, technical	769,010	120,150
Electricity Corp. of Nigeria	7,300,000	3,750,000
Geological survey	46,000	30,740
Government Press	760,000	159,480
Hotels	40,000	40,000
Industry	1,802,250	885,140
Lagos town planning	9,903,000	5,599,590
Medical and health	3,463,940	1,933,500
Meteorology	136,500	67,500
National Archives	175,600	44,200
Natural resources research	973,430	265,260
Nigerian Ports Authority	2,000,000	954,000
Nigerian Coal Corp.	120,000	—
Nigerian Railway Corp.	18,630,000	7,928,960
Government offices, in Nigeria	1,679,170	1,247,640
Government offices, outside Nigeria	519,000	127,730
Police	3,857,530	1,206,170
Ports and inland waterways	14,754,950	6,314,220
Post and Telegraph services	15,035,250	10,422,970
Prisons	940,970	552,130
Highways and bridges	22,954,010	15,041,810
Other public works	8,094,970	3,518,180
Social welfare	216,800	30,000
Central bank	4,495,360	2,861,180
Survey	453,450	313,680
Senior staff housing and minor works	7,065,770	5,578,270
Cooperatives	3,000	—
Miscellaneous	17,636,530	6,520,090
Margin for increased costs	600,000	—
Total	164,683,620	85,545,220

Source: Nigeria, *Progress Reports.*

Science, and Technology, money was allocated for capital work, pharmacy training, and the construction of a hostel and laboratory.

The Electricity Corporation of Nigeria (ECN) was to receive a loan of £7.1 million to develop electricity supplies, especially in areas where demand made new investments profitable. The ECN proposed linking its Aba and Port Harcourt undertakings and interconnecting Lagos, Abeokuta, and Ibadan.

A number of institutions would be expanded by increasing their labor force, equipment, and office space. These included the Government Press in Lagos, the Kano Central Hotel, the Nigerian Coal Corporation, police, port authorities, Post and Telegraph services, prisons, and the Railway Corporation. In addition to new highways and bridges, existing structures would be widened and resurfaced. Expenditures on water supplies would concentrate on Lagos, while the regional administrations were expected to service the rest of the country. A central bank would be established.

Although the federal government decided to let the regions dominate the industrial sector and provided technical advice to them, it nevertheless decided to promote some large industrial schemes. The Institute of Applied Technical Research would be organized at Osodi, Lagos province, to investigate "the technical problems inherent in enlarging the scope of industrialisation," including the possible uses of several raw materials and appropriate industrial processes. In addition, an industrial estate would be created to assist industrialists in the federal territory. The estate would lease small factory units to tenants with limited financial resources to build and equip their factories. Some financial assistance would be provided for industrial ventures to aid small enterprises, provide loans to a few major projects, and underwrite the share capital of the Nigerian Cement Company at Nkalagu in Ogoja province.

Other principal projects included a grant to the Lagos Executive Development Board to clear slums, complete housing projects, and start new housing units. The city of Lagos, the seat of the federal government, would also benefit from expansion of medical and social facilities. Research would continue on natural resources at various centers, while the geological survey of the country would provide accurate maps.

While the capital expenditures were larger than the previous plan, the schemes were fewer in number because the regions had their own separate programs. Communications of all kinds received 56 percent of total expenditures because the federal government believed that this was the best way to accelerate the country's overall development. Productivity was expected to increase in agriculture through research and in industry by spending on coal and electricity production. The widespread shortage of staff would be solved by increased access to higher education. Improvements for police and prisons would assure order, and those to customs would generate revenues.

Table 6.4. Key proposals and projects, 1955–1960

	Estimates (£)
Industry	
Federal Loans Board[a]	300,000
Major projects[b]	500,000
Nigerian Cement Company[c]	175,000
Lagos town planning	
Lagos Housing Scheme (1955)[d]	1,000,000
Loan expenditures[e]	3,260,000
Other expenditures[f]	1,050,000
Medical and Health	
Mainland hospital[g]	1,750,000
Other hospital improvements, including a maternity hospital and Sisters' quarters at Chest Clinic Creek Hospital	450,000
Dispensary services, including 3 outpatient dispensaries	12,000
and 3 clinics	78,000
Training facilities, notably School of Medical Laboratory and	42,500
School of Dental Hygiene	17,500
Vaccine production	23,000
Other projects, including	60,000
blood transfusion services,	84,000
Lagos Ambulance Services, and	36,000
acquisition of hospital site at Apapa	20,000
Meteorology[h]	76,000
Natural resources research	
Agriculture, fisheries, forestry, and veterinary projects	1,442,000
Nigerian Coal Corp.[i]	1,000,000
Police	
Expansion of facilities	1,000,000
Ports and inland waterways	
Extension of Port Harcourt Wharf	3,250,000
Escravos Bar Project[j]	6,500,000
Improvements of ports[k]	314,000
Reclamation vessel	150,000
Post and Telegraphs services	
Engineering and equipment (mainly telecommunications equipment)	6,720,000
Buildings in Lagos and regional capitals	5,470,000

(*Table continues*)

Table 6.4. (*Continued*)

	Estimates (£)
Miscellaneous (e.g., vehicles, building stores)	700,000
Prisons (mainly new buildings)	500,000
Public works	
New construction outside of Lagos	2,883,000
Lagos-Apapa approach roads	1,750,000
Bituminous surfacing[l]	4,447,000
Strengthening bridges (mainly on the federal highway system)	2,000,000
Completion of projects in previous programs	1,503,000
Equipment	1,050,000
Other[m]	5,339,000
Railway Corporation	
System improvements	10,020,000
Borno extension	9,480,000
Social welfare[n]	52,000
State Bank[o]	350,000
Survey[p]	250,000
West African Airways Corporation	
Additional aircraft	280,000

Source: Nigeria, *Economic Programme.*

[a]A separate board for Lagos.

[b]Large industrial projects that were the responsibility of the federal government.

[c]The federal government was to underwrite the share capital to build a cement company at Nkalagu.

[d]For mortgages for individuals as well as for the government to build housing for civil servants.

[e]To clear slums on Lagos Island ("a disgrace to the capital"); to develop housing at Surulere; to build facilities for the Lagos Executive Development Board.

[f]To build housing and to embark on a reclamation project at Victoria Island.

[g]To expand hospital facilities in Lagos.

[h]To purchase equipment and build staff quarters and maintenance and repair workshop.

[i]To expand coal production for domestic use and export by opening new mines and introducing new technology.

[j]To dredge the Forcados estuary to allow passage of vessels up to fourteen feet (at high water).

[k]To dredge the Sheba bank and to improve ports at Sapele, Warri, and Koko, and at Lagos Customs Wharf.

[l]To adapt Trunk A roads for heavier traffic.

[m]Includes projects under £25,000, such as Lagos water supply and sewage system, offices, and Public Works Department requirements.

[n]Mainly to build a departmental headquarters and a school for female juvenile offenders in Lagos.

[o]To supplement existing commercial banks.

[p]Mainly to accelerate survey work, complete existing projects, and enlarge the federal topographical survey.

The Performance of the Economic Programme

True to the program's commitment to flexibility, 1955–60 was marked both by progress in execution and by constant revisions. The program was extended to 1962.[36] All estimated funds were not spent, as table 6.5 shows. This was attributed to problems of obtaining materials and staff. Annual revisions occurred but finances were not totally unpredictable, since the major projects were long-term. Although failure to raise projected funds (especially from loans) forced the reduction of estimates, none of the individual schemes was completely abandoned. In general, there was more success in raising domestic loans than external ones. Only small sums of money—about £200,000—were received as gifts from three foreign companies for projects on education and public records. In 1958, a central bank was established and a Banking Ordinance coordinated the operations of commercial banks with the central.

Individual projects were executed as funds were released for the fiscal year. New terminal buildings were constructed and opened at Kaduna, Enugu, and Port Harcourt, the runways and taxiways at Kano and Lagos were upgraded to accommodate larger airplanes. To produce technical staff, work began on the Aviation Ground Services Training School and the Flying Training School, both in Lagos. Telecommunications equipment was installed to improve air traffic control.

The performance of the Building Society was mixed: it recorded losses in its first two years but turned a profit of £57,000 at the end of December 1960. The mortgage assets had increased threefold from £503,818 in 1955 to £1,471,960 in 1960, and shareholders received a 2.5 percent dividend (shareholders included the Colonial Development Corporation, federal government, and eastern region government). The Building Society expanded its

Table 6.5. Expenditures, 1955–1960

Area of Expenditures	*Estimated total cost*	*Actual expenditures*
Loans	30,375,000	14,149,960
Highways and bridges	23,054,010	15,041,810
Public Works Extraordinary	29,071,720	16,362,830
Post and Telegraph services	15,135,250	10,422,970
Other capital expenditures	67,047,640	29,587,650
Total	164,683,620	85,565,650
1955–56	n/a	2,299,590
1956–57	n/a	8,775,350
1957–58	n/a	15,424,560
1958–59	n/a	26,993,950
1959–60	n/a	32,071,770

Source: Nigeria, *Progress Reports.*

office, established a regional one at Enugu, invited public investment, and provided a rather limited mortgage service for home construction.

Several government departments expanded their physical infrastructures. The Customs and Excise Department completed facilities at Port Harcourt, Maiduguri, Yola, Edib Nyok, and Mbonzie in the Eastern Frontier Control Stations. The Government Press completed its new building at Apapa in 1960. The army and navy also concentrated on building quarters and offices. In 1960 the army completed its Military Training School at Kaduna, while the newly formed navy spent its money on bases at Calabar and Lagos.

Education received a great boost. Primary school enrollment in Lagos more than doubled to 72,000 in 1960. Seventy primary schools were built or expanded, in addition to completing needed repairs. Thirteen post-primary schools were completed, increasing the number of placements to 2,350.

The University College at Ibadan completed many new buildings and purchased books for its library. Criticisms of the college continued, voiced by Nigerians who accused the school of financial recklessness and of failure to contribute to national unity by admitting more northern students and to reflect national aspirations.[37]

The three sites of the Nigeria College of Arts, Science, and Technology (Enugu, Ibadan, and Zaria) expanded their facilities and were upgraded to university level soon after the country's independence. Indeed, education underwent a major expansion. An expanded scholarship scheme for post-secondary education awarded 526 scholarships in 1960. In mid-1960 the Commission on Post School Certificate and Higher Education submitted its report projecting the needs of the country over a period of twenty years. The Shell BP Company gave £500,000 for the expansion of Yaba Technical Institute with two new teaching buildings.

In spite of the expansion, schools were not yet available in all areas; there was no balance between primary and secondary school enrollments; most teachers were not certified; and two-thirds of teachers had no more than primary school education. Unequal access to education over the years had created regional inequalities (with the north lagging far behind) and class inequalities (as those with the relevant qualifications obtained employment and lived a different lifestyle).

The Electricity Corporation (ECN) began a new development program to supply electricity to twenty-seven towns. By the end of 1960, twelve of the schemes had been commissioned and major extension works were completed at Oji and Ijora in Lagos.[38] In 1958, the ECN initiated the Niger Dam project to generate electricity and improve navigation, agriculture, and fisheries.

In general, the research projects were beset by a lack of skilled staff although they were able to build some offices and laboratories. At the Federal Institute of Industrial Research, the mechanized production of gari from cassava was successful, and equipment was installed to experiment with the possibilities of the production of pulp and paper. At the Lagos industrial estate, about twenty-four new factory units were leased by small-scale industrialists. A great exhibition of the products from the research centers and other sectors of the economy was held in 1960, "the largest ever staged in West Africa."

In spite of its detailed projection for staff requirements and expenditures for recruitment, the execution of the Economic Programme was affected by a shortage of professional staff. Contractors also faced the problem of scarcity of skilled personnel. Foreigners were recruited, while the number of qualified Nigerians was gradually increasing. Construction programs were delayed and a number of regional projects were deferred to the 1960s. A general shortage of steel for construction was reported. The preparation of technical specifications, tenders, and contract documents took much time and caused delays. In projects that required loans, there was a lot of anxiety. In general, external loans fell far short of expectations, affecting the pace of development.[39]

While the accomplishments did not meet expectations, there was fatigue with respect to criticism of the colonial regime. A lot of economic and political activities occurred in the regions, diverting attention from the development program. After 1958, when it became clear that the country would soon be independent, this political transition became far more important than the ongoing implementation of the Economic Programme.

Beyond the Economic Programme: The Private Sector and the Regional Governments

No comprehensive program existed for the private sector. This was a deliberate omission: the development strategy was to allow the private sector to operate freely within the law. During the 1950s the federal government decided to actively promote foreign investments. In the transition years, there was a need to ensure a continuity of ties between Nigeria and Britain. With independence, Britain thus sought a new way to continue its domination of the country. The strategy entailed the retention of the capitalist system. The government's laws, regulations, and policies favored private, foreign investments.

In 1958, the federal government issued a major statement welcoming outside participation, assuring investors that there were no plans for nationalization, except for public utilities such as the railways, telecommunications, and electricity. The government insisted that it would not require joint participation and also promised to share the cost of a business that might be of special significance to the public. When the government intervened, it was not a departure from an ideology of free enterprise but to fill an important vacuum.

The federal government used its power over taxation and tariffs to provide special incentives to foreign investors.[40] Five major acts were passed to provide these: the Industrial Development (Import Duties Relief) Act (1957), the Industrial Development (Income Tax Relief) Act (1958), the Customs Duties (Dumped and Subsidized Goods) Act (1958), the Customs (Drawback) Regulations (1958), and the Income Tax (Amendment) Act (1959).[41] These acts represent the most comprehensive package of the 1950s to link the Nigerian economy to the international market.

The Income Tax Relief Act made relief from income tax possible in the early years of pioneer industries (limited liability companies that manufactured important items for domestic use). A successful company could operate for five years without paying tax. The Import Duties Relief Act offered a new industry both relief from import duties and tariff protection. The Customs Duties Act permitted the imposition of a special duty on goods dumped in Nigeria or being subsidized by any foreign government or authority, in order to protect local industry from unfair price competition. The second customs regulation allowed importers to claim repayment of import duties if goods were exported in the same condition or state as they had been imported or if materials were imported for use in the manufacture of goods and then exported.

There were no legal restrictions to prevent foreigners from owning businesses, and all companies, indigenous or foreign, were governed by the same laws. In places where land was difficult to obtain (notably in the western and eastern regions), the government could acquire and lease land to a company. Creating industrial estates had become part of the program in the 1950s. By 1960 about 930 acres of industrial estates had been developed in Lagos at Apapa, Ijora, and Iganmu, towns that became the earliest industrial centers in the country. In the north, 2,100 acres were developed for industries at Kaduna, Kano, Zaria, Jos, Ilorin, Gusau, and Maiduguri. On the whole, the terms were more than generous, allowing the free transfer out of the country of profits and dividends arising from an investment.[42]

The regional governments pursued their own plans, drawing on funds from the federal government, locally generated revenues, and limited external aid. Nigeria was crowded with plans and ideas; a few were new and reflected the views of those in power and the IBRD's committee. To oversimplify, rapid industrialization, agricultural mechanization, mass education, infrastructures, and communications were the leading schemes in the regional development plans.[43]

The regions continued to fund research, the provision of water and electricity supplies to new areas, medical services, and roads. They instituted regional development corporations that became active in establishing agricultural plantations to increase the output of export crops. All regions desired industrialization, and they considered many proposals, sent fact-finding committees abroad, and made small inroads in establishing agro-allied factories. The regional production development boards, too, committed money to projects such as road construction, research, and scholarships.

The marketing and regional development boards continued to award loans to individuals, cooperative societies, and local government councils.[44] In 1954, existing boards, with countrywide jurisdiction over different crops, had been broken into four (one for each region and another for the Southern Cameroons), each with power over regionally produced commodities. A central marketing board was established to set standards of quality and organize transportation and marketing overseas. The regional boards, with the advice of the central body, determined price and stabilization policies.

The regional boards relentlessly pursued the old policy of underpaying farmers in order to accumulate reserves. If the producers were deceived in the 1940s as to the intention of the marketing boards, this was no longer the case in the 1950s; resounding complaints of being cheated and receiving an inequitable share of higher prices were registered against the state. The government dismissed the complaints, arguing that stabilization was necessary to form reserves to guarantee producers stable prices, to lend money for development purposes, and to mitigate the severity of inflationary pressures.

Community grants for self-help became the sole responsibility of the regional governments, and they all budgeted funds accordingly. Whether a community was lucky enough to receive part of a grant was irrelevant in focusing the aspirations and desire of the people. Self-help, which began as a small idea early in the 1940s to organize change on the basis of deliberate long-term planning, had become an entrenched value by 1960. Ever since, as far as Nigerians have been concerned, the first responsibility of any concerned government is to plan for change. Moreover, the only way successive governments have been judged is by the extent of their commitment and contribution to development.

To avoid any infringement on the regional powers, the federal plan provided guidelines on coordination of activities. The ministries responsible for similar subjects engaged in ad hoc consultations, in addition to conferences convened by all government levels to discuss subjects of common interest. Bodies such as the Council of Natural Resources (to discuss natural resources research) and the Loans Advisory Board became permanent consultative groups that brought the regional and federal governments together. The National Economic Council, recommended by the IBDR's committee, became the highest level of interaction where top officials discussed common economic problems. The Federal Loans Board loaned funds to thirty-six projects sponsored by the regions, in addition to those awarded to indigenous entrepreneurs.[45]

The Colonial Development Corporation continued to enter into joint partnerships with regional governments in the areas of agriculture, mining, and commerce, and by 1956 the CDC had invested £2.8 million in sawmills, housing projects, and light engineering.[46] In 1959 the Investment Company of Nigeria was formed from the Commonwealth Development Finance Company by British and Nigerian businesses to recruit skilled foreign workers and promote new industries.

Coordination between federal and regional institutions notwithstanding, the plans were too numerous and duplicative. Mimicking the political situation, each region was more concerned with protecting its rights and obligations than with collaborating on a joint or common economic goal. By the time the National Economic Council was organized, the regions had already decided on their course of action, and each was functioning relatively autonomously. A common dependence on export crops meant that the agricultural sector had to be promoted—which at least united the plans. In addition, by concentrating its own activities on the provision of utility services and infrastructures, the federal government ensured a minimum level of cohesiveness.

public records. Customs services, police, and higher education were also expanded. The regional governments and the private sector generated activities that also contributed to the changes of this decade.

By 1960, Nigeria had accepted planning as a government function. Full political power was transferred in that year, expectations about change were high, and the independent government, while new, was no stranger to the theory and practice of long-range economic planning. Planning as a function of the state was, however, an unintended outcome of a series of colonial policies and reactions to changing political circumstances. All the major colonial plans and revisions had been formulated in response to a crisis or a major political change. The 1929 Act was in response to the worldwide economic depression while those of 1940 and 1945 owed their origins to World War II and to demands by colonial subjects for progress. The changes of the 1950s were imposed by far-reaching constitutional reforms that introduced federalism and regional autonomy and assured independence. A unitary planning system was abandoned. While the regions basked in the glory of their new found power, the center, that is, the federal government, retained its power. The IBRD's committee provided a much needed answer to the problem of intergovernmental relations between the powerful regions and the center by recommending a group of plans for the country.

The ideas of planning were relatively consistent over the two decades. The state became interventionist, moving away from the previous doctrine of laissez-faire to that of "development planning." The control measures of the war years gave enormous power to bodies such as the marketing boards and the Department of Commerce and Industries. Planning became an exercise in determining the direction of the economy and accelerating the pace of social programs in education and health. The objectives were modified from time to time. At the start, planning was limited to material development, excluding such things as technical education. In the 1940s, the government included virtually everything. This new approach determined all available resources without limiting spending; it included all potential major development projects on the expenditure side, and important increases in the recurrent expenditures of the existing Health and Agriculture Departments and other services.[1] In the 1950s, planning emphasized avoiding heavy expenditures on social programs that would consume recurrent capital but yield no profit. Import-substitutions and the promotion of local industries became part of planning.

The Colonial Office clearly instructed that planning in the colonies must benefit the "mother country." The wording of the plans contained the rhetoric of philanthropy and external aid, but their policies ensured the survival of the colonial economic structure. Features of the pre-1940 economy were easily carried forward. Agriculture remained the bedrock of planning, and projects and research were focused on export crops. The interest in food crops was also connected to that of exports, as the case of rice demonstrates: "If it is possible to increase the acreage under rice it would not only be of direct benefit to the rice farmers, but by increasing the amount of food available, would allow other farmers to grow more groundnuts for export."[2]

The country remained dependent on external trade, and foreign firms retained their domination. Communications co-opted resources because of the need to ensure the mobility of goods. In revising its policy in 1940, the Colonial Office linked economic planning to increased productivity. The assumption was that if the people's social and economic well-being were improved, they would produce more and have more purchasing power. Enhanced purchasing power would increase the volume of exports and imports, all to the benefit of the British economy. Even in the 1950s when small-scale attempts were made in manufacturing and promotion of local industries and import-substitution, planning was focused on the participation of private foreign investments and diversion of local resources to the Colonial Development Corporation.

To assure control, the officers of the colonial government and the Colonial Office played a leading role in the formulation of development plans, stressing their own importance as the so-called "trustees" of a backward region. Although development committees (with Nigerian members) were established in the provinces and districts, the colonial administrators maintained control over the plan formulation process. In some cases, as in the Plateau towns and villages, British officers wrote all the proposals, acting on an alleged basis of "superior knowledge." As an example, in 1944 the District Officer stressed the need for closer European supervision of the Plateau, if there was to be "any immediate progress in the matter of development and social welfare. Little or no co-operation can be looked for from the people themselves."[3]

In the same year at Ogoja a citizen who proposed a cooperative plantation like the Soviet collective farm was quickly dismissed as a layman without any knowledge of agriculture.[4] The Ogoja case was not an isolated one: the officers were contemptuous of ordinary people's ideas. Thus, to guarantee control, plan implementation was carried out and supervised by government officers.

This approach was not without grave consequences for planning. Many project designs ignored people's aspirations. For example, the model houses and settlements that attempted to change lifestyles and even architecture all ultimately failed. Suggestions for change were arrogantly insensitive to Nigerians' needs.

Typically, an all-wise officer of the state was sent to train farmers in production, women in child care, and elders in village administration, while purposefully avoiding a dialogue or exchange of ideas. The result was that many people chose not to listen—or pretended enthusiasm and then carried on with their old habits. The officers continually complained about the people's apathy, conservatism, and resistance to change.

In some cases, the definition and direction of development differed between the government and the people. In the early 1950s when the majority of communities wanted piped water supplies and electricity, the officers were talking about community development and public hygiene. When people preferred to live in towns and cities, the government focused on village planning.

Many experiments with different aspects of agriculture and livestock, such as the importation of foreign stocks and crops, failed partly because farmers were not involved. For most of the 1940s, the population was kept in the dark. Propaganda was utilized to ensure that the people's support for the government's political activities (for example, its World War II campaign for support for the war effort). In such major innovations as the erection of mills and the use of tractors, details and expectations were scarcely examined. The government expected people to show instant gratitude and to keep any reservations to themselves. In cases involving the people or community, the results were generally positive. Midway through the plan's implementation, the government had realized that there was a missing link in the planning process—the involvement and mobilization of the people.[5]

To most senior administrators, however, funding was the core of planning, not mass participation.[6] The Colonial Office felt that as long as it increased monetary grants in absolute terms, it had fulfilled its own side of the bargain. True to its words, from 1929 to 1960, the fund for development increased from time to time with each enabling act. In 1940 the fund stood at £5.5 million, in 1945 it was £120 million, and in 1950, £140 million. From 1946 to 1956, the financial commitment of Britain to its colonies was between £17.5 million and £25 million per annum. T. R. Batten has calculated this as between three and four shillings per head, if the total population in the colonies was sixty million.[7] It is noteworthy, however, that over the twenty-year period covered by this study only 25 percent of development funds for Nigeria were externally generated.

For Nigeria, funds were always too little and actual expenditures were lower than estimates. Until 1945, money not spent in one year could not be carried forward. Although all the plans made long-range projections and the Colonial Office made long-term monetary promises, the implementation was dependent on short-term considerations. In addition, between 1940 and 1945, monetary promises went unfulfilled because of British wartime domestic problems. Thereafter, the loans and grants were severely limited while the market for loans became so competitive that in the 1950s Nigeria's applications were denied.

Planning was beset by other problems. The planners' knowledge of the country and its domestic economy was miniscule. Technical knowledge and the understanding of the environment were limited. Scarce labor was a constraint in cases where money was available for specific projects. For instance, the adult education program and expansion of schools in the northern region did not falter because of a lack of enthusiastic learners or funds but because of an inadequate supply of teachers. Capital goods and equipment were also in short supply. The expansion of the regional bureaucracies in the 1950s and the various new programs pushed available resources to their limits.

Rapid expansion of economic activities demanded more qualified labor and capital than the country could offer. The cost of projects rapidly increased, with inflation and adjustments to salaries and wages. Spreading the benefits to most people was never achieved, mainly due to the preference for projects for towns and administrative centers. Projects were conceived too quickly, with minimum consideration for visibility, suitable locations, and technical issues. For instance, many of the feeder roads to the provincial and district capitals were built hurriedly and had to be rebuilt in later years. In the early 1950s in the eastern region, a number of bridges and embankments collapsed due to faulty construction and the underestimation of the rise and fall of rivers.[8]

The magnitude of Nigeria's problems was not often appreciated by the planning committees, which always exaggerated the potential of every proposal. For instance, the proposal for a small cattle ranch of less than two hundred animals was praised for its anticipated consequences of improving the health and standard of living of several hundred people.[9] Most of the new projects, such as in the livestock industry in the south, resettlement of people, and promotion of local industries, failed. In cases where technology provided a solution, such as the use of mechanical plows, success was limited by poor reception by the people and limited amounts of equipment.

Projects were not always adequately evaluated, and new ones were added without completing those already begun. In the 1950s, the regional and federal plans lacked coordination, and there was minimal consultation with the private sector. Moreover, planning completely excluded the informal sector that supported thousands of urban dwellers.[10] Finally, even if planning entailed the mobilization and allocation of resources for accelerated development, the colonial state was in a poor position to undertake it, since one of its own major roles was to ensure the transfer of wealth to Britain.

To confine discussions to the planning process in explaining the post–World War II economy and society is somewhat misleading, as these plans did not exhaust the range of government activities: the financial budget for the plans was less than half of total public expenditures. Contributions by the private sector, public agencies, and the regional governments in the 1950s enlarged receipts from exports, and the many last-minute reforms of the departing colonial government also influenced changes.

The leading Nigerian nationalists and emerging scholars promoted development ideas both similar to and different from those of the colonial government. Those who were privileged to preside over their regions in the 1950s began to pursue the ways and means they thought would facilitate rapid change. In addition, there was a great desire by individuals to take part in the private sector of the economy. Pressure came from several directions: from the farmers and traders who wanted the marketing boards to function in such a way that it would be easier to obtain licenses and make profits and from the entrepreneurs who wanted startup loans for manufacturing businesses.[11] Some called for indigenization to empower Nigerians. Finally, self-help projects were intensified in the 1950s. Schools, community centers, post offices, and other facilities, as well as roads, became projects that communities undertook either with their own contributions or with small government grants.

Planning and the Limits of Change

Some of the achievements of planning were major, such as increased research in agriculture, livestock, and forestry, which aided understanding of the effects on crop productivity of improved hybrids, insecticides, fertilizers, and storage, expansion of communications abilities, vaccine production, rural and preventative medicine in selected locations, and the establishment of hospitals and schools (including a university and a teaching hospital, plus the Colleges of Arts, Science, and Technology). Many were minor, such as the introduction of technology to rural areas and the production sector (for example, using mills to extract oil and power looms for weaving). Some areas benefited greatly from the new facilities and projects, notably the provincial headquarters and administrative centers. A few individuals benefited from loans from the loan development boards, contracts awarded by departments, and government sale of mills at reasonable prices. Small beginnings were made to improve the condition of women and children with new maternity and female wards in hospitals and welfare clinics.

In general, state intervention in many sectors of the economy injected more capital into the system. The bureaucracy expanded in the 1950s, providing opportunities for employment, promotion, and privileges. Changes were recorded by way of expansion of infrastructures, domestic markets, production of certain goods like rice and dairy products, export trade levels, and social services (for example, water and electricity supplies, hospitals, and schools). Ideas about planning spread to the new regional governments. Moreover, the ability to analyze the economic situation improved, as well as an understanding of ideological debates and obstacles to development.

Nigeria's economy changed substantially during the years of planning. In 1940, the plan's first year, Nigeria had the lowest per capita revenues in British West Africa. Public expenditures had increased in the 1930s but fluctuated disturbingly. Development received limited attention: expenditures on so-called development schemes ranged from zero to £18,000 per annum until the early 1940s.

Some important changes were recorded after 1940. The colonial economy expanded. Economic decline ended; import and export markets increased, with the most substantial revenues from exports. After World War II, exports expanded dramatically, due to increases in market prices, rising consumption, and demand for materials for postwar reconstruction in Europe. In Nigeria, the domestic economy was expanding and modernizing, due to the combined impact of infrastructure, urbanization, the wage economy, better integration of regional trade, and a population increase. The expenditures generated by the normal activities of government and programs executed under the plans (and by such bodies as the marketing boards) ensured measurable expansion in social services, infrastructure, research, and education. The provision of electricity and water supplies quadrupled. More roads were constructed, and over a thousand miles of roadway were tarred to aid transportation and, therefore, growth of the domestic market.

The private sector benefited from the export expansion by enlarging its operations, while many Nigerians found some areas in which to participate in foreign trade. In the 1950s, manufacturing increased by 500 percent: it was still very small though, contributing less than 8 percent to the GDP. The major industries were a cement factory, three cotton factories, three cigarette factories, two breweries, a plastic factory, and one factory producing steel drums and other goods. Oil exports also started in 1958, but the full potential of this export was yet to be tapped.[12]

The regional governments added to the tempo of change through public expenditures for capital investment and expansion of public services. The private sector benefited from these basic services as well. Gross investment by the major companies increased from £11.7 million in 1954 to £20.5 million in 1959–60. In the early 1950s, there were high demands on the international market for raw materials, food products, and luxuries. In Nigeria the total production averaged a 4 percent growth per annum, prices rose rapidly, and this sector alone yielded 85 percent of the foreign exchange, which paid for the imports. Agricultural production grew by 30 percent, owing to a combination of such factors as external demands, creative response by the farmers, and transportation improvements.

In spite of their severe limitations, and perhaps unreliability,[13] all official figures concluded that aggregate indicators of economic change witnessed an upward trend. The GDP grew at 4.1 percent from 1950 to 1957 and at 5.7 percent in the closing years of that decade. Agriculture contributed at least 64 percent of the GDP.

Table 7.1 (from the IBRD's report in mid-1955) indicates some economic gains between 1934 and 1955. The table conveys an impression of rapid growth and expansion, yet, the exaggeration notwithstanding, it illustrates the nature of the changes. Among the major increases were the revenues of the federal government, the amount of currency in circulation, Post Office Savings Bank deposit levels, personal income, and consumption. The volume of railway freight traffic tripled, and passenger traffic doubled, indicating the extent of infrastructure growth. National income estimates in the 1950s indicated that per capita income increased in real terms at a rate of about 2 percent while capital formation was approximately 10 percent of the gross national product. Capital formation increased with better highways, additional locomotives and rolling stock, public school buildings and hospitals, manufacturing plants, permanent housing, garages, lorries, automobiles, sewing machines, oil presses, and bicycles, as well as in the form of external assets.[14] The government expenditures and gross domestic investments expanded, due to increased yields in indirect taxation, private overseas investment, and a small utilization of past savings.[15]

Tables 7.2 to 7.8 present additional data on the 1950s, indicating important changes during the last decade of colonial rule. The amount of private consumption increased as the GDP grew. The value of domestic merchandise exports doubled during the decade. Until the mid-1950s, the value of exports exceeded that of imports, and there was a 50 percent increase in domestic consumption. After 1954, there was a faster increase in imports than exports, and after 1955 there was a decline in prices for export crops.

These changes convincingly indicate economic growth, stressing the increase in per capita income over time. The country witnessed a precarious, "slowly transforming" economy, but the changes obscured significant problems. Because the colonial government established the criteria, the sectors used for the computation are in general the "modern," externally oriented ones such as imports and exports or the formal sector components of banking, post offices, and railways. We have little data on the informal sector to indicate the nature and character of change.

Table 7.1. Economic indicators

	Units and period	*1934*	*1939*	*1944*	*1949*	*1951*	*1953*
Financial data							
Central government							
Total revenues	£ million	4.9	5.8	10.9	23.8	32.8	50.9
Customs and excise		2.2	2.5	4.9	12.6	18.2	33.9
Direct taxes		0.8	0.9	2.4	3.8	5.3	6.8
Revenue of NAs		n.a.	1.5	2.8	4.9	5.9	8.2
Currency in circulation		n.a.	5.9	13.5	31.8	39.2	51.4
Bank deposits with major Nigerian banks	£ million	n.a.	n.a.	9.9	13.5	22.4	31.2
Post Office Savings	£ thousand						
Bank deposits	1,000	71	185	879	2,254	3,239	4,059
No. of accounts		21	45	86	169	169	198
Foreign trade	£ m/calendar yr.						
Exports, total	1,000 tn.	8.9	10.5	17.2	81.1	120.1	125.3
Cocoa	1,000 tn.	78.0	113.8	70.1	103.6	121.5	104.7
Palm kernels	1,000 tn.	289	300	314	376	347	403
Palm oil	1,000 tn.	113	126	125	170	150	201
Groundnuts	1,000 tn.	245	147	156	378	141	327
Cotton	Million lbs.	5.9	4.4	4.3	10.0	15.4	17.7
Bananas	Million lbs.	51.0	138.5	—	145.5	160.9	202.4
Rubber	£ m/calendar yr.	3.6	6.2	21.1	15.4	46.7	47.6
Imports, total	1,000 tn.	5.4	6.8	15.7	58.2	84.6	108.2
Iron sheet	1,000 tn.	6.9	5.8	1.4	14.4	19.0	34.3
Sewing machines	1,000	2.5	3.2	0.3	19.5	32.4	37.9
Bicycles	Million sq. yd.	5.2	6.6	14.1	129.6	153.4	217.0
Cotton piece goods	Million sq. yd.	63.2	60.7	106.6	185.2	121.3	172.0
Rayon piece goods	Thousand tn.	5.1	3.1	5.2	15.0	40.7	64.8
Cement	Million gal.	35.1	51.1	45.8	161.9	261.1	297.4
Kerosene consumption		1.7	2.0	2.3	4.7	9.0	12.0
Transport and communications							
Nigerian Railway	Thousand mi.	148	198	266	326	352	351
Passenger traffic	Thousand mi.	293	315	513	658	672	827
Freight traffic	Thousand mi.	n.a.	21.0	24.6	26.3	27.2	28.8
Roads, total							
Tarred roads	Mi.	n.a.	n.a.	533	937	1.114	1,631
Commercial vehicles, new registrations	Calendar yr.	538	559	663	2,356	2,901	4,159
Cars and taxis, new registrations	Calendar yr.	439	572	61	2,112	3,457	3,873
Motor fuel, consumption	Million gal.	3.0	4.9	9.9	17.6	23.7	33.3
Telephone and telegraph	1,000 wire mi.	21.5	26.7	30.6	31.8	37.6	42.1

Source: IBRD, *Economic Development*, 9.

Table 7.2. Gross domestic product of manufacturing, in constant prices (£1,000)

	1950	*1954*	*1957*	*1960*	*% increase*
Bakeries	19.0	66.0	210.0	316.0	1,550
Oil milling	363.6	356.9	2161.6	2610.0	618
Margarine	2.5	12.0	18.2	18.2	630
Beer and soft drinks	275.9	741.1	1683.7	2800.0	911
Tobacco	1395.8	2226.4	2100.6	2190.0	57
Textiles	4.5	50.0	377.0	613.0	1,350
Rubber processing	19.5	137.8	594.8	1378.0	7,080
Tanning	5.9	16.7	39.2	40.5	586
Saw milling	498.7	1304.4	1531.4	1800.0	261
Cement	0.0	0.0	372.4	1160.0	—
Total	3129.3	6474.0	10924.7	15650.0	398

Source: Nigeria, *National Development Plan,* 9–13.

Even in the sectors used as the indices of change, there were several serious limitations. The percentage and level of revenues available for local governments failed to keep pace with those of the central and regional bodies. While the mileage of tarred roads increased, it did not accommodate the increase in traffic. The roads and railways projects did not have as their priorities the convenience of rural dwellers, promotion of internal trade, or even travelers' safety. For example, a direct link between the western and eastern regions would have reduced the traveling distance considerably but was not considered. The railway was retained as a traditional single-track system, but track mileage was not extended in any appreciable way. The trains' slow speed discouraged its use by many people.

Economic growth was unevenly spaced, because it was affected by the performance of the agricultural sector that in turn was subject to price fluctuations and weather conditions. The so-called increase in standards of living was paid for by export proceeds spent on imported items consumed by the urban middle class. For example, a fivefold increase in flour and sugar imports in the 1950s and a tenfold increase in the fish imports reveal a rising level of consumption and changing tastes that were funded with export revenues. Overall, imports grew from 10.7 percent in 1950 to 24.7 percent in 1960.

Cash reserves accumulated in the early 1950s due to favorable export prices were carelessly and quickly dissipated to finance consumption and some investments of the late 1950s. Ninety percent of those reserves were used for consumption purposes. The increase in private savings noted in table 7.1 was gradually offset by a steep rise in government consumption, estimated in 1960 at 7.5 of the GDP, compared to 3.5 in 1950. Manufacturing grew, but in

Table 7.3. Crops grown primarily for domestic use (million tons)

	1950	*1957*
Yams	6.63	6.69
Cassava	3.61	4.66
Cocoyams	0.60	0.67
Guineacorn	1.38	2.14
Millet	0.92	1.79
Maize	0.47	0.66
Rice	0.19	0.26
Kolanuts	0.08	0.11
Beans	0.07	0.23
Other	0.76	5.00

Source: Nigeria, *National Development Plan,* 9–13.

Table 7.4. Major export products, 1950–1960

	Volume (1,000 tn.)		*Value (£ m.)*	
	1950	*1960*	*1950*	*1960*
Cocoa	100	180	19	35
Palm kernels	420	420	16.5	25
Groundnuts	143	619	15.2	22.0
Palm oil	167	197	12.1	13.2
Benniseed	9.0	27.5	0.7	1.8
Cotton	42	151	3.0	5.9
Petroleum	0	847	nil	4.4
Sawn timber	548	2,000	0.22	1.1
Timber	9,218	22,00	02.2	5.9
Rubber	13.7	58.0	2.8	14.2

Source: Nigeria, *National Development Plan,* 9–13.
Notes: Cocoa, palm kernels, groundnuts, palm oil, benniseed, and cotton were purchased by marketing boards for the marketing years 1950–51 and 1960–61 for export use (export values refer to calendar years); petroleum exports in 1958 totaled 245,000 tons.

absolute terms it constituted only a small proportion of the GDP. The few established industries were first-stage, bulk-reducing processes or small to medium finishing facilities, such as print shops and bakeries.

The colonial government, throughout the last decade, was conscious of the impending transfer of power and assessed most policies and decisions with posterity in mind. Except when expressing concern about how Nigerians would govern themselves in the future, they refused to allow any negative thinking or any admission of guilt. A number of senior administrators admitted that the success of planning was limited, but they insisted that it was not a failure. As with other changes, time would tell.

In spite of the severe limitations imposed by World War II, the official position in the 1940 CDWA was that it "contributed even in those difficult times, with faith and assurance, to the future development and welfare of Nigeria."[16] The performance of the first half of the Ten-Year Plan was described as remarkable, as laying the foundations upon which advancement could proceed "with an ever increasing tempo."[17] Critics were reminded that "human progress through education and social services cannot be measured by arithmetic or the expenditure of money, but only through the inexorable processes of time."[18] Some officers, however, were more realistic in their assessment. For instance, Governor J. S. MacPherson, after a depressing evaluation of the economy, concluded in the late 1950s that although the Ten-Year Plan had contributed to the country's progress, it "cannot be regarded as more than the framework on which the Nigeria of the future must build."[19]

In general, development plans did not change the face of the country or alter the living standards of the majority of the population. Planning did not have an immediate impact in the 1940s; not until 1949 did some areas see the very first signs of growth. Frustration was evident everywhere in 1950: ten years later, while some were able to point to water and electricity supplies or a few new roads, the majority could point to nothing at all. While the plans were forward-looking in quantifiable terms, actual implementation quickly assumed the character of short-term measures in response to emergency

Table 7.5. Government services

	1950	*1960*
Mileage of roads maintained by governments		
Bituminized	1,025	5,267
Unsurfaced	27,021	41,494
Number of telephones in service	7,760	38,690
Electricity output KWh	61.1	448.3
Expenditures on health and medical services, capital and recurrent (£ m.)	2.2	10.8
Expenditures on education, capital and recurrent (£ m.)	3.1	26.3
Railway freight (m. tons)	711	1,250
Port cargo (m. tons)	3.16	7.31

Source: Nigeria, *National Development Plan,* 9–13.

Table 7.6. Gross domestic product by category of expenditure (1957 prices; in million £)

	1950	*1951*	*1952*	*1953*	*1954*	*1955*	*1956*	*1957*	*1958*	*1959*	*1960*
Consumers' expenditures	609.4	650.2	695.9	717.3	774.6	805.5	798.9	815.5	830.0	830.0	870.0
Government expenditures on goods and services	24.4	26.8	33.5	29.9	31.2	45.5	43.8	47.6	56.7	70.0	77.0
Gross fixed deposit in Nigeria	48.4	59.7	75.0	79.9	92.9	102.6	108.0	113.0	122.3	136.7	158.0
Increase in market, British Stocks	–7.3	6.3	1.5	–0.1	–6.2	4.6	–4.8	9.1	–0.3	n.a.	n.a.
Plus Exports (f.o.b.)	99.9	93.6	111.7	114.8	131.9	126.9	138.5	129.1	144.0	163.0	171.0
Final Expenditures	774.4	836.6	917.6	941.8	1024.4	1085.1	1084.41	114.3	1163.2	1208.9	1276.0
Minus imports (c.i.f.)	75.1	82.6	108.3	114.1	131.6	163.3	180.9	175.6	182.0	212.0	253.0
GDP at market price	699.3	754.0	809.3	827.7	892.8	921.8	903.5	938.7	970.7	84.0%	85.0%
Consumers' exp. as % of GDP	87.1%	86.2 %	86.0%	86.7%	86.8%	87.4%	88.4%	86.9%	85.5%	7.1%	7.5%
Govt. expenditures as % of GDP	3.4%	3.6%	4.1%	3.6%	3.5%	4.9%	4.8%	5.1%	5.8%	13.8%	15.4%
Gross fixed invest. in Nigeria	6.9%	7.9%	9.3%	9.7%	10.4%	11.1%	12.0%	12.0%	12.6%		

Source: Nigeria, *National Development Plan*, 9–13.

Table 7.7. Postwar economic changes

	Units	1947	1953	1958
Government revenues (excluding overseas grants)	£ 1,000	14,193	51,110	81,288
Currency in circulation	£ 1,000	23,429	51,365	55,118
Bank deposits	£ 1,000	13,697	31,238	58,056
Exports and re-exports	£ 1,000	44,314	124,232	135,690
Imports	£ 1,000	32,636	108,290	167,074
Cement, imported and local	tons	107,306	297,436	573,119
Railway freight traffic	ton mi. in 1,000s	571,000	827,000	1,232,000
Commercial vehicles registr.	no.	n/a	10,700	17,900
Private vehicles licensed	no.	n/a	12,300	24,150
Telephones in use	no.	6,544	13,279	31,000
Electricity generated	units in 1,000s	85,836	164,756	331,125
Gross capital formation	£ 1,000	n/a	52,157	108,938

Source: National Economic Council, *Economic Survey of Nigeria,* 11.

situations and to meet the demands of the normal activities of existing government departments.

Although the federal government (and the regions in the 1950s) desired external aid, Nigeria's role in international politics was limited. Until its independence, the country could not seek aid beyond what the Colonial Office allowed. For example, the country had no independent monetary base, as the currency board was controlled from London. Several aspects of the currency board system and banking, highlighted in a number of studies, indicate a steady flow of capital out of the country, the prevention of the country from using its foreign exchange to buy from a market of its choice, and the resultant difficulty of generating sufficient domestic capital for development.

The economy was backward at independence in 1960, although there was an impressive push toward growth; despite pervasive poverty, the economy was not stagnant. Nigeria's economic base remained the export of raw materials produced by an army of small-scale poor farmers and mine workers. Occupational groups still reflected the structure of the 1940s, although the modern sector of the economy had expanded. Food production was declining, especially in the south where it was less than the annual population growth of nearly 2 percent.

Agriculture, the dominant sector, was beset by problems of capital shortages and poor access to credit for farmers, continued use of simple implements, small, scattered land holdings, and poor production techniques in general. There were farmers without land in the cocoa belt of western region, either because they were migrants or because wealthy people had purchased more land to the detriment of others. Landlessness pushed many people into poverty and migration. Inequality was becoming pronounced in the north, too, partly due to land dispossession. When conditions were too harsh, farmers migrated elsewhere, as in the case of the Igbo of the eastern region who moved to other places, including the Spanish territory of Fernando Póo. The farmers were also exploited: the government, through the marketing boards, squeezed producers by underpaying them.

Urban unemployment increased in the late 1950s, fueled by rural-urban migrations and the high turnover of primary school graduates. The movement to urban areas for better incomes and social lives became uncontrollable, in spite of the fact that there were fewer jobs, increasing poverty, and social adjustment difficulties. In addition, such migration meant the withdrawal of necessary labor from the farms and villages.

In education, the majority of primary school teachers were not highly trained, elementary and higher teacher training centers were inadequate, and the space for ambitious and talented students in the colleges was too limited.

The problems identified as obstacles to development in the 1940s were repeated in the early 1960s: a low level of productivity in agriculture, the existence of large-scale underemployment and the fear of rising unemployment, the dependence on external sources for heavy equipment and even simple consumer goods, with the consequent loss of wealth to the country, lack of technical know-how within the country, and a shortage of capital for development purposes.[20]

In addition, new problems appeared. The population increased at an annual rate of not less than 1.5 percent,[21] the rate of urbanization was high, the literacy rate was too low in spite of previous advances in the 1950s, the standard of living was low (per capita income was £21), and the GDP was only £680 million in 1952. From businessmen and manufacturers, there were increasing complaints that the economic environment (including, for example, problems of obtaining equipment within a reasonable time, adequate markets for products, acquiring trained staff, and good working conditions) was hostile, in addition to the long-standing difficulty of access to capital.

Dependence was recognized as problematic, but the ties with Britain and some other parts of the developed world only strengthened in the fifties and early sixties. The colonial government entered into bilateral economic agreements and enacted trade laws to benefit foreign firms and governments. The Nigerian elite, who inherited power, was very friendly to Britain, in spite of a so-called policy of nonalignment. External domination persisted in all key sectors: foreign trade, commercial banking, insurance companies and allied institutions, mining and petroleum investigation, and building and construction.

Table 7.8. Gross domestic product, 1950–1960 (1957 prices, £ million)

Activities	*1950*	*1951*	*1952*	*1953*	*1954*	*1955*	*1956*	*1957*	*1958*	*1959*	*1960*
Agriculture	385.8	423.2	438.7	454.2	479.5	492.1	468.0	479.6	542.2	526.2	549.4
Livestock	60.1	57.7	52.5	53.5	55.7	56.5	57.6	57.7	52.3	58.7	61.0
Fishing	9.7	9.8	9.9	10.0	10.3	10.3	12.6	13.3	15.0	15.0	15.0
Forest products	9.4	12.0	10.1	11.9	12.3	13.4	13.6	14.6	10.4	13.1	14.6
Mining	7.6	7.6	7.9	7.9	8.1	9.0	9.6	9.4	7.0	6.6	8.4
Manufacturing and public utilities	3.9	4.0	5.8	6.3	7.9	8.7	12.0	13.1	25.4	30.6	36.1
Communications	2.7	2.7	3.0	2.9	2.6	2.4	2.6	3.1	2.9	3.1	3.2
Building and civil engineering	20.3	25.4	19.4	25.9	37.8	38.3	36.5	43.0	22.9	32.1	33.3
Ownership of buildings	8.9	9.1	9.2	9.4	9.4	9.7	9.8	10.3	7.9	8.6	9.3
Transport	28.6	34.0	35.3	45.4	50.9	60.2	65.1	74.6	29.1	32.2	37.3
Craft	15.8	15.9	16.0	16.1	16.2	16.4	16.5	16.7	20.4	20.4	20.4
Missions	6.9	7.0	7.6	7.8	8.7	11.4	12.7	15.9	18.1	21.6	23.3
Government	15.0	16.4	19.9	16.5	17.6	23.4	28.7	30.5	29.1	36.3	35.0
Marketing boards	41.0	10.5	28.0	28.8	42.7	25.0	44.9	11.7	0.7	11.6	5.8
Banking, insurance and professionals	1.5	1.2	1.3	1.7	1.7	2.1	2.5	3.1	3.7	3.7	3.7
Domestic services	4.4	4.4	4.4	4.7	4.8	5.0	5.7	5.5	3.7	3.9	4.0
Miscellaneous services	0.9	1.0	1.1	1.1	1.2	1.5	1.9	2.0	1.8	2.1	3.7
Distribution, residual error	66.2	99.5	123.4	107.5	104.7	109.8	73.7	106.5	108.0	112.6	117.8
GDP at factor cost	688.7	741.4	793.5	811.6	872.1	895.2	873.7	910.0	900.0	938.5	981.3

Source: Federal Office of Statistics, *Annual Abstract of Statistics,* 1966.

The Legacy of Planning

By the 1950s development planning had become a key function of the state. The Nigerian elite accepted planning as a strategy of transforming the economy and society. The framework and ideology of development for the postindependence era were defined by the colonial plans of the 1940s and 1950s. In this closing section, I shall examine the key elements of this framework and ideology, which have shaped modern Nigeria for almost fifty years.

First, the primary objective of development was to improve the standard of living. Paradoxically, every individual was to have a minimum standard, although what constituted this minimum was never defined. Planning would involve the exploitation of the country's resources, natural and human, in order to increase wealth. The wealth generated would be used to improve the people's situation. It was easy for individuals to assess the extent to which they thought their lives had been improved. Increasingly, popular assessment focused on the availability of cheap food, employment, schools, medical facilities, housing, and transportation.

Second, the generation of capital was a development goal, especially in the 1950s and in particular for the regional governments, but the plans only glibly touched upon it. Planners generally assumed that rapid changes in other sectors would bring about the necessary capital and that, in the interim, more and more funds should be devoted to projects, even if they were unrelated to one another. Until this occurred, there were two sources of money: internal and external. The use of external funding was regarded as inevitable since internal resources were inadequate and taxation was not yet a useful tool. It was not until the late 1950s that prominent Nigerians began to question the wisdom of reliance on external financial sources, complaining that such funding was difficult to obtain and carried too many unacceptable requirements. They proposed to pay greater attention to local capital formation by raising the level of local investments. The radical option was to seek a rapid transfer of economic power to Nigerians: "Unlike the position in developed and developing countries, only a negligible percentage of the wealth of the country is in the hands of or is controlled by the nationals of the country."[22]

Third, while the problems of development were recognized, there were ideological debates about which issues were most important. The radical/socialist school did not agree with any of the colonial plans (or with the postindependence plans). They regarded the colonial, imperialist domination of the economy, reckless waste of natural and human resources, corruption in public and private life, and inequality in wealth distribution as the key problems.

There was consensus between the government officers and orthodox economists on many points. In agriculture, dependence on traditional farming methods was seen as the main barrier to progress (for example, poor implements, lack of irrigation, and inadequate marketing), in addition to reliance on only a few export crops and limited research. Industrialization was in its infancy, thus limiting capital formation and the development of the other sectors. Gross investment, savings, and aggregate consumption spending were low. Institutional requirements for education, banking, and health care were substantial.[23] These were the problems that the postindependence plans needed to address.

Fourth, real economic development could not proceed with a policy of laissez-faire (which theorizes that an economy left to the direction of individual entrepreneurs will obey laws of growth and development). Planning was variously portrayed as accelerating growth, organizing and reorganizing the economy, providing facilities for private sector functions, nationalization and indigenization of industry and manufacturing, increasing the standard of living, westernization and modernization, industrialization, and advancing technology. Most members of the post–1950 ruling elite were persuaded that development was a process of imitating the West by way of industrialization, urbanization, advanced technology, and the adoption of universalist values.

Regardless of its interpretation, planning involved state intervention in economic management. The state became less a spectator and more an initiator of change, although in subsequent years it also constituted an obstacle. The state, too, played the role of a manager and entrepreneur of business and welfare programs, although its incompetence would become increasingly apparent after 1960.

Discussions of the desirable degree of state intervention generated intense ideological debate. The socialists wanted a radical intervention that would turn the state into a central planning agency, terminate imperialist control, and stop wealth transfer. The capitalists wanted minimum interference and a limit to state control.[24] An efficient free market economy has not yet emerged, and the pattern of state intervention launched by the colonial state has been largely retained.

Free enterprise is allowed to function within an accepted policy whereby the state dictates policies and infrastructure, maintains law and order, funds education and industrial ventures, and conducts international diplomacy. In all these, the state has been very active by using public funds to initiate changes, promote the interests of the ruling class, and distribute scarce resources. Since 1940, the state, as an interventionist mechanism and as an engine of growth and instrument of modernization, has grown larger and stronger. The state became more centralized and the center dominated revenue collection after the mid-1960s. In the 1970s, the state's role was vigorously questioned, together with many of its assumptions on planning.[25] Since the 1980s, the interventionist state has been criticized for over-governance, stifling the free market, and preventing the emergence of a dynamic private sector. More recently, as the society moves in the direction of economic and political liberalism—a commitment to political pluralism and market forces—some of the characteristics of the interventionist colonial state are finally being shed.

A fifth legacy is the assumption that for development to occur, the key sectors that required attention were infrastructure, agriculture, industry, education, research and surveys, and the generation of capital. The colonial plans covered all sectors, but in determining their priority in the 1950s, they chose infrastructure, as this most directly affected export levels. However, there were debates in the regions and among other interested elite as to the correct priorities.

Most agreed that there was a need to increase production. How to do it, what to emphasize, and which social services to provide varied slightly from one person to the next and among the regions. The consensus was that the major sector requiring transformation was agriculture, but there was no agreement on how to bring this about. The best explanation was offered by the eastern region:

> It is the one sector which we can develop from our own resources without external assistance, capable of yielding immediate results and which involves activities in which the majority of the population can participate. Industrialisation takes a long time. Experts and technicians have to be trained and money has to be found from somewhere. Furthermore, little will be achieved in any other field if we do not produce sufficient food for the population, if the diet is unbalanced or if we have to spend money in importing such food items as meat, fish, etc. A well-fed man will be able to indulge in other activities. How can we industrialise without the development of commercial crops to meet the requirements of both the proposed industries and of exports?[26]

All the regions were enthusiastic about industrialization. While the governing elite thought that agriculture would bring rapid improvements in the economy, the farmers believed in the power of education. Moreover, most people tended to associate development with industrialization. They wanted to see factory smoke and vehicles, in addition to more yams and cutlasses: "We have to become like Liverpool and Birmingham" is a famous line from the testimony of a keen observer.[27]

Just as with improved agriculture, there was a consensus on the need for industrialization. Debates centered on whether to emphasize it above agriculture or vice versa. Whereas the colonial regime was interested in small crafts and local agro-allied industries in the 1940s, the Nigerian elite of the 1950s believed that the starting point should be establishing the basic heavy industries, such as steel, fuel, power, and machine tools, on a large scale to ensure further industrialization. They felt Nigeria had rich resources and a large population with which to sustain heavy industries and that industries should be subsidized at the expense of agriculture. For long-term solutions to famine, dependence on the West, and technological backwardness, rapid industrialization was the only solution. Nigeria—and indeed most African countries—put their faith in industrialization, though this turned out to be an unsuccessful policy.

Another priority of the people was education. While the north and east placed this third on their priority list, the west believed it should rank first. To the colonial regime, education was a "social sector" that consumed too much money. Moreover, there was no agreement on the type of education to provide. In the eastern region, the priority was technical training for workers for industries, rather than the general education desired by the western and northern regions.

Many other planning issues were secondary to agriculture, infrastructure, industrialization, and education, although funds were committed to them, and some projects addressed them. One exception was research, consistently funded since 1940. There was a desire to know more about agriculture and local industries, although the money devoted to research was limited. The regions did not support research at the same level as the federal government. In the east, the belief was that agricultural research must be the last priority because "the industries must be established and the men trained, if the results of research are to be profitably applied."[28]

Finally, people increasingly accepted that economic problems must be tackled and solved within a democratic framework, defined in both practical and constitutional terms. As the eastern regional government put it in 1961, all economic programs must receive the sanction of the people's representatives and all citizens must be active "if not in the formulation at least in the implementation of those development projects." However, democracy has not been equated with egalitarianism. The cornerstone of the democratic framework was "a sense of participation" whereby the rich would invest, the poor would work harder, and "everyone [would be] willing, where required, to make sacrifices, suffer financial privations, for the common objectives."[29]

The connection between mass participation, democratic institutions, and planning was recognized in the 1950s, even by the colonial state. The government began to admit the need to explain its programs to the public, to involve Nigerians in actual policy formation, to remove the feeling that the central government was remote and unapproachable, and to cooperate with the people through voluntary work.[30]

In reality, for the colonial government the involvement of the people was more or less a rhetorical issue, and democratization was limited to the transfer of power to a few elite. In formulating its last economic program the government involved only highly educated people, senior administrators, and politicians. The traffic of ideas that was established in the 1940s, from the district to provincial to the central levels, was gradually abandoned, in spite of its potential for improvement. What emerged was a cult of experts and technocrats, as a few Nigerians replaced the few colonial officers to lay claim to a monopoly of knowledge and power to control the future of the general populace.

Alternative suggestions on planning models have always emphasized the virtues of democracy as an influence on economic development. The nationalist attacks on the colonial state and its plans touted empowerment over and over again. Since independence, the point has been repeated, justified by the fact that the military had dominated the country's politics and that external influences (lately the World Bank and International Monetary Fund [IMF]) exert a noticeable impact on policies.

This study raises several pertinent issues on democracy and planning. The colonial state was authoritarian, but it set up central, provincial, and district committees to discuss proposals. Through these committees, discussions on planning activities reached the indigenous authorities and local elite. The development committees offered an enormous potential of creating a viable democratic network that was never fully explored. After 1955, the federal government opted for a central secretariat, dominated by civil servants. In the regions, several bodies emerged, creating confusion and overlap that foiled efficiency and public trust. The civil service was gradually consumed by issues unrelated to development, was unable to determine the final contents of plans, and was a victim of constant tailoring to shifting agendas and purposes by the government in power.

The colonial government was supervised by the Colonial Office in London. One advantage of this was that Lagos had to report the progress of planning projects and its other activities to London. For this, it established some procedures to monitor performance and public finance. This monitoring function was inherited in 1960 but, again, its potential for the creation of enduring democratic structures was unexplored. With independence, the mechanisms of accountability were weakened. Military rule, less tolerant of critical public opinion and the media, further eroded the mechanisms of accountability and evaluation that are important to all development planning.

The Nigerian state itself is a victim of external control. This study demonstrates the role of the Colonial Office in the planning process. In the 1950s, the International Bank for Reconstruction and Development became London's partner. The trend of involving powerful external agencies has continued, with implications for the democratization of planning. In some instances, the colonial state was in fact more responsive than the postcolonial state. Both the colonial and postcolonial states recognized the conflict between what people want and what experts think is good for the economy. Whereas the British tried somewhat to straddle the two forces, the external agencies that currently control the postcolonial state, notably the World Bank and the IMF, do not always care. In the colonial state, Nigerians were quick to realize that they could influence policy, a major stimulant to nationalism. In the postcolonial state, the opportunity to influence the World Bank, IMF, and military regimes has been more constrained.

When the colonial state was terminated in October 1960, most Nigerians associated the transition with progress and thought that the end of underdevelopment was in sight. While no one denied the enormity of the problem, most people, including the departing British officers, were optimistic about the potential for rapid development. Most of the economic and social indicators were interpreted as positive: Nigeria was Africa's largest country, with a population of 55.6 million; it was Africa's largest single market, with a strategic location and an endowment of rich mineral and agricultural resources on which many industries could be built; it had a rapidly expanding population with an increasing standard of living and a definite demand for "sophisticated products of science and industrialization"; the people were innovative, enterprising, and ready for change; the marketing boards had been established to build reserves for the government; the currency was stable; and all sectors of the economy were capable of expansion.[31]

The last decade of colonial rule was not a period for most Nigerians to lament the problems of colonial subordination or the inadequacies of planning since 1940. Many Nigerians were expecting rapid change through planning. The new government was more optimistic even than its citizens; it saw Nigeria as a potentially rich country, soon to attain the "takeoff" stage through stupendous planning and the dedication of the populace.[32] Independence foreshadowed a bright dawn, with the opportunity to use political sovereignty for economic transformation. Few could see far enough ahead to foretell that the journey would be rough and that their dreams might not come true for a very long time. Perhaps "the limitlessness of time"—to repeat the positive remark that opens this chapter—will complete the long process of Nigeria's development, "whatever may be the vagaries in the short span of human memory."

Notes

Abbreviations

ACEDSW	Advisory Committee on Economic Development and Social Welfare
CDA	*Colonial Development Act, 1929*
CDAC	Colonial Development Advisory Committee
CDB	Central Development Board
CDC	Colonial Development Corporation
CDF	Colonial Development Fund
CDWA	*Colonial Development and Welfare Act, 1940*
CEAC	Colonial Economic Advisory Committee
CSE	Chief Secretary, Enugu
CSO	Chief or Central Secretary's Office, Lagos
EP	*Economic Programme of the Government of the Federation of Nigeria, 1950–60*
IBRD	International Bank for Reconstruction and Development
NAE	National Archives, Enugu
NAI	National Archives, Ibadan
NAK	National Archives, Kaduna
NLCD	Nigeria Legislative Council Debates
NLDB	Nigerian Local Development Board
NYM	Nigerian Youth Movement
PDC	Provincial Development Committee
PW	Public Works Department
RP	*Revised Plan of Development and Welfare for Nigeria, 1951–56*
SNP	Secretary or Secretariat, Northern Provinces
TYP	*A Ten-Year Plan of Development and Welfare for Nigeria, 1946*
UN	United Nations
WIRC	West Indian Royal Commission

Introduction

1. For a wide-ranging criticism of development economics, see Hill, *Development Economics.* See also, Toye, *Dilemmas of Development;* Adelman, "On the State," 3–5.

2. Books on the contemporary economy depicting these and other features are many. See for instance, World Bank, *Sub-Saharan Africa;* Bates, *Beyond the Miracle;* Onimode, *Political Economy.*

3. See for instance, Rostow, *Theorists of Economic Growth,* 426.

4. The idea of planning as an exercise in progression from one stage to another received validity in the theoretical literature of the post–World War II years. See for instance, Rostow, *Stages of Growth; Lewis, Development Planning;* Meir and Seers, *Pioneers in Development.*

5. Adedeji, "Economic Planning," 8.

6. This is not the place for an elaborate discussion of the early theories on development and development planning. For fuller details, see among others, Rostow, *Stages of Growth;* Lewis, *Theory of Economic Growth.*

7. Lewis, "Economic Development," 139.

8. UN, *Measures for the Economic Development.*

9. See for instance, Scitovsky, "Two Concepts."

10. Rostow, *Stages of Growth.*

11. The comprehensive model, used after 1962, included the entire national goals, an assessment of available resources for planning, the required investment, public sector projects, and a package of incentives to stimulate the private sector. See for instance, Seidman, *Planning in Subsaharan Africa,* chap. 4.

12. Lewis, "On Assessing a Development Plan," 21.

13. See for instance, Coleman, *Nigeria;* Sklar, *Nigerian Political Parties;* Awa, *Federal Government in Nigeria.*

14. These, too, tend to be sketchy on the historical background to the Ten-Year Plan. See for instance, Wicker, "Colonial Development."

15. See for instance, Hopkins, *Economic History;* Akinjogbin and Osoba, *Topics on Nigerian Economic and Social History.*

16. Among others, see Aboyade, *Issues in the Development;* Ake, *Political Economy;* Stolper, *Planning without Facts.*

17. See for instance, Ayo, *Development Planning in Nigeria;* Mehta, *Development Planning,* 48–52.

18. See for instance, Nnoli, *Path to Nigerian Development;* Oni and Onimode, *Economic Development;* Osoba, "Colonial Antecedents," chap. 1.

19. Osoba, "Colonial Antecedents," 117–18.

20. Hopkins, "Clio-Antics."

21. Among others see, Frank, *Capitalism and Underdevelopment;* Holland, *Beyond Capitalist Planning;* Jalee, *Pillage of the Third World;* Rodney, *How Europe Underdeveloped Africa.*

22. Ekundare, *Economic History,* 400.

23. Nigeria, *National Development Plan.*

24. Schatz, "Nigeria's First" and "Two Years of Progress"; Stolper, "How Bad"; Dean, "Planning Nigeria's Development."

Chapter One: Investment in Colonial Nigeria before World War II

1. On the conquest and evolution of territory, see for example, Flint, *Sir John Goldie;* Ikime, *Fall of Nigeria;* Okafor, *Indirect Rule;* Okonjo, *British Administration.*

2. Smith, *Wealth of Nations,* 69.

3. *Parl. Deb.*, Commons, ser. 5, vol. 200 (1926), cols. 1317–18.

4. Helleiner, *Peasant Agriculture,* 5.

5. See, Freund, *Capital and Labour;* Perham, *Mining, Commerce and Finance;* Godfrey, "Mining Industry"; Grace, "Tin Mining"; Bello, "Some Remarks."

6. Ekundare, *Economic History,* 103.

7. Nicolson, *Administration of Nigeria,* 216.

8. White, *Central Administration,* chap. 10.

9. Frankel, *Capital Investment in Africa,* 182, table 37.

10. Nigeria, *Annual Report, 1938,* 38.

11. Bourdillon, *Economic Development,* 12.

12. NLCD, 17th sess., Dec. 4–7, 1939.

13. See for instance, Osuntokun, "Post–First World War."

14. On the depression, see for instance, Helleiner, *Peasant Agriculture,* 18; Oyemakinde, "Impact of the Great Depression."

15. Hopkins, *Economic History,* 238, 254–67.

16. Pim, "Public Finance," 252.

17. NLCD, 17th sess., Dec. 4–7, 1939.

18. Watts, *Silent Violence,* chap. 6.

19. Agricultural workers were trained "scientists," knowledgeable in different aspects of production and farm work. Cooperative societies, usually sponsored or encouraged by the government, comprised many people who united and contributed money and time to achieve specific economic objectives to benefit their members. The Forestry Department was in charge of the creation and conservation of forest reserves located in different parts of the country. The Veterinary Department was responsible for developing the livestock industry in the country.

20. Macmillan, *Road to Self-Rule,* 258.

21. *Parl. Deb.,* Commons, ser. 4, vol. 36 (August 22, 1895), cols. 641–42.

22. MacPhee, *Economic Revolution,* 229.

23. See for instance, Wicker, "Colonial Development and Welfare," 173.

24. *Parl. Deb.,* Commons, ser. 4, vol. 36 (August 22, 1895), col. 642.

25. *Parl. Deb.,* Commons, ser. 5, vol. 200 (1926), cols. 1317–18.

26. Morgan, *British Aid-5.*

27. Pim, *Financial And Economic History,* 226.

28. Ibid., 193; Lawal, "Sharing Profits."

29. Bourdillon, *Economic Development,* 1.

30. UK, CDA, chap. 5.

31. UK, CDA, chap. 5.

32. *Parl. Deb.,* Commons, vol. 229, col. 45 (May 21, 1940); Bourdillon, *Economic Development,* 2.

33. See for instance, Niculescu, *Colonial Planning,* 61.

34. NAI, CDF, General Papers, Estimates, vol. 1; CDAC, *Fifth Annual Report,* 7.

35. Ibid., vol. 1.

36. Ibid., vol. 2.

37. Ibid., vol. 3.

38. Ibid., vol. 4; NAI, CDF, Sanitary Development.

39. NAI, CDF, General Papers, Estimates, vol. 3.
40. Ibid., vol. 4.
41. NAE, CDF, EP 6269, vol. 2.
42. CDAC, *Fifth Annual Report; Seventh Annual Report; Ninth Annual Report.*
43. NAE, CDF, EP 6269, vol. 2.
44. CDAC, *Eleventh and Final Report,* table 1.2, p. 8.
45. NAI, Oyo Prof, 2/1/OY26663, vol. 1.
46. NAI, CDF, General Papers, Estimates, vol. 2.
47. NLCD, Jan. 30, 1930.
48. Bourdillon, *Economic Development,* 3–4.
49. Ibid., 4.
50. CDAC, *Statement of Policy,* 3.
51. CDAC, *Eleventh and Final Report,* 8–10.
52. NLCD, 17th sess., Dec. 13, 1939.
53. Bourdillon, *Economic Development,* 4.
54. Ibid., 9.
55. Zachernurk, "Lagos Intelligentsia."
56. See for instance, Campbell, *Observations;* Martins, "New Spirit"; "Wake Up Nigeria," *African Messenger,* Jan. 30, 1927; NAI, Relations between Government and European Firms.
57. Coleman, *Nigeria;* Sklar, *Nigerian Political Parties;* Hopkins, "Some Economic Aspects"; Hodgkin, *Nationalism.*
58. *Colonial Empire,* 98.
59. Nigeria, *Digest of Statistics,* 2, 3.
60. WIRC, *Report.*
61. Hancock, *Wealth of Colonies,* 45.
62. Perham, "Restatement of Indirect Rule"; Coupland, *Empire in These Days;* Macmillan, *Warning from the West Indies;* Hailey, *African Survey;* McLean, "Economic and Social Development."
63. Hargreaves, *Decolonization in Africa,* 40.
64. Ibid., 42.
65. Bourdillon, *Economic Development,* 9–10.
66. Ibid., 15.
67. See for instance, Olusanya, *Second World War,* chap. 3; Njoku, "Contributions."
68. Hancock, *Survey of British Commonwealth,* 292.

Chapter Two: Colonial Development and Welfare, 1940–1945

1. CDAC, *Statement of Policy.*
2. Ibid., 2.
3. Ibid.
4. Not all government functionaries were originally committed to it. The 1940 Act was a compromise between the "welfarist" ideas of those in the Colonial Office and the "productionist" ideas in the Treasury. For details, see Lee and Petter, *Colonial Office,* 208–14.

5. WIRC, *Recommendations*, 30.

6. NAI, CDF, General Papers, Estimates, vol. 3.

7. For the technical details of the application procedure, see NAI, CDF, Oyo Prof, 2/1/OY26663, vol. 1.

8. Ibid.

9. Ibid., Colonial Development Scheme (minutes of Ibadan Native Administration Inner Council Meeting, May 27, 1940).

10. Ibid., Colonial Office to the government of Nigeria, April 30, 1940.

11. NAE, Central Development Committee, Og Prof 2/1/2783.

12. NAI, CEAC.

13. NAI, Economic and Social Development Committee proposals.

14. NAI, CDF, Economic Development and Social Welfare, vol. 1.

15. NAI, CEAC.

16. NAI, ACEDSW, Kuku div., Advisory Committee.

17. NAI, CDF, Economic Development and Social Welfare, vol. 1.

18. See for instance, NAE, PDC (Minutes); NAI, Extension of Medical Facilities; NAE, Calabar PDC.

19. See for instance, NAE, Owerri PDC (1944); NAE, Onitsha PDC; NAE, Ondo PDC.

20. NAI, CDB.

21. NAE, Inspection Notes; NAE, Onitsha PDC, Water Supply (1944); NAE, Colonial Development Committee, Public Works (1940); NAE, Calabar PDC, minutes (1944); NAE, Provincial Development and Welfare Board.

22. Trunk B roads connected provincial capitals and large towns with the skeleton Trunk road system, with one another, or with a convenient station on the railway. Trunk A roads formed a skeleton system consisting of two main north-south roads from Lagos and Port Harcourt and four east-west roads.

23. NAE, Public Works (1940).

24. Ibid.

25. Oral interviews with A. Dantata, J. Olokun, M. Labinjo, O. Ajimoke, and B. Olawale.

26. See for instance, NAK, Plateau PDC, Major Development Schemes.

27. NAE, Owerri PDC, CSO.

28. NAI, Ilorin PDC.

29. NAI, CDB.

30. See for instance, NAI, ACEDSW, Ondo Prof; NAI, ACEDSW, Ondo div.

31. See for instance, NAK, Plateau PDC, Major Development Schemes, where this was clearly stated and put before the development boards.

32. NAE, Onitsha PDC, EP, (1943–45).

33. NAI, ACEDSW, CSO.

34. See for instance, NAI, ACEDSW, Ondo div.; NAE, Central Development Committee, Og Prof 2/1/2789.

35. NAI, Local Industries.

36. Falola, "Cassava Starch."

37. NAI, CDB.

38. NAI, ACEDSW, Kuku div.

39. NAI, ACEDSW, Ondo Prof.

40. NAI, Local Industries.

41. The estimates for 1940 were 5 million cattle, 10 million goats, and 4 million sheep. See NAI, Economic Development of the Livestock Industry.

42. Ibid, Lagos Area.

43. Ibid.; see also, vol. 1, Livestock Development.

44. Ibid., Zaria province.

45. Ibid., see also vols. 1 and 2.

46. Ibid., Zaria province.

47. Ibid.

48. NAI, Economic Mission to the Belgian Congo.

49. NAI, Oyo Prof 2/1/OY2663, vol. 1.

50. Hancock, *Survey of British Commonwealth,* 324.

51. CDAC, *Statement of Policy.*

52. NAI, Oyo Prof 2/1/OY2663, vol. 1.

53. NAI, Economy in the Use of Stationery.

54. Colonial Office, "Effects of War-Time Changes."

55. NLCD, March 1940.

56. Niculescu, *Colonial Planning,* 62.

57. CDWA (Cmd. 6457); CDWA (Cmd. 6532).

58. See for instance, NAE, Inspection Notes.

59. See Njoku, "Contributions"; NAI, Nigerian War Relief Fund; Olusanya, *Second World War,* chap. 3.

60. See for instance, NAK, NA's Contributions.

61. Coleman, *Nigeria,* 255.

62. See for instance, NAI, Economy in the Use of Stationery; NAI, CSO 26/36027, Economy Measures; NAE, War Measures: Production, vol. 3.

63. Bauer, *West African Trade,* 315–16.

64. See for instance, NAI, Economic Mission to the Belgian Congo; NAI, Economic Relations with Ivory Coast; NAI, British Economic Mission; NAI, Economic Co-operation with French Territories.

65. NAI, Development of Local Industries, vol. 2.

66. PW, *Report on the Highways,* 40.

67. NAK, Mining Activities.

68. NAI, Sugar Production; NAK, Zaria province, Annual Report (1945).

69. See for instance, NAK, Report on Nigeria by Lord Hailey.

70. Coleman, *Nigeria,* 252. For a neglected but useful examination of the war's impact on nationalism, see Mbadiwe, *British and Axis Aims.*

71. See for instance, *West African Pilot,* Jan. 15, 1941; *Nigerian Eastern Mail,* Mar. 6, 1943; NLCD, 1945, 179–87.

72. NAI, ACEDSW, CSO.

73. NAI, ACEDSW, Kuku div.

74. See for instance, NAK, Bornu province, Annual Report (1945).

75. NAK, Plateau province, Annual Report (1945).

76. The Sokoto and Adamawa provinces are good examples where there was a lot of resentment. See NAK, Sokoto province, Annual Report (1945); NAK, Adamawa province, Annual Report (1945).

77. See for instance, *Nigerian Eastern Mail,* Sept. 20, 1941; *Daily Times* (Lagos), May 20, 1943; *West African Pilot,* Sept. 15, 1941.

78. For a study of this, see Watts, *Silent Violence.*

79. NAK, Ilorin province, Annual Report (1945).

80. NAK, Benue province, Annual Report (1945).

81. Ibid.; NAK, Zaria province, Annual Report (1945); NAK, Sokoto province, Annual Report (1945).

82. NAK, Kabba province, Annual Report (1945).

83. NAK, Zaria province, Annual Report (1945).

84. Ibid.

85. The official report admitted that the dangers brought about by the strike were substantial. See NAK, Niger province, Annual Report (1945).

86. NAK, Plateau province, Annual Report (1945).

87. Coleman, *Nigeria,* 238.

Chapter Three: The Ten-Year Plan: Contents, Philosophy, and Development Institutions

1. TYP.

2. An important document on this is Colonial Office, "Effects of War-Time Changes."

3. NLCD, Aug. 1948.

4. See Lee and Petter, *Colonial Office;* Meyer, *Britain's Colonies.*

5. "Planning of Social and Economic Development."

6. Ibid., 6.

7. Ibid., 2.

8. Ibid.

9. *Colonial Development and Welfare,* 1.

10. Ibid.

11. W. W. Rostow, *Stages of Growth,* 143.

12. CDAC, *Statement of Policy,* 3.

13. Ibid.

14. Ady, "Britain and Overseas Development," 563.

15. NAI, CDB.

16. *Colonial Territories,* 53.

17. *Colonial Development and Welfare,* Cmd. 6713.

18. Ibid., 11.

19. Mikesell and Allen, "Economic Policies," 142.

20. Lewis, "Policy for Colonial Agriculture," 72.

21. Collins, "Economic Problems," 128.

22. See Hancock and Gowing, *British War Economy.*

23. Jones, "Labour's Colonial Policy," 13.

24. Dosser, "Formulation of Development Plans."
25. *Colonial Development and Welfare,* Cmd. 6713, p. 7.
26. *Colonial Development and Welfare Acts: Report.*
27. NLCD, Mar. 1940.
28. NAI, Ten-Year Plan.
29. See for instance, NAK, Regional Estimates (1949–50).
30. *Colonial Development and Welfare* (m.d. 6713), 11–13.
31. *Preliminary Statement.*
32. TYP, 9, 33.
33. NAI, CDB, vol. 3 (Economic Development and Social Welfare).
34. Caine, "Colonial Development," 82.
35. TYP, 2.
36. Ibid., 37.
37. Ibid., 3.
38. Ibid., 114.
39. Galbraith, *Economic Development,* 37.
40. Higgins, *Economic Development,* 636.
41. NAI, ACEDSW, Ondo div. 1/3/D.24, Development General.
42. Ibid.
43. NAI, ACEDSW, Kuku div.
44. H. O. Davies, *Daily Service,* June 3, 1940.
45. NYM, *Nigerian Youth Charter,* 3–10.
46. For representative opinions, see issues of the *Nigerian Worker* from the 1940s.
47. Ojike, *My Africa,* 114–15.
48. Azikiwe, "Post War Nigerian Economics."
49. See Olusanya, "Zikist Movement."
50. See for instance, Okoye, *Letter to Dr. Nnamdi Azikiwe,* 6–7.
51. See for instance, Balogun, *Existence of Virtual Monopoly,* 7–8.
52. Awolowo, *Path to Nigerian Freedom,* 19–20.
53. *Preliminary Statement.*
54. Ibid.
55. NAK, Bornu PDC, Development Scheme (1943–49); NAI, CDB, vol. 3; NAI, Development Proposals.
56. See for instance, the minutes in NAK, Borno PDC, Development Scheme.
57. NAI, CDB, vol. 1.
58. NAK, Kano PDC, Rural Development Schemes.
59. *West African Pilot,* May 17, 1946.
60. NAI, ACEDSW, Ondo div. 1/3/D.24, Development General.
61. NAI, CDB, vol. 3.
62. *Nigeria Local Development Board Ordinance.*
63. NAI, ACEDSW, Ondo div. 1/3/D.24, Development General.
64. NAI, CDB, vol. 1.
65. NLDB, *Annual Report,* 1947.
66. NAI, PDC and Welfare Boards, General Instructions.
67. NLDB, *Annual Report,* 1948.

68. Ibid.

69. NAI, General Progress of Development and Welfare Schemes.

70. NLCD on budget, Mar. 1948.

71. Sessional paper no. 20, 1948. *Annual Report of the Nigeria Local Development Board, 1948.* For the activities of the regional boards, see Schatz, *Economics, Politics, and Administration.*

72. NAI, Application for Development Loan; NAI, Granting of Loans.

Chapter Four: The Ten-Year Plan: Implementation and Evaluation, 1946–1950

1. Among others see, UN, *Measures for the Economic Development; Review of Economic Conditions; Economic Survey.*

2. Nigeria, *Annual Report on the General Progress,* Lagos, 1949.

3. NAI, CDB, minutes of Nov. 13, 1947.

4. NAI, ACEDSW, CSO.

5. NAI, ACEDSW, Ondo Prof, vol. 2 (see District Officer to the Resident, Apr. 10, 1947).

6. Ibid.

7. Oral interviews with B. K. Macaulay, M. Ichaver, and C. Bulama.

8. Oral interviews with O. Ogbon, N. Jella, and A. Maina.

9. Oluwasanmi, *Agriculture and Nigerian Economic Development,* 225.

10. Nigeria, *Statement of Agricultural Policy.*

11. NAI, Possibilities of Livestock; NAI, Economic Development of the Livestock Industry, Lagos Area.

12. Nigeria, *Half-Yearly Report.*

13. NAI, Economic Survey of the Cocoa Producing Areas.

14. NAI, Annual Report on the General Progress.

15. NAI, General Progress of Development and Welfare Schemes.

16. Ibid.

17. NAI, Agricultural Development, vol. 2.

18. NAK, Quarterly Reports (1945–46 onwards).

19. NAK, Development Scheme: Agriculture.

20. NAI, CDB, Economic Development and Social Welfare PDC, Other Provinces.

21. NAK, Area Development Committees (1945–48).

22. NAI, Economic Development of the Livestock Industry.

23. NAI, General Progress of Development and Welfare Schemes.

24. Nigeria, *Annual Report on the General Progress, Lagos,* 1950.

25. Ibid.

26. NAI, General Progress of Development and Welfare Schemes.

27. NAI, Quarterly Report on General Progress.

28. Richards, *Indigenous Agricultural Revolution,* chap. 1.

29. Nigeria, *Half-Yearly Report.*

30. Nigeria, *Annual Report,* 1949.

31. Oral interviews with K. Morgan, S. Olomo, and P. Tango.

32. NAI, Colonial Economic Research, Ondo Prof; NAI, Colonial Economic Research, Com Col.

33. NAI, Economic Missions.

34. NAI, Colonial Economic Research, Oyo Prof.

35. NAI, Economic Survey of the Colonial Empire.

36. NAI, ACEDSW, Ondo div. 1/3/D.24, Development General.

37. NAI, ACEDSW, Kuku div.

38. NAK, Quarterly Reports on Development and Welfare Schemes (1945–46).

39. *Preliminary Statement.*

40. Ibid.

41. Oral interviews with O. Ajimoko, A. Okoye, and B. Olawale.

42. Nigeria, *Annual Reports,* 1948–1950.

43. NAI, ACEDSW, Ondo Prof 1/3/D. 2, vol. 2.

44. NAI, General Progress of Development and Welfare Schemes.

45. Nigeria, *Half-Yearly Report.*

46. NAI, Community Development; NAI, Development Returns, vol. 2.

47. NAI, CDB, vol. 3.

48. NAI, CDB, minutes, Mar. 21, 1947.

49. The objectives of the Centre, as outlined in the Ten-Year Plan, were (1) to provide a vocational education that would encourage and train youths of school-leaving age to return to their homes, become established on the land or in some other worthwhile rural occupation, and take a responsible part in the welfare and development of the community of their origin, (2) to train in sound rural practices selected families, who could then return to their communities to serve as basic family units for future improvement projects, (3) to demonstrate the practices advocated for community improvements, and (4) to provide a center for all rural development activities sponsored by the missions.

50. NAK, Quarterly Reports on Development and Welfare Schemes (1945–46).

51. See NAK, Rural Development (1945–48).

52. NAI, Ilorin PDC.

53. NAI, ACEDSW, Ondo Prof 1/3/D.2; NAI, ACEDSW, CSO.

54. NAI, CDB, vol 3.

55. Ibid.

56. Among others, see NAK, Bornu PDC, Development Schemes.

57. NAE, Colonial Annual Development and Welfare Schemes (1946–53).

58. NAE, Development Works; NAE, Owerri PDC, minutes; NAE, Development Committee.

59. Nigeria, *Annual Report,* 1949, 1950.

60. NAI, ACEDSW, Ondo Prof 1/3/D.2, vol. 2.

61. See for instance, NAI, CDB, vol. 3.

62. NAI, General Progress of Development and Welfare Schemes, vol. 1.

63. Oral interviews with S. Jacobs, M. Obi, J. Olokun, and C. Beatrice.

64. Ibid.

65. NAI, Quarterly Report on General Progress of Development and Welfare.

66. Nigeria, *Progress Report.*

67. NAK, Quarterly Reports on Development and Welfare Schemes (1945–46 onwards).

68. Nigeria, *Progress Report.*

69. NAI, Colonial Economic Research, Oyo Prof.

70. Ibid.

71. NAI, Palm Produce Marketing Board.

72. Nigeria, *Annual Report, 1949–50,* 1951.

73. NAI, CDB, vol. 3 (Economic Development and Social Welfare).

74. NAI, Economic Development and Social Welfare.

75. NAI, Colonial Development Corporation.

76. NAI, Development, Com Col 1/3238.

77. *Nigeria Review,* Feb. 4, 1950.

78. Nigeria, *Annual Report, 1949–50.*

79. Nigeria, *Annual Report, 1949–50.*

80. Oral interviews with O. Ajimoko, M. Labinjo, and T. Lafe; NAI, General Progress on Development and Welfare Schemes.

81. NAI, CDB.

82. Ibid.

83. Ibid.

84. Interesting cases of petitions can be found in NAI, ACEDSW, Ondo Prof 1/3/D.2, vol. 2.

85. NAK, Kano PDC, CSO.

86. NAI, ACEDSW, CSO.

87. Ibid.

88. NAI, CDB.

89. Nigeria, *Annual Report, 1948–50.*

90. Nigeria, *Report of the Accountant-General,* 119.

91. NAI, CDB, minutes, Nov. 13, 1947.

92. Nigeria, *Annual Report,* for 1946–50.

93. See for instance, RP, 7.

94. NAK, Kano PDC, CSO.

95. Ibid.; Nigeria, *Annual Report,* 1947 and 1948.

96. NAI, ACEDSW, Ondo div. 1/3/D.24, Development General; NAK, Kano PDC, CSO.

97. PW, *Annual Report, 1947–48,* 5.

98. PW, *Annual Report, 1945–46* and *1947–48.*

99. NAK, Major Development Schemes.

100. NAI, CDB, vol. 3 (Economic Development).

Chapter Five: Midterm Reflections and Revisions, 1950–1955

1. TYP, 2, 9.

2. NAI, CDWF, Annual Audited Report Returns.

3. RP.

4. Ibid.

5. Nigeria, *Annual Report, 1949–50.*

6. NAI, CDB.

7. NAI, Colonial Economic Research, Com Col.

8. See Phillipson, "Administrative and Financial Procedure."

9. See for instance, *Western House of Assembly Debates.*

10. NAI, ACEDSW, CSO.

11. NAI, ACEDSW, Ondo Prof 1/3/D.2.

12. NAI, ACEDSW, Kuku div.

13. Ibid.

14. NAI, Economic Development in West Africa.

15. Samuel, "Economic Potential," 18.

16. Ibid.

17. The most famous theoretical exposition on this is the so-called "need for achievement theory" (or the n Achievement) in McClelland, *Achieving Society.* See also, Higgins, *Economic Development.* For a critique of this orthodoxy, see Schatz, "n Achievement and Economic Growth."

18. NAI, Economic Development in West Africa.

19. Ibid.

20. Ibid.

21. NAI, ACEDSW, CSO.

22. Ibid.

23. Ibid.

24. RP, 5.

25. NAI, ACEDSW, Ondo Prof 1/3/D.2, vol. 2; NAI, Adamawa PDC.

26. *Memorandum on the Revision,* 1.

27. RP, 7.

28. Ibid., 7–8.

29. Ibid., 9.

30. Ibid.

31. Nigeria, *Annual Report, 1951–52,* 4.

32. NAI, General Progress of Development and Welfare Schemes.

33. NAK, Revision of Ten-Year Development Plan: Textile Industry (1950–51).

34. NAK, Revision of Ten-Year Development Plan.

35. Eastern Regional Production Development Board, *Third Annual Report, 1951–52,* 2.

36. Nigeria, *Annual Report, 1951,* 1.

37. A list of all research works can be found in Nigeria, *Annual Report, 1952–53,* 144.

38. Oral interviews with S. F. Adepoju, O. Chukwuemeka, A. Olabiyi, and S. Akinlalu.

39. Oral interviews with J. Olowu, L. Banwo, S. Akinola, and F. Adeola.

40. Nigeria, *Annual Report, 1953,* 6.

41. Oral interviews with S. Ojike, F. Mbonu, M. Lawal, and S. Abdulahi.

42. Nigeria, *Annual Report, 1953,* 7.

43. For details, see Baldwin, *Niger Agricultural Project.*

44. NAK, Food Production (1951–55).

45. Nigeria, *Annual Report, 1953,* 12.
46. Oral interviews.
47. Nigeria, *Half-Yearly Report.*
48. NAI, Development of Fishing Industry.
49. NAI, Livestock Industry; NAI, Development of Livestock.
50. Oral interviews with O. Ojiodon, A. T. Awe, O. Tukur, S. Takar, and F. Olu.
51. NAI, Community Development Grants, vol. 2.
52. Nigeria, *Annual Report, 1951–52,* 54.
53. NAI, Owo Div 1/787 A.
54. *Nigeria Trade Journal,* 1, 3, 1953.
55. Mellamby, *Birth of Nigeria's University.*
56. *Daily Service,* July 28, 1952; *West African Pilot,* Editorial, Oct. 26, 1953; Ikejiani, *Nigerian Education,* 147–48; Nigeria, House of Representatives Debates, Aug. 1954, 265.
57. Nigeria, *Annual Report, 1951–52,* 51–53.
58. Nigeria, *Annual Report, 1951–52,* 38.
59. Nigeria, *Half-Yearly Report, 1951.*
60. NAI, Agricultural Development; NAK, Colonial Annual Reports (1946–52).
61. Oral interviews with F. Ekpeyong, K. Johnson, B. Olurin, and Z. Akpamgbo.
62. *Commerce in Nigeria,* 1, 2, 1950.
63. Nigeria, *Annual Report, 1953–54.*
64. *Nigeria Trade Journal* 3, no. 1 (1955).
65. NAK, Textile Industry; Nigeria, *Half-Yearly Report, 1951–52.*
66. Nigeria, *Half-Yearly Report* [Oct. 1, 1951 to Feb. 15, 1952].
67. Nigeria, *Annual Report, 1953-54.*
68. Nigeria, *Western House of Assembly Debates,* Feb. 26, 1952.
69. NAI, Owo div. 1/787, vol. 2.

Chapter Six: "An Integrated Development Programme," 1955–1960

1. EP, 3.
2. IBRD, *Economic Development of Nigeria.*
3. NAI, Sessional paper no. 6, 1951.
4. NAK, Provincial Conference (1953).
5. EP, 4.
6. NAK, Colonial Economic Research (1953).
7. For brief notes on the members see, ibid.; NAK, Economic Survey by the International Bank.
8. IBRD, *Economic Development.* The reports were published in two forms: a comprehensive one of more than four hundred pages, and an abridged edition that omitted the third part with appendices.
9. IBRD, *Economic Development,* 10.
10. Oral interviews with T. Esan, K. Majekodunmi, M. Abayomi, and O. Anderson.
11. Oral interviews with Z. Adepegba, O. Douglas, S. Zaccheus, and K. F. Tarr.

12. Oral interviews with L. F. Ogedengbe, S. J. Dike, D. Uche, F. Enobong, T. Nwokorie, and S. O. Nyiam.

13. See for instance, Oyenuga, "Latest Development in Marxist Ideology"; Ikoku, *Nigeria for Nigerians.*

14. IBRD, *Economic Development,* 7.

15. Ibid., 8.

16. Ibid., 10.

17. See for instance, Onukaogu, "Conditions Affecting the Administration."

18. Oral interviews with J. Adebayo, T. Okolie, M. Adelegan, O. Adeyemi, O. Rasaki, and O. L. Agbakoba.

19. IBRD, *Economic Development,* 14.

20. Ibid., 14.

21. Ibid., 15.

22. EP, 6.

23. "Stormy Corner by 'Goddie.'" *Nigerian Statesman,* June 11, 1955.

24. Udegbunam, *West African Pilot,* Feb. 14, 1955); Awolowo, *Some Aspects of Our Economic Problems.*

25. See for instance, Njoku, *Commerce and Industry,* 9; Awolowo, "Speech to Foreign Industrialists."

26. Nigeria, House of Representatives Debates, Mar.–Apr. 1960.

27. NAI, ACEDSW, Ondo Prof 1/3/D.4, vol. 3.

28. NAI, Economic Programme (1955–60).

29. Final annual recurrent cost was defined as the recurrent cost that would arise in the first full year after the project had reached completion (e.g., in the case of a hospital, when all construction was completed, all staff positions were filled, and all beds were occupied).

30. NAI, Economic Programme (1955–60).

31. Capital requirements covered loans or grants from the resources of the federal government, exclusive of other funds that the bodies could utilize from their sources or reserves.

32. NAI, New Five-Year Development Plan (1955–60).

33. EP, 8.

34. Zaria was chosen because of its proximity to the Nigerian College of Arts, Science, and Technology. The institute was to study the problems of traditional building techniques, such as improving the durability and fire-resistance of thatched roofs and wall finishes, methods of constructing grain stores, and standards of village hygiene.

35. The building of a Command Headquarters became necessary with the dissolution of the West African Command Headquarters in July 1956 and given the need to have a separate one to serve Nigeria in preparation for the Nigerian government's assumption of responsibility for its army.

36. Expenditures increased to £157.7 million. See, Nigeria, *Second Progress Report.*

37. See for instance, "Action Group Paper on Higher Education."

38. Bailey, "Report on the Electricity Corporation."

39. Nigeria, *Progress Report on the Economic Programme.*

40. See for instance, Oyejide, *Tariff Policy.*

41. Nigeria, *Establishing a Business.*

42. Nigeria, *Policy for Industrial Development.*

43. See for instance, Nigeria, *Northern Progress.*

44. NAI, SAP DIST 1/171, vol. 2, CDF.

45. Federal Loans Board. *Annual Reports, 1956–60.*

46. CDC, *Annual Reports.*

Chapter Seven: Two Decades of Planning: An Overview

1. *Colonial Development and Welfare,* 1.

2. *Northern Regional Production Development Scheme, Annual Report, 1950–55.*

3. NAK, Plateau PDC, Major Development Schemes.

4. NAE, Ogoja PDC.

5. See for instance, NAK, *Community Development* (1947–56).

6. NLCD, 17th session, Dec. 1959.

7. Batten, *Problems of African Development,* 17.

8. NAE, Annual Report on the General Progress.

9. Oyo Prof 1/4670.

10. These were occupations that employed less than ten people per workshop, in which the entrepreneur had little or no education and relied on limited capital. Several studies conducted after 1960 confirm that this sector was large in many urban areas. See for instance, Fapohunda, *Informal Sector.*

11. NAI, Cocoa Marketing.

12. The real transformation of this sector did not come until the huge revenues from petroleum beginning in the late 1960s. See for instance, Schatzl, *Petroleum in Nigeria.*

13. The methods of data compilation in the 1950s were crude, and no rigorous means were established to test their accuracy. For these problems and for useful data on national accounts and other important statistics, see the pioneering work of Okigbo, *Nigerian National Accounts.* See also, Helleiner, *Peasant Agriculture,* Statistical Appendix, 384–591.

14. IBRD, *Economic Development,* 16.

15. National Economic Council, *Economic Survey.*

16. RP, 1.

17. Ibid.

18. Ibid.

19. NAI, Colonial Economic Research, Com Col 1/3487.

20. See for instance, Nigeria, *Report of the Economic Mission, 1961;* Nigerian Institute of Social and Economic Research, "Socio-Economic Factors."

21. IBRD, *Economic Development,* 4.

22. Ibid.

23. See for instance, *National Development Plan, 1962–68,* 14–18.

24. One point of agreement in this productive debate is that everyone believes that planning works—although the model can be faulty. The relevance of this consensus is to sustain the intellectual discussion on planning and the controversy on the models.

25. There is a rich literature on this. Among others, see Seidman, "Changing Theories"; Diaku, "Capital Surplus."

26. Nigeria, *Report of the Economic Mission,* 3.

27. Oral interview with A. Elere.

28. Nigeria, *Report of the Economic Mission,* 4.

29. Ibid.

30. NAK, Community Development.

31. IBRD, *Economic Development;* Nigeria, *National Development Plan, 1962–68,* 18–20.

32. Nigeria, *National Development Plan,* chap. 1; Stapleton, *Wealth of Nigeria.*

Bibliography

Oral Interviews

(all dates refer to the final interview session in a series)

Abayomi, M. (local historian). Ikorodu. July 11, 1993.
Abdulahi, S. (politician/trader). Minna. Jan. 12, 1993.
Adebayo, J. (clerk). Kaduna. July 19, 1991.
Adelegan, M. (journalist). Maiduguri. Sept. 18, 1992.
Adeola, F. (produce dealer). Jebba. Aug. 4, 1991.
Adepegba, Z. (civil servant). Aug. 17, 1992.
Adepoju, S. F. (bookshop manager). Ile-Ife. Aug. 1, 1992.
Adeyemi, O. (contractor). Zaria. July 15, 1992.
Agbakoba, O. L. (contractor). Epe. Aug. 3, 1991.
Ajimoke, O. (community leader). Kaduna. Aug. 14, 1992.
Akinlalu, S. (contractor). Aug. 8, 1993.
Akinola, S. (farmer/trader). Mokwa. Oct. 11, 1992.
Akpamgbo, Z. (federal clerk). Aba. May 6, 1991.
Anderson, O. (member of Development Community). Aba. Aug. 25, 1992.
Awe, A. T. (farmer). Owerri. July 24, 1991.
Banwo, L. (Native Administration clerk). Gbaja. Oct. 8, 1992.
Beatrice, C. (produce merchant). Enugu. July 18, 1992.
Bulama, C. (contractor). Aug. 11, 1991.
Chukwuemeka, O. (Development Officer). Aug. 13, 1991.
Dantata, A. (trader). Zaria. Aug. 23, 1992.
Dike, S. J. (community leader). Nsukka. Aug. 5, 1991.
Douglas, O. (trader). July 30, 1991.
Ekpeyong, F. (community leader). Uyo. July 12, 1992.
Elere, A. E. (Native Administration staff). Dec. 12, 1992.
Enobong, F. (trader/fisherman). Uyo. May 11, 1992.
Esan, T. (community leader). Osu. Aug. 11, 1992.
Ichaver, M. (ex-serviceman). July 8, 1992.
Jacobs, S. (local historian). Asaba. May 15, 1992.
Jella, N. (local leader). July 11, 1991.
Johnson, K. (civil servant). Uyo. Aug. 13, 1991.
Labinjo, M. (civil servant). Kaduna. Aug. 14, 1992.
Lafe, T. (ex-serviceman). Okitipupa. Aug. 17, 1992.
Lawal, M. (clerk). Iwo. July 4, 1991.

Macaulay, B. K. (federal officer). Dec. 5, 1991.
Maina, Alhaji. (local historian). July 11, 1991.
Majekodunmi, K. (federal officer). Ijebu-Ode. Aug. 19, 1992.
Mbonu, F. (dispenser). Enugu. Sept. 18, 1992.
Morgan, K. (local historian). Ibadan, July 16, 1991.
Nwokorie, T. (baker). Owerri. May 15, 1992.
Nyiam, S. O. (ex-serviceman). Uyo. July 10, 1991.
Obi, M. (Native Administration clerk). Onitsha. July 3, 1991.
Ogbon, O. (scholar/trader). June 10, 1991.
Ogedengbe, L. F. (project supervisor). Aug. 17, 1992.
Ojike, S. (schoolteacher). Nsukka. Mar. 2, 1993.
Ojiodon, O. (Native Administration police). Makurdi. Jan. 10, 1993.
Okolie, T. (planning officer). Onitsha. July 13, 1991.
Okoye, A. (civil servant). Enugu. Aug. 15, 1992.
Olabiyi, A. (local historian). Ikare. Jan. 12, 1993.
Olawale, B. (Native Administration police). Zaria, July 23, 1991.
Olokun, J. (Native Administration staff). Kaduna. July 19, 1991.
Olokun, M. (market woman). Kaduna. July 19, 1991.
Olomo, S. (farmer/trader). Kaduna. Feb. 1, 1993.
Olowu, J. (farmer/trader). July 17, 1993.
Olu, F. (Native Administration staff). Kaduna. Aug. 14, 1992.
Olurin, B. (Native Administration staff). Sokoto. July 29, 1991.
Rasaki, O. (entrepreneur). Zaria. Aug. 29, 1992.
Takar, S. (Native Administration staff). Makurdi. July 11, 1991.
Tango, P. (clerk/trader). Kaduna. Feb. 1, 1993.
Tarr, K. F. (contractor). Sept. 13, 1992.
Tukur, O. (teacher). Zaria. July 23, 1991.
Uche, D. (clerk/farmer). Nsukka. July 15, 1992.
Zaccheus, S. (community leader). Aug. 14, 1992.

Unpublished Sources

Dissertations and Theses

Edozien, G. C. "The Impact of Direct Foreign Investment on an Underdeveloped Economy: The Nigerian Case, 1924–64." Ph.D. diss., University of Michigan, 1966.

Odumosu, F. O. "Credit Facilities for Farmers and Traders in Nigeria." M. Litt. thesis, Trinity College, Dublin, 1962.

Onitiri, H. M. A. "Nigeria's Balance of Payments and Economic Policy, 1946–1960." Ph.D. diss., University of London, 1963.

Onukaogu, G. U. "Conditions Affecting the Administration of Technical Assistance Programs in Nigeria." Ph.D. diss., Indiana University, 1955.

Osoba, S. O. "The Colonial Antecedents and Contemporary Development of Nigeria's

Foreign Policy: A Study in the History of Social, Economic, and Political Conflict." Ph.D. diss., Moscow State University, 1967.

National Archives, Enugu

Annual Report on the General Progress of Development and Welfare Schemes, Og Prof 2/1/2917.
Calabar PDC. Minutes, Og Prof 2/1/2787.
Calabar PDC. Minutes, Og Prof 3279 (1944).
Central Development Committee. Og Prof 2/1/2783.
———. Og Prof 2/1/2789.
Colonial Annual Development and Welfare Schemes: Quarterly and Annual Reports, Cal. Prof 3804/4 (1946–53).
Colonial Development Committee. Public Works, EP 6219/5 (1940).
Colonial Development Fund. EP 6269, vol. 2, 1930–31.
———. Public Works, EP 6291/5 (1940).
Development Committee, CSE 1/85/9766.
Development Works, Og Prof 2/1/2785.
Inspection Notes, Onitsha Province, CSE 1/85/8620.
Ogoja PDC, CSE 1/85/9776.
Ondo PDC. Ondo Prof 1/3, D.1.
Onitsha PDC. EP/19655/4/C.6.
Onitsha PDC. Water supply, EP/19655/4/C.5 (1944).
Owerri PDC. CSO 26/35817/S.23.
Owerri PDC. EP/9655/5 (1944).
Owerri PDC. Minutes, Og Prof 3281.
PDC and Welfare Boards. General Instructions, Ben Prof 1/2188, vol. 3.
Progress Report on the Nigerian Plan of Development and Welfare: The First Five Years in Eastern Nigeria. CSE 1/75/1950.
Provincial Development Committee. Og Prof 2/1/3287.
War Measures: Production, Ogoja province, EP 18038/71, vol. 3 (1944–45).

National Archives, Ibadan

Adamawa PDC. CSO 26/35817/S.1.
Advisory Committee on Economic Development and Social Welfare. CSO 26/41955.
———. Kuku div., 2/K 771.
———. Ondo Prof 1/3/D.2.
———. Ondo div., 1/696/E.
Agricultural Development in the Badagry Division, Com Col 1/2862/S.2, vol. 2.
Annual Report on the General Progress of Development and Welfare Scheme, War Prof 146/G.
Application for Development Loan, Ben Prof 1/2464/59.
British Economic Mission, CSO 26/37875.
Colonial Economic Advisory Committee. CSO 26/41537.
Central Development Board. Oyo Prof 1/3980, vols. 1 and 3.

Cocoa Marketing, Oyo Prof 1/4363, vol. 1.

Colonial Development and Welfare Fund (CDWF). Annual Audited Report Returns and Excesses to Secretary of State, CSO 26/27372/S.4 and S.2.

———. Economic Development and Social Welfare, Western Provinces Area and Development Committee and Central Development Board, Oyo Prof 1/3980, vol. 1.

———. General Papers and Estimates, CSO 26/23668, vol. 2.

———. Sanitary Development, Kwale district 1/344.

———. SAP DIST 1/171, vol. 2.

Colonial Development Corporation. Ben Prof 1/2665.

Colonial Economic Research, Com Col 1/3487.

Colonial Economic Research, Ondo Prof 1/3/D.45.

Colonial Economic Research, Oyo Prof 1/4730.

Community Development, Kwale district, 1/344/4.

Community Development Grants, Ondo Prof 1/3/D.81, vol. 2.

Development, Com Col 1/3238.

Development of Fishing Industry, Ile div. 1/1/995A/5.

Development of Livestock: Ilesa Dairy Scheme, Ile div. 1/1/1565.

Development of Local Industries, Owo div. 1/597, vol. 2.

Development Proposals, War Prof 146/1.

Development Returns, War Prof 146/G, vol. 2.

Economic and Social Development Committee. Proposals, CSO 26/40805.

Economic Co-operation with French Territories, CSO 26/37300/S.29/T.

Economic Development and Social Welfare, Ondo div. 1/696 D.

Economic Development in West Africa, Oyo Prof 1/4427.

Economic Development of the Livestock Industry, CSO 26/37095.

Economic Missions, CSO 26/37819.

Economic Mission to the Belgian Congo, CSO 26/37499.

Economic Programme, Com Col 1/3926 (1955–60).

Economic Relations with Ivory Coast, CSO 26/38166.

Economic Survey of the Cocoa Producing Areas of Nigeria, Ekiti div. 1/959.

Economic Survey of the Colonial Empire, Com Col 1/3700.

Economy in the Use of Stationery and Information on Annual Requirements, Oyo Prof 2/1/2456.

Economy Measures, CSO 26/36027.

Extension of Medical Facilities, CSE 1/85/3332.

General Progress of Development and Welfare Schemes: Half Yearly Report for Publicity Purposes, Oyo Prof 1/4504/5.

Granting of Loans under Development Schemes, Ile div. 1/1/995/4.

Ilorin PDC. CSO 26/35817/S.5.

Livestock Industry, Com Col 1/1021.

Local Industries and Agriculture Research Development, Ben Prof 1/B.P.2058.

New Five-Year Development Plan, Abe Prof 2/2218/2 (1955–60).

Nigerian War Relief Fund, Summarized Accounts of Receipts and Payments. NAI, CSO 26/6/36026.

Owo Div 1/787 A. Colonial Development Plan—Quarterly Reports.

Oyo Prof 1/4670. Colonial Development Scheme—Livestock.
Oyo Prof 2/1/OY26663, vol. 1.
Palm Produce Marketing Board. Ben Prof 1/2635.
Possibilities of Livestock. Com Col 1/1021.
Provincial Development and Welfare Board. CSE 1/85/9780.
Quarterly Report on General Progress of Development and Welfare, Abe Prof 2/1613/24.
Relations between Government and European Firms, Oyo Prof 2/3/C.85.
Sugar Production, Oyo Prof 2/3/C.230.
Ten-Year Plan of Development and Welfare for Nigeria, Abe Prof 2/2218.

National Archives, Kaduna

Adamawa province. Annual Report, SNP 17/5/6531 (1945).
Area Development Committees, Zar Prof 1/4035 (1945–48).
Benue province. Annual Report, SNP 17/5/6525 (1945).
Bornu province. Annual Report, SNP 17/5/6520 (1945).
Bornu PDC. Development Schemes, SNP 17/4/5795 (1943–49).
Colonial Annual Reports, SNP 17/5/6735 (1946–52).
Colonial Economic Research, and International Bank Mission, Ilor Prof 2798/5098 (1953).
Community Development, Jos Prof 5121 AM 8033 (1947–56).
Development Scheme: Agriculture, Zar Prof 1/3937.
Economic Survey by the International Bank, Com Col 1/3794. Food Production, Zar Prof 3354/16 (1951–55).
Ilorin province. Annual Report, SNP 17/5/6515 (1945).
Kabba province. Annual Report, SNP 17/5/6504 (1945).
Kano PDC. CSO 26/35817/S.7.
Kano PDC. Rural Development Schemes, SNP 17/4/5797.
Major Development Schemes: Public Buildings, SNP 17/4/6165.
Mining Activities, Mineral Statistics' Report, SNP 32793.
NA's Contributions from Direct Taxation to Government Revenue, SNP 17/4/5589 (1942–46).
Niger province. Annual Report, SNP 17/5/6501 (1945).
Plateau province. Annual Report, SNP 17/5/6505 (1945).
Plateau PDC. Major Development Schemes, SNP 17/4/5787 (1945).
Provincial Conference, SNP 17/9 AM 53516/S.2 (1953).
Quarterly Reports on Development and Welfare Schemes, SNP 17/5/6740 (1945–46).
Quarterly Reports on Development and Welfare Schemes, SNP 17/5/6741 (1945–46 onwards).
Regional Estimates, SNP 17/5/6994 (1949–50).
Report on Nigeria by Lord Hailey, Zar prof 51/1943.
Revision of Ten-Year Development Plan, SNP 17/4/37711/S.21.
Revision of Ten-Year Development Plan: Textile Industry, SNP 17/4/AM 38422/S.1 (1950–51).

Rural Development: Model Settlements and Compounds, Zar Prof 3354/S.7B (1945–48).

Sokoto province. Annual Report, SNP 17/4/6502 (1945).

Textile Industry, Zar Prof 1/3892.

Zaria province. Annual Report, SNP 17/5/6511 (1945).

Other

Awolowo, O. "Speech to Foreign Industrialists." Unpublished MS, 1957.

Nigeria. House of Representatives Debates. Aug. 1954.

———. Legislative Council Debates (NLCD). Various dates, Jan. 30, 1930, through Aug. 1948.

Nigerian Institute of Social and Economic Research, "Socio-Economic Factors Affecting the Productivity of Agriculture." Unpublished MS, Ibadan, 1963.

Oyenuga, V. A. "Latest Development in Marxist Ideology." Unpublished MS. Ibadan: Summer School Lecture Action Group, 1956.

Published Sources

Abbot, G. C. "British Colonial Aid Policy during the 1930s." *Canadian Journal of History* (1970): 73–89.

———. "A Re-examination of the 1929 Colonial Development Act." *Economic History Review* 24 (1971): 68–81.

Aboyade, O. *Foundations of an African Economy: A Study of Investment and Growth in Nigeria.* New York: Praeger, 1972.

———. *Issues in the Development of Tropical Africa.* Ibadan: Ibadan University Press, 1976.

"Action Group Paper on Higher Education in Nigeria." *Daily Service,* Sept. 5 and 6, 1958.

Adedeji, A. "Economic Planning in Theory and Practice." *Nigerian Journal of Economic and Social Studies* 4, no. 1 (1962): 7–15.

Adelman, I. "On the State of Development Economics." *Journal of Development Economics* 1, no. 1 (1974): 3–5.

Ady, P. H. "Britain and Overseas Development." In *The British Economy, 1945–50,* edited by G. D. N. Worswick and P. H. Ady, 547–69. Oxford: Clarendon Press, 1952.

Ake, C. *A Political Economy of Africa.* London: Longman, 1981.

———. *Social Science as Imperialism.* Ibadan: Ibadan University Press, 1979.

Akinjogbin, I. A., and S. O. Osoba, eds. *Topics on Nigerian Economic and Social History.* Ife, Nigeria: University of Ife Press, 1980.

Alder, J. H. "The Economic Development of Nigeria: Comment." *Journal of Political Economy* 64, no. 5 (1956): 435–41.

Anababa, W. *The Trade Union Movement in Nigeria.* London: Hurst, 1969.

Anjorin, A. O. "The Background to the Amalgamation of Nigeria in 1914." *ODU: A Journal of African Studies* 3, no. 2 (1967): 72–86.

Awa, E. O. *Federal Government in Nigeria.* Berkeley and Los Angeles: University of California Press, 1964.

Awolowo, O. *Path to Nigerian Freedom.* London: Faber and Faber, 1947.

———. *Some Aspects of Our Economic Problems.* Address to Lagos Chamber of Commerce, Feb. 2, 1955. Lagos: Government Printer, 1955.

Ayo, E. J. *Development Planning in Nigeria.* Ibadan: Ibadan University Press, 1988.

Azikiwe, N. *The Economic Reconstruction of Nigeria.* Lagos: African Book Co., 1948.

———. "Post War Nigerian Economics." *West African Pilot,* June 11, 1942.

Bailey, A. E. "Development Plans in Nigeria: Rapid Advance with Government Aid." *Electrical Review* 8 (July 1960): 53–55.

———. "Report on the Electricity Corporation of Nigeria." *Electrical Review* 10 (July 1961): 12–19.

Baldwin, K. D. S. *The Niger Agricultural Project: An Experiment in African Development.* Oxford: Basil Blackwell, 1957.

Balogun, J. O. *The Existence of Virtual Monopoly in the British Colony of Nigeria.* Lagos: Published by the author, 1944.

Bates, R. H. *Beyond the Miracle of the Market: The Political Economy of Agrarian Development in Kenya.* Cambridge: Cambridge University Press, 1989.

Batten, T. R. *Problems of African Development, Part I: Land and Labour.* Oxford: Oxford University Press, 1954.

Bauer, P. T. *Dissent on Development.* London: Weidenfeld and Nicolson, 1971.

———. "The Economic Development of Nigeria." Journal of Political Economy 63, no. 5 (1955): 398–411.

———. *West African Trade.* London: Routledge and Kegan Paul, 1954.

Bello, A. *My Life.* Cambridge: Cambridge University Press, 1962.

Bello, Sule. "Some Remarks on the Development of Raw Material Production in the Colony of Kano, c. 1912–1919." In *Studies in the History of Kano,* edited by B. M. Bakindo, 173–85. Ibadan: Heinemann, 1983.

Biersteker, T. *Multinationals, the State, and Control of the Nigerian Economy.* Princeton, N.J.: Princeton University Press, 1987.

Bourdillon, B. H. *Economic Development of Nigeria.* Lagos: Government Printer, 1939.

Bower, P. A. *The Balance of Payments of Nigeria in 1936.* Oxford: Basil Blackwell, 1949.

Caine, Sidney. "Colonial Development: A British Contribution to World Progress." *Progress* 46, no. 256 (1957): 82.

Cairncross, A. "The Postwar Years, 1945–77." In *Africa Today,* edited by C. G. Haines, 420–30. Baltimore: Johns Hopkins University Press, 1955.

Campbell, J. G. *Observations on Some Topics in Nigeria during the Administration of His Excellency Sir Frederick Lugard G.C.M.G.* Lagos: Published by the author, 1918.

Carland, J. M. *The Colonial Office and Nigeria, 1898–1914.* Stanford, Calif.: Hoover Institute Press, 1985.

Carney, D. E. *Government and Economy in British West Africa.* New York: Bookman Associates, 1961.

Central Bank of Nigeria. *Twenty Years of Banking in Nigeria.* Lagos: Central Bank of Nigeria, 1979.

Charle, E. G. "An Appraisal of British Imperial Policy with Respect to the Extraction of

Mineral Resources in Nigeria." *Nigerian Journal of Economic and Social Studies* 6, no. 1 (1964): 13–24.

Chukwuemeka, N. *Industrialization of Nigeria.* New York: William Fredrick, 1952.

Coleman, J. S. *Nigeria: Background to Nationalism.* Berkeley and Los Angeles: University of California Press, 1965.

Collins, H. "Economic Problems in British West Africa." In *The New West Africa,* edited by B. Davidson and A. Ademola, 94–101. London: Allen and Unwin, 1963.

Colonial Development Advisory Committee (CDAC) (Cmd. 4634). *Fifth Annual Report.* London: H.M.S.O., 1934.

———. *Seventh Annual Report* (Cmd. 5202). London: H.M.S.O., 1936.

———. *Ninth Annual Report* (Cmd. 5789). London: H.M.S.O., 1938.

———. *Eleventh and Final Report* (Cmd. 6298). London: H.M.S.O., 1941.

———. *Statement of Policy on Colonial Development and Welfare* (Cmd. 6175). London: H.M.S.O., 1940.

Colonial Development Corporation (CDC). *Annual Reports.* London: H.M.S.O., various years.

The Colonial Empire, 1947–49 (Cmd. 7433). London: H.M.S.O., 1950.

Colonial Office. "Effects of War-Time Changes in Colonial Economic Structure and Organization." *Papers on Colonial Affairs,* no. 4. London: H.M.S.O., 1944.

Coupland, R. *The Empire in These Days.* London: Macmillan, 1935.

Dean, E. R. "Planning Nigeria's Development: A Study of Alternative Techniques." Ibadan: NISER Research Project no. 3, 1965, 18–28.

Diaku, I. "A Capital Surplus Illusion: The Nigerian Case Revisited." *Nigerian Journal of Economic and Social Studies* 14, no. 1 (1972): 47–62.

Diamond, L., J. L. Linz, and S. M. Lipset, eds. *Democracy in Developing Countries: Africa.* Boulder, Colo.: Lynne Rienner, 1988.

Dosser, D. "The Formation of Development Plans in British Colonies." *Economic Journal* 69, no. 274 (1959): 255–66.

Eastern Regional Production Development Board, *Third Annual Report, 1951–52.* Enugu: Government Printer, 1953.

Economic Commission for Africa. *Comprehensive Planning in Africa.* Addis Ababa, Ethiopia: Economic Commission for Africa, 1962.

Eicher, C. K., and C. Liedholm, eds. *Growth and Development of the Nigerian Economy.* Michigan, 1970.

Ekundare, R. O. *An Economic History of Nigeria.* London: George Allen, 1973.

Ergas, Z., ed. *The African State in Transition.* London: Macmillan, 1987.

Falola, Toyin. "Cassava Starch for Export in Nigeria during the Second World War." *African Economic History* no. 18 (1988): 73–98.

———. "The Lebanese in West Africa." In *People and Empire in Africa,* edited by Ade Ajayi and J. Peel, 121–41. London: Longman, 1992.

———. "The Lebanese Traders in Colonial Southwestern Nigeria." *African Affairs* 89 (October 1990): 523–53.

———. "'An Ounce Is Good Enough': The Gold Industry in Colonial Southwestern Nigeria." *African Economic History* no. 20 (1992): 27–50.

———, ed. *Britain and Nigeria: Exploitation or Development?* London: Zed, 1987.

Fapohunda, O. J. *The Informal Sector of Lagos: An Inquiry into Urban Poverty and Employment.* Ibadan: University Press Ltd., 1985.

Federal Loans Board. *Annual Reports.* Lagos: Government Printer, 1956–60.

Federal Office of Statistics. *Annual Abstract of Statistics, 1966.* Lagos, F.O.S., 1967.

Fieldhouse, D. K. "The Economic Exploitation of Africa: Some British and French Comparisons." In *France and Britain in Africa,* edited by P. Gifford and William R. Louis, 593–662. New Haven, Conn.: Yale University Press, 1971.

Filani, M. "Nigeria: The Need to Modify Centre-down Development Planning." In *Development from Above or Below?* edited by W. B. Stohr and D. R. Taylor, 84–93. New York: Wiley, 1981.

Flint, J. E. *Sir John Goldie and the Making of Nigeria.* London: Oxford University Press, 1960.

Folarin, A. *A Short Historical Review of the Life of the Egbas from 1829 to 1930.* Abeokuta, Nigeria: Published by the author, 1931.

Fortes, M. "The Impact of the War on British West Africa." *International Affairs* 21, no. 2 (1945): 218.

Frank, A. G. *Capitalism and Underdevelopment in Latin America.* New York: Monthly Review Press, 1967.

Frankel, H. *Capital Investment in Africa.* London: Oxford University Press, 1938.

Freund, B. *Capital and Labour in the Nigerian Tin Mines.* London: Longman, 1981.

Galbraith, J. K. *Economic Development in Perspective.* Cambridge, Mass.: Harvard University Press, 1982.

Godfrey, F. "The Mining Industry in Nigeria." *Journal of the Royal African Society* 38 (1938–39): 247–59.

Grace, J. J. "Tin Mining on the Plateau before 1920." In *Studies in the History of Plateau State,* Nigeria, edited by E. Isichei, 111–27. London: Macmillan, 1982.

Greaves, Ida. *Colonial Monetary Conditions.* London: H.M.S.O., 1953.

Green, R. H. "Four African Development Plans: Ghana, Kenya, Nigeria, and Tanzania." *Journal of Modern African Studies* 3 (1965): 249–79.

Hagin, E. R., ed. *Planning Economic Development.* Homewood, Ill.: Irwin, 1963.

Hailey, Lord. *An African Survey.* London: Oxford University Press, 1956.

Hancock, W. K. *Survey of British Commonwealth Affairs.* Vol 2. London: Oxford University Press, 1962.

———. *Wealth of Colonies.* Cambridge: Cambridge University Press, 1950.

Hancock, W. K., and M. M. Gowing. *British War Economy.* London: H.M.S.O., 1949.

Hargreaves, J. D. *Decolonization in Africa.* London: Longman, 1988.

Hazlewood, A. "Sterling Balances and the Colonial Currency System." *Economic Journal* 62, no. 248 (1952): 942–45.

Helleiner, G. K. "The Fiscal Role of the Marketing Boards in Nigerian Economic Development, 1947–1961." *Nigerian Journal of Economic and Social Studies* 73, no. 295 (1964): 582–610.

———. *International Trade and Economic Development.* London: Penguin, 1972.

———. *Peasant Agriculture, Government, and Economic Growth in Nigeria.* Homewood, Ill.: Irwin, 1966.

Higgins, B. *Economic Development: Principles, Problems, and Policies.* New York: Norton, 1959.
Hill, P. *Development Economics on Trial: The Anthropological Case for a Prosecution.* Cambridge: Cambridge University Press, 1986.
Hirschman, A. O. *The Strategies of Economic Development.* New Haven, Conn.: Yale University Press, 1958.
Hodder, B. W. *Economic Development in the Tropics.* London: Methuen, 1968.
Hodgkin, T. *Nationalism in Colonial Africa.* London: Muller, 1956.
Holland, S., ed. *Beyond Capitalist Planning.* Oxford: Basil Blackwell, 1979.
Hopkins, A. G. "Clio-Antics: A Horoscope for African Economic History." In *African Studies since 1945: A Tribute to Basil Davidson,* edited by C. Fyfe, 31–48. London: Longman, 1976.
———. *The Economic History of West Africa.* London: Longman, 1973.
———. "Some Economic Aspects of Political Movements in Nigeria and in the Gold Coast, 1918–1939." *Journal of African History* 7, no. 1 (1966): 133–52.
Ikejiani, O., ed. *Nigerian Education.* London, 1964.
Ikime, O. *The Fall of Nigeria: The British Conquest.* London: Heinemann, 1977.
Ikoku, S. G. *Nigeria for Nigerians: A Study of Contemporary Nigerian Politics from a Socialist Point of View.* Lagos, 1963.
International Bank for Reconstruction and Development (IBRD). *The Economic Development of Nigeria: Report.* Lagos: Government Printer, 1954.
Jalee, P. *The Pillage of the Third World.* New York: Monthly Review Press, 1970.
Jones, A. C. "Labour's Colonial Policy." London: Fabian Publications Ltd., 1947.
Kilby, P. *Industrialisation in an Open Economy: Nigeria, 1945–1966.* Cambridge: Cambridge University Press, 1969.
Knowles, L. C. A. *The Economic Development of the British Overseas Empires.* Vol. 1. London: Routledge and Sons, 1924.
Landauer, C. *The Theory of National Economic Planning.* Berkeley and Los Angeles: University of California Press, 1947.
Lawal, Bayo. "Sharing Profits with Subjects: The Colonial Fiscal Policy." In *Britain and Nigeria,* edited by Toyin Falola, 186–222. London: Zed, 1987.
Lee, J. M., and M. Petter. *The Colonial Office, War, and Development Policy.* London: Maurice Temple Smith, 1982.
Leibenstein, H. *Economic Backwardness and Economic Growth.* New York: Wiley, 1957.
Lewis, A. "On Assessing a Development Plan." *Economic Bulletin of the Ghana Economic Society* (June–July 1959): 21–32.
Lewis, W. A. *Development Planning: The Essentials of Economic Policy.* London: Allen and Unwin, 1966.
———. "Economic Development with Unlimited Supplies of Labour." *Manchester School* 20 (May 1954): 139–92.
———. "A Policy for Colonial Agriculture." In *Attitude to Africa,* edited by W. A. Lewis et al. Middlesex: Allen and Unwin, 1951.
———. *The Principles of Economic Planning.* Washington, D.C.: Public Affairs Press, 1951.
———. *The Theory of Economic Growth.* London: Allen and Unwin, 1961.

———, ed. *Tropical Development, 1880–1913.* London: Oxford University Press, 1956.

Loynes, J. B. *The West African Currency Board, 1912–62.* London: West African Currency Board, 1962.

Lugard, F. J. D. *The Dual Mandate in British Tropical Africa.* London: Cass, 1965.

Macmillan, W. W. *The Road to Self-Rule: A Study in Colonial Evolution.* London: Faber and Faber, 1959.

———. *Warning from the West Indies.* Rev. ed. Harmondsworth: Penguin, 1949.

Macphee, A. *The Economic Revolution in British West Africa.* London, 1926.

Martins, Olatunji. "A New Spirit of Collectivism." *Service* 1, no. 3 (1935): 18–19.

Mbadiwe, K. O. *British and Axis Aims in Africa.* New York: Wendell Malliet, 1942.

McClelland, D. C. *The Achieving Society.* Princeton, N.J.: Van Nostrand, 1961.

McLean, W. H. "Economic and Social Development in the Colonies." *Journal of the Royal African Society* 35, no. 139 (1936): 191–201.

Mehta, S. C. *Development Planning in an African Economy: The Experience of Nigeria.* Delhi, India: Kalinga Publications, 1990.

Meir, G., ed. *Leading Issues in Development Economics.* New York: Oxford University Press, 1964.

Meir, G., and D. Seers, eds. *Pioneers in Development.* New York: Oxford University Press, 1984.

Mellamby, K. *The Birth of Nigeria's University.* London: Methuen, 1958.

Melson, R. *Nigeria: Modernization and the Politics of Communalism.* East Lansing: Michigan State University Press, 1971.

Meredith, D. "The British Government and Colonial Economic Policy, 1919–1939." *Economic History Review* 28, no.3 (1975): 484–98.

Meyer, F. V. *Britain's Colonies in World Trade.* London: Oxford University Press, 1948.

Mikesell, R. F., and R. L. Allen. "Economic Policies toward Less Developed Countries." Chap. 7 in *Leading Issues in Developing Economics,* edited by G. Meir. New York: Oxford University Press, 1964.

Morgan, D. J. *British Aid-5: Colonial Development.* London: Overseas Development Institute, 1964.

———. *The Official History of Colonial Development.* 5 vols. London: Macmillan, 1980.

Mortimore, M. *Adapting to Drought: Farmers, Famines, and Desertification in West Africa.* Cambridge: Cambridge University Press, 1989.

Myint, H. *The Economics of Developing Countries.* London: Hutchinson, 1967.

National Economic Council [of Nigeria]. *Economic Survey of Nigeria, 1959.* Lagos: Government Printer, 1959.

Newlyn, W. T., and D. C. Rowan. *Money and Banking in British Colonial Africa.* Oxford: Clarendon, 1954.

Nicolson, I. F. *The Administration of Nigeria, 1900 to 1960: Men, Methods, and Myths.* Oxford: Oxford University Press, 1969.

Niculescu, B. *Colonial Planning: A Comparative Study.* London: Allen and Unwin, 1958.

Nigeria. *Annual Report on the Social and Economic Progress of Nigeria, 1938.* Lagos: Government Printer, 1939.

———. *Annual Report on the General Progress of Development and Welfare Schemes in Nigeria, 1949–50.* Lagos: Government Printer, 1951.

———. *Annual Report on the General Progress of Development and Research Schemes in Nigeria, 1951–52.* Lagos: Government Printer, 1952.

———. *Digest of Statistics.* No. 1. Lagos: Government Printer, 1951.

———. *Economic Programme of the Government of the Federation of Nigeria, 1955–60.* Sessional paper no. 2. Lagos: Government Printer, 1956.

———. *Establishing a Business in Nigeria.* Lagos: Government Printer, 1961.

———. *Half-Yearly Report on the General Progress of Development and Welfare Schemes* [Oct. 1, 1949 to Feb. 15, 1950]. Lagos: Government Printer, 1950.

———. *Half-Yearly Report . . .* [Oct. 1, 1951 to Feb. 15, 1952]. Sessional paper no. 3. Lagos: Government Printer, 1952.

———. *Memorandum on the Revision of the Ten-Year Development Plan: Submitted to the Northern Regional Area Development Committee.* Kaduna: Government Printer, 1950.

———. *National Development Plan, 1962–68.* Lagos: Federal Ministry of Economic Development, 1962.

———. *Northern Progress.* Kaduna: Government Printer, 1957.

———. *Northern Regional Production Development Scheme, Annual Report, 1950–55.* Kaduna: Government Printer, 1955.

———. *Policy for Industrial Development.* Enugu: Government Printer, 1955.

———. *Preliminary Statement on Development Planning in Nigeria.* Sessional paper no. 6. Lagos: Government Printer, 1945.

———. *Progress Report on the Economic Programme.* Lagos: Government Printer, 1958.

———. *Report of the Accountant-General for the Year Ended 31st March 1955.* Lagos: Government Printer, 1957.

———. *Report of the Economic Mission, 1961.* Official document no. 5. Enugu: Government Printer, 1962.

———. *A Revised Plan of Development and Welfare for Nigeria, 1951–56.* Sessional paper no. 6. Lagos: Government Printer, 1951.

———. *Second Progress Report on the Economic Programme, 1955–62.* Lagos: Government Printer, 1958.

———. *Statement of Agricultural Policy.* Lagos: Government Printer, 1946.

———. *A Ten-Year Plan of Development and Welfare for Nigeria, 1946.* Sessional paper no. 24. Lagos: Government Printer, 1946.

Western House of Assembly Debates, Feb. 13–18, 1950; Feb. 26, 1952. Lagos: Government Printer, 1950.

Nigeria Local Development Board (NLDB). *Annual Report.* Lagos: Government Printer, 1947.

———. *Annual Report.* Lagos: Government Printer, 1948.

Nigeria Local Development Board Ordinance, 1946. Lagos: Government Printer, 1946.

Nigerian Youth Movement (NYM). *Nigerian Youth Charter: The Official Programme of the Nigerian Youth Movement.* Lagos, 1938.

Njoku, O. N. "Contributions to War Efforts." In *Britian and Nigeria,* edited by Toyin Falola, 164–81. London: Zed, 1987.

Njoku, R. A. *Commerce and Industry in Nigeria.* Lagos: Government Printer, 1955.

Nnoli, O., ed. *Path to Nigerian Development.* Dakar: Codesria, 1981.

O'Connell, J. O. "Some Social and Political Reflections of the Plan." *Nigerian Journal of Economic and Social Studies* 4, no. 2 (1962): 131–40.

Ofonagoro, W. I. *Trade and Imperialism in Southern Nigeria, 1881–1929.* New York: Nok, 1979.

Ogunsheye, A. "Nigerian Nationalism, 1919–1952." In *Nigerian Year Book, 1953.* Lagos: Daily Times, 1953.

Ojike, O. My Africa. New York: Day, 1946.

Okafor, S. O. *Indirect Rule: The Development of Central Legislature in Nigeria.* Walton/Thames: Nelson, 1981.

Okigbo, P. N. C. *National Development Planning in Nigeria, 1900–92.* London: Currey, 1989.

———. *Nigerian National Accounts, 1950–57.* Lagos: Federal Ministry of Economic Development, 1961.

———. *Nigerian Public Finance.* Evanston, Ill.: Northwestern University Press, 1965.

Okonjo, I. M. *British Administration in Nigeria, 1900–1950: A Nigerian View.* New York, 1974.

Okoye, M. *A Letter to Dr. Nnamdi Azikiwe.* Enugu: Fourth Dimension, 1979.

Olusanya, G. O. *The Second World War and Politics in Nigeria, 1939–1953.* London: Evans, 1973.

———. "The Zikist Movement: A Study of Political Radicalism." *Journal of Modern African Studies* 4, no. 3 (1966): 323–33.

Oluwasanmi, H. O. *Agriculture and Nigerian Economic Development.* Ibadan: Oxford Univeristy Press, 1966.

Oni, O., and B. Onimode. *Economic Development in Nigeria: The Socialist Alternative.* Ibadan: Nigerian Academy of Arts, Sciences, and Technology, 1975.

Onimode, B. *Imperialism and Underdevelopment in Nigeria.* London: Macmillan/Zed, 1983.

———. *A Political Economy of the African Crisis.* London: Zed, 1988.

Osuntokun, Jide. "Post–First World War Economic and Administrative Problems in Nigeria and the Response of the Clifford Administration." *Journal of the Historical Society of Nigeria* 7, no. 1 (1973): 35–48.

Oyejide, T. A. *Tariff Policy and Industrialization in Nigeria.* Ibadan: Ibadan University Press, 1975.

Oyemakinde, Wale. "The Impact of the Great Depression on the Nigerian Railway and Its Workers." *Journal of the Historical Society of Nigeria* 8, no. 4 (1977): 143–60.

Padmore, G., and D. Pizer. *How Russia Transformed Her Colonial Empire.* London: Dobson, 1946.

Peel, J. D. Y. "Olaju: A Yoruba Concept of Development." *Journal of Development Studies* 14, no. 2 (1978): 135–65.

Perham, M. *The Colonial Reckoning.* London: Fontana, 1963.

———. "Restatement of Indirect Rule." Africa 7, no. 3 (1934): 321–34.

———, ed. *Mining, Commerce, and Finance in Nigeria.* London: Faber and Faber, 1948.

———, ed. *The Native Economies of Nigeria.* London: Faber and Faber, 1946.

Phillipson, S. "Administrative and Financial Procedure under the New Constitution: Financial Relations between the Government of Nigeria and the Native Administrations." Lagos: CMG, 1947.

Pim, A. W. *The Financial and Economic History of the African Tropical Territories.* Oxford: Clarendon, 1940.

———. "Public Finance in Nigeria." In *Mining, Commerce, and Finance in Nigeria,* edited by M. Perham, 112–29. London: Faber and Faber, 1948.

"The Planning of Social and Economic Development in the Colonial Empire." *Papers on Colonial Affairs,* no. 3. London: H.M.S.O., 1944.

Prest, A. R., and I. G. Stewart. *The National Income of Nigeria, 1950–51.* London: H.M.S.O., 1954.

Public Works Department (PW). *Annual Report, 1945–46.* Lagos: Public Works Department, 1947.

———. *Annual Report, 1947–48.* Sessional paper no. 1. Lagos: Government Printer, 1950.

———. *Report on the Highways of Nigeria.* Technical paper no. 15. Lagos: Government Printer, 1953.

Richards, P. *Indigenous Agricultural Revolution: Ecology and Food Production in West Africa.* London: Hutchinson, 1985.

Rodney, W. *How Europe Underdeveloped Africa.* Dar-es-Salaam: Tanzania Publishing House, 1972.

Rostow, W. W. *The Stages of Growth: A Non-Communist Manifesto.* Cambridge: Cambridge University Press, 1960.

———. *Theorists of Economic Growth from David Hume to the Present: With a Perspective on the Next Century.* New York: Oxford University Press, 1990.

Rothschild D., and M. Chazan, eds. *The Precarious Balance: State and Society in Africa.* Boulder, Colo.: Westview, 1988.

Royal Empire Society. *The Crucial Problem of Imperial Development.* London: Longman, Green, 1938.

Samuel, F. "Economic Potential of Colonial Africa." Address to the Royal Empire Society Summer School at Ashridge, May 1949.

Schatz, S. P. *Economics, Politics, and Administration in Government Lending: The Regional Loans Boards of Nigeria.* Ibadan: Oxford University Press, 1970.

———. "The Influence of Planning on Development: The Nigerian Experience." *Social Research* 27 (Winter 1960): 451–68.

———. "n Achievement and Economic Growth: A Critique." *Quarterly Journal of Economics* 79 (May 1965): 234–47.

———. "Nigeria's First National Development Plan (1962–68): An Appraisal." *Nigerian Journal of Economic and Social Studies* 5, no. 2 (1963): 221–35.

———. "Obstacles to Nigerian Private Investment." *Nigerian Journal of Economics and Social Statistics* 4, no. 1 (1962): 66–73.

———. *Petroleum in Nigeria.* Ibadan: NISER, 1969.

———. "Two Years of Progress of Planning." *West Africa* no. 2510 (July 1965): 773–74.

Schumpeter, J. A. *The Theory of Economic Development.* Cambridge, Mass.: Harvard University Press, 1934.

Scitovsky, T. "Two Concepts of External Economies." *Journal of Political Economy* 62 (Apr. 1954): 143–51.

Seidman, A. "Changing Theories of Political Economy." In *African Studies since 1945,* edited by C. Fyfe, 49–65. London: Longman, 1976.

———. *Planning in Subsaharan Africa.* New York: Praeger, 1974.

Shenton, R. *Studies in the Development of Capitalism in Northern Nigeria.* Toronto: University of Toronto Press, 1986.

Sklar, R. L. *Nigerian Political Parties: Power in an Emergent African Nation.* Princeton, N.J.: Princeton University Press, 1963.

Smith, A. *The Wealth of Nations.* Vol. 2, book 4. London: Dent, 1910.

Stapleton, G. B. *The Wealth of Nigeria.* Ibadan: Oxford University Press, 1958.

Stewart, F., S. Lall, and S. M. Wangwe, eds. *Alternative Development Strategies in Sub-Saharan Africa.* London: Macmillan, 1992.

Stolper, W. F. "How Bad Is the Plan?" *Nigerian Journal of Economic and Social Studies* 6, no. 3 (1964): 261–73.

———. *Planning without Facts: Lessons in Resource Allocation from Nigeria's Development.* Cambridge, Mass.: Harvard University Press, 1966.

Tamuno, T. N. *The Evolution of the Nigerian State: The Southern Phase, 1898–1914.* London: Longman, 1972.

Toye, J. *Dilemmas of Development: Reflections on the Counter-Revolution in Development Theory and Policy.* Oxford: Basil Blackwell, 1987.

Udegbunam, G. *West African Pilot,* Feb. 14, 1955.

United Kingdom (UK). *Colonial Development Act, 1929* (CDA). London: H.M.S.O., 1929.

———. *Colonial Development and Welfare.* Sessional paper no. 21/45. London: H.M.S.O., 1945.

———. *Colonial Development and Welfare Act, 1940* (CDWA, Cmd. 6457). London: H.M.S.O., 1943.

———. *Colonial Development and Welfare Act, 1940* (CDWA, Cmd. 6532). London: H.M.S.O., 1944.

———. *Colonial Development and Welfare Acts: Report on the Administration and Use of the Funds Provided under the Colonial Development Acts* (Cmd. 9375). London: H.M.S.O., 1955.

———. *The Colonial Territories (1950–51)* (Cmd. 8243). London: H.M.S.O., 1951.

———. *Parliamentary Debates,* Commons, 5th ser., vol. 200 (1926).

———. *Parliamentary Debates,* Commons, ser. 4, vol. 36 (August 22, 1895), cols. 641–42.

United Nations (UN). *Community Development and National Development.* New York: UN, 1963.

———. *Economic Development and Planning in Asia and the Far East.* New York: UN, 1961.

———. *Economic Development of Under-Developed Countries.* Various issues, 1949–50.
———. *Economic Survey of Africa since 1950.* New York: UN, 1959.
———. *Enlargement of the Exchange Economy of Tropical Africa.* New York: UN, 1954.
———. *Measures for the Development of Underdeveloped Countries.* New York: UN, 1951.
———. *Measures for the Economic Development of Underdeveloped Countries.* New York: UN, 1951.
———. *Measures for the Economic Development of Underdeveloped Countries.* New York: UN, 1954.
———. *Report of the First National Conference on International Economic and Social Development.* New York: UN, 1952.
———. *Review of Economic Conditions in Africa.* New York: UN, 1951.
———. *Technical Assistance Administration: Formulation and Economic Appraisal of Development Projects.* New York: UN, 1951.
———. *World Economic Report for 1948.* New York: UN, 1949.
U.S. Bureau of Foreign Commerce. *Investments in Nigeria: Basic Information for U.S. Businessmen.* Washington, D.C.: Government Printing Office, 1957.
"Wake Up America." *African Messenger,* Jan. 30, 1927.
Watts, M. *Silent Violence: Food, Famine, and Peasantry in Northern Nigeria.* Berkeley and Los Angeles: University of California Press, 1983.
West India Royal Commission (WIRC). *Recommendations, 1938–39* (Cmd. 6174). London: H.M.S.O., 1940.
———. Report (Cmd. 6607). London: H.M.S.O., 1945.
White, J. *Central Administration in Nigeria, 1914–1948.* London: Cass, 1981.
Wicker, E. R. "Colonial Development and Welfare, 1929–1957: The Evolution of a Policy." *Social and Economic Studies* 7, no. 4 (1958): 170–82.
World Bank. Background Papers: The Long-Term Perspective Study of Sub-Saharan Africa. Vol. 2, *Economic and Sectoral Policy Issues.* Washington, D.C.: World Bank, 1990.
———. *Sub-Saharan Africa: From Crisis to Sustainable Growth.* Washington, D.C.: World Bank, 1990.
Yesufu, T. M. "Nigerian Manpower Problems: A Preliminary Assessment." *Nigerian Journal of Economic and Social Studies* 4, no. 3 (1962): 207–27.
Zachernurk, P. S. "The Lagos Intelligentsia and the Idea of Progress, ca. 1860–1960." In *Yoruba Historiography,* edited by Toyin Falola, 147–65. Madison: University of Wisconsin, African Studies Program, 1991.

Index